Oliver Stone's America

Oliver Stone on the set of his 1991 release *JFK*. Copyright © 1991 Warner Bros. Inc., Regency Enterprises V.O.F. and Le Studio Canal+.

oliver stone's
AMERICA

"Dreaming the Myth Outward"

Susan Mackey-Kallis

WestviewPress
A Division of HarperCollinsPublishers

To my father,
whose words of praise, although few,
have always meant the most

Film Studies

Copyright © 1996 by Westview Press, A Division of HarperCollins Publishers, Inc.

Published in 1996 in the United States of America by Westview Press, 5500 Central Avenue, Boulder, Colorado 80301-2877, and in the United Kingdom by Westview Press, 12 Hid's Copse Road, Cumnor Hill, Oxford OX2 9JJ

A CIP catalog record for this book is available from the Library of Congress
ISBN 0-8133-2662-1 (cloth)—ISBN 0-8133-2663-X (paper)

The paper used in this publication meets the requirements of the American National Standard for Permanence of Paper for Printed Library Materials Z39.48-1984.

10   9   8   7   6   5   4   3   2   1

Contents

6 Final Thoughts

Photographs

Acknowledgments

In any scholarly undertaking, one never works completely alone. Accordingly, there are a number of people who have supported me and offered much-needed guidance and friendship throughout. I extend my thanks to Tom Frentz for his critical but supportive review of two chapters of this book in draft form. I deeply appreciate the efforts of Janice Hocker Rushing, who took the time to meet and speak with me about my work and who offered sections of her recent book manuscript to aid in the development of my thinking about Stone's films. I give my heartfelt thanks to my editor Gordon Massman for believing in this book and doing all in his power to bring it to fruition. I humbly thank Oliver Stone for taking the time to meet with me and share some of his own ideas about his work. I will forever be indebted to Mr. Stone for his warm words of praise and his continued belief in my critical insights into his films. I also want to acknowledge Villanova University for its support in the form of a summer research grant that enabled me to write this book. Finally, I want to thank my husband, Kyriakos Kallis, for pushing me to work harder and better, particularly during the times I felt like slacking off or giving up. And thanks, Mom and Dad—you always believed in me, even when I sometimes forgot to believe in myself.

Susan Mackey-Kallis

Introduction

It may be hard for some to admit that Oliver Stone, with $40 million per film at his disposal and virtually unlimited media access, can be a subversive force, but there is no question that he has recast the idols in the heart of the Temple.

—Andrew Kopkind[1]

Oliver Stone is one of the most successful directors currently working in Hollywood. He is also a polemicist with a liberal perspective who is making films about recent U.S. history and culture. That Stone is a successful mainstream filmmaker with an overtly leftist agenda seems surprising, if not counterintuitive, given the history of political filmmaking in Hollywood and conventional wisdom's understanding of the mass media appetite of most Americans. This book is an attempt to account for Stone's success as a filmmaker, to critique his major films, and to place them inside the tradition of political filmmaking in Hollywood.

Oliver Stone, like everyone else a member of Marshall McLuhan's global village, is a storyteller, like the bards of old, weaving parables for the millions of Americans sitting around the international mass-mediated campfire. Like the philosopher king in Plato's allegory of the cave and the Biblical prophets who spoke to the people through parables, Stone has been interpreting three decades of "the shadow play upon the wall,"[2] so that anyone who has eyes may see, and anyone who has ears may hear.[3] Bard, "philosopher king," propagandist, rhetorician, revisionist historian, the Charlie Chaplin and D. W. Griffith of our age[4]—Stone is all of these. But most of all he is a passionate, if "flawed," moralist who has found a way to sustain a popular and powerful leftist vision of American life. Sometimes Stone's camera is as explosive as a gunshot, designed to startle us out of a naive or politically complacent stupor. At other times it serves as an eviscerating scalpel that leaves us bloodless and drained but somehow better for the cleansing. And often his work weaves a psychedelic love song or Rimbaud-like verse that seduces us, turns us on, and lets us see visions and dream dreams, in turn, of other places, other worlds, other possibilities.

Oliver Stone's major release films, *Salvador, Born on the Fourth of July, Platoon, The Doors, JFK, Talk Radio, Wall Street, Heaven and Earth*, and

Natural Born Killers, are aesthetic experiences and social commentaries. They are also mythological constructions based upon historical events and personae. As such, they draw upon the "inevitable tension between social actuality and film form,"[5] which often prompts critics to decry them either as pollutions and distortions of history or as blatantly overworked propaganda. In this book, I account for critics' and audiences' responses to Stone's films by teasing out some of the tensions that exist between film form and social actuality, investigating the way the interaction between these factors may contribute to the social dis-ease that Stone's films often invite. I begin, however, with the assumption that although filmmakers may work from social actuality, they "necessarily impose form upon that actuality, turning it into what may be implied by the terms *art* or *fiction*."[6] Part of that fictionalizing for Stone involves universalizing historical events and individuals. In order to convey his political perspective, Stone's films create arguments out of images and icons out of individuals. His use of mythological constructions to represent social actualities accounts, in part, for the controversy that surrounds his films, as well as contributing to their power and popularity.

My approach to Stone's work can broadly be defined as rhetorical. Rhetorical criticism of film is a mode of analysis that "regards the work not so much as an object of aesthetic contemplation but as an artistically structured instrument for communication."[7] This concern places the emphasis not on the work itself but on the way it interacts with an audience inside of a context to produce meaning. Such a "meaning-centered approach brings to the text a curiosity not simply about the structure of the text, nor about the clues to the author revealed by the text, nor about the extent to which the text mirrors 'reality,' but also about the ways in which the text invites an audience to make meanings."[8] This type of criticism starts with the assumption that films contain persuasive potential; however, whether viewers respond to the codes and symbol systems invoked by the film is influenced by how meaningful those codes are for them in a given situation. Close readings of films are implicitly rhetorical through their emphasis on a film's invitations to meaning making.[9]

Specifically, my analysis of Stone's films is sociopolitical and psychomythological in focus. Sociopolitical critics of mass media identify the larger pictures that films both draw upon and reflect about the sociological and political structures in society. Critics explore how mass media reflect and create particular political ideologies or mythologies; they also examine how ideology and mythology constrain meaning making.[10] Sociopolitical critique of film from a rhetorical perspective often goes beyond this, however, to inquire into the politics of a film's structure and form. From this perspective, film aesthetics and style are important because they are part of a film's working system of signs and are often a basis for its arguments.

Psychomythological criticism explores the mythic dimensions of film, focusing on archetypes, both historical and literary, in their relation to the viewers' experiences. Critics explore how a film's mythic structures, viewed as cultural or universal, draw upon the audiences' unconscious (psychoanalytic) structures as they are played out in a larger social context.

Because Stone's films are rhetorical arguments, powerful mythopoetic polemics that speak eloquently about the problems with American economic, political, and social life, it is particularly useful to explore not simply what they say but also the cinematic means by which they speak. Additionally, it is helpful to understand how the films were received by the critics and the public, and what effects, if any, they may have had on American political life. Oliver Stone's *JFK,* for example, although not the first film to adopt a conspiracy perspective regarding the assassination of President John F. Kennedy, has certainly been the most popular and most widely criticized conspiracy film. It also has the distinction of being one of only a few films in U.S. history that has prompted political action as a result of its release.[11]

In Chapter 1, I consider at length Oliver Stone's history as a screenwriter and filmmaker working inside mainstream Hollywood. I also explore the critical response, both positive and negative, to Stone's screenplays and films as a way to begin revealing the sociopolitical and mythological polemic to which audiences are invited to respond.

Chapters 2 through 5 take an audience-centered approach in the analysis of nine of Stone's major-release films. Chapter 2 focuses on Stone's critically acclaimed and widely criticized film *JFK.* I start with *JFK* for a number of reasons. First, it represents Stone's argument regarding America's betrayal and expulsion from the Garden of Eden/Camelot. Hence, it is a reasonable mythological starting point. Second, *JFK,* in many ways, is the most sophisticated and complicated of Stone's films, taking as its theoretical polemic the search for the "truth" with the realization that there is no single, ultimately knowable truth. Finally, *JFK* is a good place to begin because it allows us to consider at some length the circumstances surrounding the film's production, its critical and popular response, and the political actions resulting from its release. The debate surrounding *JFK*'s portrayal of the Kennedy assassination provides an unusual opportunity to explore the issues of filmic representation, historical accuracy, journalistic integrity, and artistic license played out against the background of this controversial film.

Chapters 3 and 4 continue the exploration of Stone's various sociomythological themes and their rhetorical constructions in his portrayal of American cultural history from the 1960s through the late 1980s. Chapter 3 provides partial readings of Oliver Stone's "Vietnam trilogy": *Platoon, Born on the Fourth of July,* and *Heaven and Earth.* These films, I argue, invite audiences to explore America's loss of innocence after the assassination of John F. Kennedy. Stone, in various interviews, has stated that he firmly believes that if President Kennedy had not been killed the Vietnam War would not have occurred.[12] Thus, Kennedy's death represents for Stone America's "fall from grace" and the "descent into hell" that was Vietnam. These three films, together, make up a large part of Stone's perspective on the 1960s and 1970s.

Chapter 4 focuses on three of Stone's most reflexive films to date, *The Doors, Salvador,* and *Talk Radio*. These films not only comment on the artist's responsibility to take a stance on issues of sociopolitical importance and provide prophetic vision for devotees, but they also represent the time after the Fall and detail the increasing disillusionment of Stone's prototypical heroes, grown bitter and angry about the possibilities for salvation and transcendence in the modern age.

In Chapter 5, I discuss Stone's vision of the 1980s and 1990s in his 1987 release *Wall Street* and his 1994 film, *Natural Born Killers*. Both films, despite the apparent dissimilarity in their subject matter, have much in common to say about American "soul-sickness" at the close of the millennium and point, with however shaky a finger, toward a path of future teleological development for humanity at large.

In Chapter 6, I conclude with some reflections on the body of Stone's work and a discussion of his current film about former President Richard M. Nixon.

Although the reading of each film provides a piece of the mosaic that constitutes Stone's larger vision, each analysis stands on its own. The entire book is designed to account for the various and multiple reading strategies that Stone seems to invite from his audiences; however, as a rhetorical critic, I am primarily interested in an audience-based analysis rather than an auteur critique. This assumes that Stone's audiences are unlikely to have watched all of his films in close succession. The critic's job, therefore, is to highlight each film's invitations to meaning while still arguing that American audiences, through Stone's collected films, are offered a vision of American political and cultural life that transcends individual films.

In closing, it should be mentioned that any rhetorical critic interpreting an audience's experience of a film might be faced with two questions. First, can one claim that Stone meant his films to be interpreted in a particular way? And second, what about the dangers of "overreading" a film and finding significance where none exists? To both of these questions the answer is that any analysis of a film is simply one interpretation of many possible interpretations. Although Stone has spoken at length in various interviews about what his films mean for himself and for his audiences, I cannot claim that what I say is what Oliver Stone, given the chance, would say about his films. In many cases his insights into his films have aided mine, although I am sure there are times when he would disagree with what I suggest may constitute a filmgoer's experience of a particular film. And this is fine. Although film critics and audiences might occasionally agree on similar interpretations of a film, there is no definitive reading of any film. For me, this is the beauty and fascination of film as visual argument and aesthetic experience. Although no one reading of a film is "correct" or "incorrect," there are more and less well-informed readings and more and less helpful analyses. I naturally hope, of course, that I have provided both an informed and a helpful reading of Stone's films. My work is simply one interpretation of Oliver Stone's films and is offered as a dialogue with those films and with my audience. With both humility and excitement, I acknowledge that any interpretation of a film, like any film itself, is part of a conversation about what it means to be human, to symbolize, to create ourselves and our histories, and to understand ourselves and our histories through the stories we tell and the conversations we have with one other.

Notes

1. Andrew Kopkind, "*JFK*: The Myth," *Nation*, 20 January 1992, 40.
2. Plato, "Allegory of the Cave," *The Republic,* Book 7 William Heinman, ed. (Cambridge: Harvard University Press, 1937).
3. Matt. 13:13 Standard American Version.
4. Martin Medhurst also drew a comparison between Stone and D. W. Griffith in "The Rhetorical Structure of Oliver Stone's *JFK*," *Critical Studies in Mass Communication* 10 (1993):128–143.
5. Thomas Benson and Carolyn Anderson, *Reality Fictions: The Films of Frederick Wiseman* (Carbondale: Southern Illinois University Press, 1984), 2.
6. Ibid., 1.
7. Martin Medhurst and Thomas Benson, *Rhetorical Dimensions in Media: A Critical Casebook* (Dubuque, IA: Kendall/Hunt, 1984), x.
8. Thomas Benson, "Respecting the Reader," *Quarterly Journal of Speech* 72 (1986):204.
9. According to Benson and Anderson, rhetorical critics of film "try to find words to describe what the audience experience may be like, understanding, of course, that words are only an approximation and that every person experiences the films to some degree idiosyncratically. And yet the films are social constructions and as such invite shared experiences. The rhetorical critic inquires into that shared experience, not by surveying audience response, and not simply by reporting the critic's subjective, impressionistic responses, but by interrogating the film itself, regarding the film as a constructed invitation to a complex experience of thoughts and feelings. At best, a film is an 'invitation' rather than a 'cause' of its viewer's response" (*Reality Fictions*, 2–3).
10. See, for example, Carpenter and Seltzer's analysis of the film *Patton*. They have argued that the film "functioned rhetorically to crystallize and then provided reenforcement for the developing Silent Majority sentiment about the Vietnam

War" (R. H. Carpenter and R. V. Seltzer, "Nixon, *Patton,* and a Silent Majority Sentiment About the Vietnam War: The Cinematic Basis of a Rhetòrical Stance," *Central States Speech Journal* 25 [1974]:106). See also Janice Hocker Rushing, "*E.T.* as Rhetorical Transcendence," *Quarterly Journal of Speech* 71 (1985): 188–203.

11. Senate debate about the early release of classified files pertaining to President Kennedy's assassination cites Stone's film *JFK* as a significant force in the push to open the files. This debate is discussed in greater detail in Chapter 2.

12. David Ansen, "What Does Oliver Stone Owe History?" *Newsweek,* 23 December 1991, 49.

one

Stone's Dilemma: A Platonist Seeking Postmodern "Truth," or the Quandary of the Left-Wing Intellectual in Hollywood

I believe that the highest ethic is the Socratic one, from the dialogues of Socrates, which says, "Know thyself."

—Oliver Stone[1]

We have not . . . to risk the adventure alone; for the heroes of all time have gone before us; the labyrinth is thoroughly known; we have only to follow the thread of the hero-path. And where we had thought to find an abomination, we shall find a god; where we had thought to slay another, we shall slay ourselves; where we had thought to travel outward, we shall come to the center of our own existence; where we had thought to be alone, we shall be with all the world.

—Joseph Campbell[2]

Oliver Stone's body of work provides a vision of thirty years of American political life. But more than offering a compendium of American events and political history, Stone's films combine a liberal critique with philosophical and mythical musings on the nature of the human condition and on the evolution of human consciousness. His films, individually and collectively, assert that we live in an age of fragmentation and secularization, separated from our world, ourselves, and each other. It is a world, according to Stone, where technology and bureaucracy have rationalized all gods and devils out

Oliver Stone on the set of *JFK*, a film he produced, directed, and cowrote. Copyright © 1991 Warner Bros. Inc., Regency Enterprises V.O.F. and Le Studio Canal+.

of existence.[3] Despite the fruits of modern enlightenment, we wander lost in a world without meaning. Stone's films speak to our desire for cosmic connectedness and to one of the most profound rhetorical exigencies of all, the need to transcend self and death in the belief in something more. His films long to proclaim with "conviction that the entire system of the world forms a single, integrated system united by universal principles, that all things in the world consequently share in a common 'good order,' in short that the universe or *ouranos* is 'well turned out.'"[4]

The central myth running through Stone's work is that of the fallen idealist/savior (Christ/Adam/Hector/Achilles), killed, maimed, or disillusioned in a seemingly senseless sacrifice; John Kennedy and Jim Garrison in *JFK*, Jim Morrison in *The Doors*, Richard Boyle in *Salvador*, Ron Kovic in *Born on the Fourth of July*, Barry Champlain in *Talk Radio*, Sergeant Elias in *Platoon*. The "fall" of these saviors represents America's loss of innocence, while the halfhearted resurrection offered by and to many of them represents, on one level, a sinfully unredeemable America. Jim Garrison fails to change anything with his uncovering of the plot to kill Kennedy in *JFK*. *Platoon*'s Sergeant Elias is an ineffectual Christ figure overpowered by the Devil, Sergeant Barnes. And by killing Barnes, Chris Taylor, the protagonist of *Platoon*, may himself have defected to the "bad" side. *Talk Radio*'s Barry Champlain suffers a meaningless murder. Although Ron Kovic, in *Born on the Fourth of July*, eventually finds his true political voice, he remains trapped in a crippled body for life. Richard Boyle, the classic anti-hero in *Salvador*, yearns for a salvation we are unsure he ever finds. Jim Morrison in *The Doors*, one of America's visionary "saviors" of the 1960s, self-destructs from drugs, alcohol, and excess. Mickey and Mallory Knox in *Natural Born Killers*, by their murder of the Navajo Indian shaman, lose their last chance at transformation and redemption. And even *Wall Street*'s Bud Fox, although he eventually chooses "the good," is presented as a much less fascinating figure than Gordon Gekko, the incarnation of the Devil himself.

On another level, however, Stone's archetypal heroes, willing to live life in the extreme—whether it be in a Southeast Asian jungle, on the ledge of a building, or on the edge of the psyche's unconscious abyss—offer the only hope for transcendence, for moving culture from the current age of ego consciousness into the next era of transconsciousness. It is there on the edge that Stone's archetypal heroes meet themselves in the most terrible battle of all—the internal battle of the soul. This is tricky terrain to negotiate, however, and lacking models for transcendence in an era of postmodernity, these heroes often remain rough sketches of what the next generation of heroes, given the right spiritual ammunition, may look like. As we will see, the journey outward—of action, energy, and rage—so often undertaken by Stone's protagonists is slowly being replaced over the course of his films by the journey inward, a journey marked by inaction, silence, and the slow dawning of enlightenment.

Stone's films often personify the evils to be found in the universal story of Pandora's box and their manifestation in the cultural story of America's post-Camelot fall from grace. Indeed, every film Stone has made, both before and after the release of *JFK*, dates America's political and social demise as starting with Kennedy's assassination, the event, which in Stone's view, started Vietnam. Three of Stone's films, *Platoon, Heaven and Earth,* and *Born on the Fourth of July*, are explicitly about Vietnam, whereas all of his films reference Vietnam or Kennedy's assassination. In *Talk Radio*, for example, just before radio talk-show host Barry Champlain is about to be murdered by a crazed neo-Nazi, Champlain explains to his girlfriend, Laura, why their relationship would never work: "I'm too old for you Laura. I mean, you don't know about Vietnam, *Easy Rider,* The Beatles." Laura responds, "Start over, Grandpa." Champlain replies, "I can't. I'm inside of this thing and

A seemingly fatigued yet contemplative Oliver Stone on the set of his 1991 film *The Doors.* Copyright © 1991 Tri-Star Pictures, Inc.

you're not." Stone, like his protagonist Champlain, is "inside of this [Vietnam] thing." In his films, then, this is both his and our frame of reference. Richard Boyle, in *Salvador,* in an extended diatribe against U.S. involvement in Central America, asked a U.S. colonel, "Is that why you guys are here? Some kind of post-Vietnam experience, like you need a rerun or something?" Vietnam is the backdrop for Stone's portrait of *The Doors,* and even in *Wall Street* and *Natural Born Killers,* two films seemingly divorced in time and subject matter from Vietnam and Kennedy's assassination, the turbulent events of the 1960s and early 1970s provide the critical canvas for their visions of America.

Taken as a whole, Stone's films are somewhat of an anomaly, however, in that they offer a unified mythic vision in the midst of postmodern fragmentation. His portrait of thirty years of American life, however, as we will see, draws on perennial philosophy, Jungian psychology, and universal mythology in order to critique and extend social constructions of the current postmodern condition. Before turning to the cultural and transcultural stories told individually and collectively by Stone's films, it is helpful to first explore Stone's success with negotiating a working relationship in Hollywood as a writer, producer, and filmmaker.

Oliver Stone: Screenwriter and Filmmaker

Although Hollywood routinely draws from the American cultural and political scene for ideas and perspectives, this scene usually provides no more
than a backdrop to highlight personal dramas of tragedy and triumph. It is
rare to find a filmmaker like Oliver Stone whose films do not simply allude
to historical issues and personae but actually use them as bases for persuasive arguments about the American political scene.

Drawing on Hollywood's dedication to the topical and its historical commitment to the politically mainstream "social problem film," Stone usually
manages to walk a fine line between heavy-handed propaganda and apolit-
ical entertainment by fictionalizing and universalizing historical events and
individuals. He successfully negotiates and exploits the tension in Hollywood between topicality and political centrality by infusing political and
cultural issues with his own brand of liberal critique, while creating dramatic narratives and characters that tingle and sizzle with energy and rage.
It is this ability, in part, that accounts both for Stone's success in negotiating a profitable working relationship with Hollywood and, as we will see,
for his films' power and popularity.

Stone was born in New York City on September 15, 1946, to a Jewish father and a French Catholic mother. By his own concession, he was raised
Protestant as "the great compromise."[5] His political outlook on life, however, was adopted from his stockbroker father, a man whom he describes as
a "conservative in an intelligent sense," who "ultimately . . . was an apolo-
gist—a defender of the Cold War." As a result, Stone "grew up really frightened of the Russians," whom his father had created "as a nightmare
image" for him as a child. As Stone explained it, "At the age of ten, I
thought that Roosevelt was the bad guy and John Maynard Keynes was the
Devil."[6] He considered himself a "Goldwater Republican" upon entering
Yale University. His politics, however, changed sometime thereafter.

After dropping out of Yale in 1965, Stone took a teaching position at
Free Pacific Institute in Cholon, Vietnam. He later joined the U.S. Mer-
chant Marine, volunteered for the 25th Infantry Division of the U.S. Army
in 1967, and was eventually awarded the Bronze Star for Valor and a Pur-
ple Heart for his tour of duty in Vietnam. When he returned to the States,
he reentered college, studied film at New York University under Martin
Scorsese, and graduated with a B.F.A. in 1971. Stone has said of Scorsese,
his mentor and friend, "He was someone on an equal wave of nuttiness.
And he helped channel the rage in me."[7]

Stone received his first recognition as a screenwriter. In 1978 he won an
Oscar for Best Script and the Writers' Guild Award for Best Screenplay for
his screenplay adaptation for Alan Parker's *Midnight Express* (1978). The

film was based upon the real-life story of a young American imprisoned in Turkey for drug smuggling. Stone's second produced screenplay, *Conan the Barbarian* (1982), was coscripted with the film's director, John Milius. Stone also wrote the screenplay for Brian De Palma's *Scarface* (1983) and coscripted Hal Ashby's *Eight Million Ways to Die* (1986).

Despite the awards Stone received for his screenwriting, many of these early screenplays were criticized for their racist undertones. *Midnight Express, The Year of the Dragon,* and *Conan the Barbarian,* in particular, provoked charges of racism because the protagonists' emotions were not detached from the films themselves. In recent interviews, Stone has responded to the charges made against these films, averring that "the complaints are legitimate about 'Dragon,' and certainly about *Midnight Express.* That was my fault. I was younger then. . . . 'Conan' and *The Year of the Dragon* are Fascist, but I don't really consider 'Conan' mine, because the first draft was radically changed by John Milius."[8] Speaking of his original draft for the film, Stone explains: "It dealt with the takeover of the planet and the forces of life being threatened by the forces of darkness. The mutant armies were taking over, and Conan was the lonely pagan—as opposed to the Christian hero; he was Roland at the pass, he was Tarzan, he was a *mythic* figure. I loved that he had been enslaved and suffered, and that he *rose.*"[9] Stone's unrealized mythic and messianic aspirations for Milius's *Conan,* as we will see, surfaced later in Stone's own films.

Stone's directing career began in 1973 with *Seizure,* a film about a horror-story writer haunted and ultimately destroyed by nightmares. *Seizure* was followed in 1981 by another low-budget horror film called *The Hand,* starring Michael Caine. It was not until 1986, however, that Stone released his first major film, *Salvador,* a film that marked a significant change in Stone's filmmaking style and began his career as a politically liberal and emotionally explosive filmmaker. *Salvador* (1986), about the U.S. support for the repressive and conservative military government in Nicaragua, was quickly followed by *Platoon* (1986), a semiautobiographical account of a foot soldier's experience in Vietnam; *Wall Street* (1987), a film about corporate greed in the world of high finance; *Talk Radio* (1988), about the eventual murder of late-night radio personality Alan Berg; *Born on the Fourth of July* (1989), the story of Ron Kovic, a crippled Vietnam vet who learns to cope, stateside; *The Doors* (1991), an account of the rise and fall of the still-popular 1960s rock band of the same name; *JFK* (1991), Stone's version of the Kennedy assassination and cover-up; *Heaven and Earth* (1993), a second look at Vietnam through the eyes of a South Vietnamese woman; and *Natural Born Killers* (1994), a critical assessment of violence in the American culture, family, and mass media.

Stone's nine major-release films were a radical departure from his first two low-budget horror films. Their marked difference, however, can be explained by more than Stone's growing maturity as a filmmaker. Said one writer:

> It was an open secret in L.A. during the last decade that Stone was a frustrated "cause freak" whose commercial sell-out was a disillusioned "detour into the mainstream" (his words) after more cherished projects had foundered. His long-planned adaptation of Vietnam Vet leader Ron Kovic's *Born on the Fourth of July* came asunder days before shooting was to begin, and his script about Russian dissidents was optioned but never made. . . . Around the time he finished *The Hand,* he attended a screening of Warren Beatty's *Reds* and was struck by its vision and daring. Consequently, Stone's own political and creative goals were revitalized.[10]

Particularly compelling to Stone was Beatty's ability to express his leftist politics in a big-budget, major-release film. Stone, in other words, may have remembered why he came to Hollywood in the first place.

Unable to land American backing for *Salvador,* his first major-release film, Stone eventually secured funding from Hemdale Films, a British production company. Hemdale, impressed by Stone's ability to bring *Salvador* in under budget (he spent $6 million of the budgeted $6.5 million), also signed on to produce *Platoon* before *Salvador* was even completed. The seven major films that were to follow *Platoon* were financed by American companies. For *Platoon,* Stone received Academy Awards for Best Picture, Best Director, Best Editing, and Best Sound. For *Born on the Fourth of July* he was awarded an Academy Award for Best Director.

Despite his current bankable status in Hollywood, Stone and his critics acknowledge that his success at making overtly leftist films in mainstream Hollywood is surprising. "Had he been filming in the McCarthy era," commented one journalist, "he would doubtless have been drummed out of Hollywood instead of becoming the hot property his box-office success has made him."[11] Another claimed, "Mr. Stone had to fight to win his cinematic pulpit and still worries about losing it."[12] Comparing himself to Charlie Chaplin in an interview, Stone noted that he fears the possibility of ending up in exile like Chaplin but added, "I'm not going to leave that easily."[13] Many critics have questioned whether Stone will be able to maintain his outspoken views. Stanley Weiser, speaking of the likelihood of Stone's being seduced by Hollywood mediocrity, has asserted: "Oliver's been around the block ten times and won't be seduced by money. He's not an easy lay."[14]

Critics have applauded Stone's brand of political liberalism. Robin Wood, speaking of Stone, said, "anyone attempting with any degree of success, both artistic and commercial, to make overtly political movies that sustain a left-wing position within the Hollywood cinema of the 1980s deserves at least our respectful attention."[15] "Stone is the Bruce Springsteen of the American Cinema," declared another critic, "a thinking man with his heart in the right place who skillfully translates his fundamental liberalism into a media event."[16] Stuart Klawans asserted that Stone "gives you more of one man's reality than you can easily handle, combined with more political honesty than anyone could expect from Hollywood."[17] Film critic Stanley Kauffman has claimed that "after Martin Scorsese, [Stone] is the most exciting American director. Exciting in more than a fast-action snap-editing way. Stone's directing excites with its hunger, its avidity, by the way he grabs a scene cinematically, squeezes it of its juice, and casts it aside."[18] According to many critics, Oliver Stone is a rarity simply because so few filmmakers in Hollywood have consistently and successfully made films primarily out of political conviction.

The relationship between Hollywood and politics has always been complex. Hollywood filmmakers, on the whole, have traditionally been reluctant to explicitly engage political issues and events. Because of major film studios' historical leeriness of overtly political films, the history of the American cinema is marked by few important films of notable political relevance. A brief survey of political filmmaking in America from the 1930s through the 1980s, for example, reveals, with some significant exceptions, an ideologically centrist cinematic landscape.[19] Richard Maltby pointed out that historically, "conventional Hollywood wisdom has regarded films about politics as box-office poison, since anything controversial was liable to move the cinema out of its safe and profitable territory as entertainment into more dangerous areas."[20] "Americans are uneasy with ideology, especially any ideology other than their own," asserted Terry Christensen. As a result, "most movies respect this by remaining resolutely centrist."[21] Even if the Hollywood film industry were to treat political issues or perspectives, there remains, as Stephen Prince noted, a "long-standing belief that entertainment values must take precedence over whatever social messages or values a given film might embody or convey."[22] Messages, as the Hollywood industry's wisdom reminds us, are better sent by Western Union than by movies.

Despite this oft-quoted proclamation, Hollywood cinema has historically been neither politically mute nor politically univocal. Although generally leery of making overtly political films—with the possible exception of the 1940s anti-Fascist films—the American cinema has consistently sought topicality for box-office success and has remained committed to a clearly liberal, if only populist and pragmatic, American agenda, most notably apparent in the "social problem" films of the 1930s and 1940s.[23] Political issues and events are often topical and are frequently also issues of social concern. As a result, as Robert Sklar noted, even though American movies often reflect established ideologies, they have also, on occasion, "altered or challenged many of the values and doctrines of powerful social and cultural forces in American society, providing alternative ways of understanding the world."[24]

These challenges to mainstream ideology, however, are seldom completely successful, nor are they easily accomplished. The filmmaker's task is to balance political critique with a well-developed character-centered drama, all without erring too much in either direction. An overt political critique supported by a threadbare drama would most likely result in a box-office failure, whereas a narrative too focused on the individual character and the idiosyncratic dilemma would either dull or extinguish the critical grounds the film stakes out. Prince called this "the unresolved dialectic informing American political filmmaking: topicality without sustained commitment, passion without analysis."[25] Thus, concluded Prince, "Expressing a critical politics with critical cinematic forms has always been very difficult in the American cinema."[26]

Oliver Stone is one of the most successful directors working in Hollywood today. He is also a liberal filmmaker with an overtly political agenda who is adept at balancing this critique with box-office success. Able to create passionate character-centered dramas with strong audience appeal, Stone delivers films that contain liberal assessments of thirty years of American cultural and political life. Stone is something of an anomaly in Hollywood, however, because, like a few other notables, he not only directs but also scripts or coscripts his films' screenplays. He is also able to finance and make the films he wants without "selling his soul to the company store." Although it is extremely difficult for liberal or leftist filmmakers to express an explicitly political vision inside the American commercial film industry, Oliver Stone, "with $40 million per film at his disposal and virtually unlimited media access," is, in one critic's words, the new Golden Calf, who "has recast the idols in the heart of the Temple."[27]

Since Stone's reconstruction of social actualities through mythological and rhetorical frameworks accounts, in part, for his films' power and popularity, I now turn to a discussion of the Judeo-Christian mythology, Jungian psychology, and perennial philosophy that are so central to Stone's representation of American political and cultural life.

The Perennial Journey Home

From the perspective of perennial philosophy, the "felt fragmentation" of the modern age is a result of our desire for the next stage of evolutionary consciousness being stymied by our inability either to give up ego identity or to see it as a part rather than a whole, as a transition rather than a final stage in the development of consciousness. This exigency invites individuals and cultures to search for stories that offer transcendence and freedom from the fear of ego death. Oliver Stone's films respond to this exigency by, in Carl Jung's words, *"dream[ing] the myth outward"* (emphasis mine). His films depict heroes who perennially slay the monsters of modern rationality, battle with their own shadow, and plumb the depths of the collective unconscious in a search for the next phase of teleological development, represented, in Stone's films, by either a return to the Garden (preconsciousness) or a seeking of the new Garden (transconsciousness).

Perennial philosophy asserts that the ultimate goal for the individual and the culture is unitive knowledge of Jung's divine Ground made possible by movement from preconsciousness through consciousness to transconsciousness. In this development, as Janice Hocker Rushing has explained:

> The human psyche evolves . . . from an unconscious state of absolute oneness with Spirit, through consciousness of its separation from Spirit, to conscious transcendence of boundaries in a reuniting of itself with Spirit. The evolution of consciousness matures from matter to body to mind to soul to Spirit. Or, to put it another way, it grows from *preconsciousness* (matter and body) to *consciousness* (ego/mind) to *transconsciousness* (soul and Spirit).[28]

What perennial philosophy refers to as teleological evolution, Jung called individuation—"the process by which a person becomes a psychological 'in-dividual,' that is, a separate, indivisible unity or 'whole.'"[29] For Jung, individuation is achieved by exploring our personal and collective unconscious. Whereas the personal unconscious consists of repressed personal memories and experiences, including the shadow, the collective unconscious is made up of "archaic" or "primordial types," "universal images that have existed since the remotest times."[30] "Identical in all,"[31] the collective unconscious is made available to culture and the individual through archetypes. Archetypes, manifestations of the unconscious, are expressed in cultures' myths and fairy tales.[32] Not only disseminated "by tradition, language, and migration," they can also "rearise spontaneously, at any time, at any place, and without any outside influences."[33] "Meant to attract, to convince, to fascinate, and to overpower," archetypes are links to the past and harbingers of future teleological development. In Jung's words, "That is why they always give man [sic] a premonition of the divine while at the same time safeguarding him from immediate experience of it."[34] It is through archetypes, Jung asserted, that "the union of conscious and unconscious contents is consummated. Out of this union emerge new situations and new conscious attitudes"—what Jung called the "transcendent function."[35] Individuation thus represents both an individual and a universal evolution. Jung's "transcendent function" is equivalent, in other words, to a culture's teleological movement toward transconsciousness.

In psychological terms, the collective unconscious represents that which is pre-egoic. In the language of perennial philosophy, it represents preconsciousness, the historical period before the development of civilization and rationality. The infant's developing ego, in other words, parallels the history of humanity's developing ego consciousness. Indeed, the history of teleological evolution, according to Jung, is the history of the emergence of consciousness from a pre-egoic state. Jung, for example, described primitive humanity's attempts to consolidate a newly emerging fragile consciousness and its profound fear of falling back into an unconscious state:

> The unconsciousness no sooner touches us than we *are* it—we become unconscious of ourselves. That is the age-old danger, instinctively known and feared by the primitive man, who himself stands so very close to this pleroma. His consciousness is still uncertain, wobbling in its feet. It is still childless, having just emerged from the primal waters. A wave of the unconsciousness may easily roll over it, and then he forgets who he was and does things that are strange to him. . . . All man's strivings have therefore been directed towards the consolidation of consciousness.[36]

Jung asserted that the emergence of consciousness was most likely a "tremendous experience for primeval times, for with it a world came into being whose existence no one had suspected before."[37]

From the perspective of Jungian psychology and perennial philosophy, the heroes are the ones able to try out the next stage of human consciousness—to act as philosophical test pilots for an entire culture. Jung explained that these heroes, "as bringers of light, that is, enlargers of consciousness . . . overcome darkness, which is to say that they overcome the earlier unconscious state."[38]

Reaching the next level of consciousness, however, requires the hero to slay or overcome the gods of his age. In the era of preconsciousness, for example, "the hero's main feat is to overcome the monster of darkness: it is the long-hoped-for and expected triumph of consciousness over the unconscious."[39] So in the Golden Age of heroes in Greek mythology, for example, male figures such as Pericles, Jason, Achilles, Hector, and Odysseus had to face the monsters and villains of preconsciousness in order to liberate the ego identity just beginning to emerge. These monsters or villains were represented by the "Great Mother" or "Great Goddess" worshiped during the era of preconsciousness. These female figures became the dragons to be slain, however, because they represented obstacles impeding the emergence of ego consciousness and thus the rise of civilization. Jung called the battle between consciousness and preconsciousness the "paternal principle, the 'Logos,' which eternally struggles to extricate itself from the primal warmth and primal darkness of the maternal womb; in a word, from the unconsciousness. . . . Unconsciousness is the primal sin, evil itself, for the 'Logos.' Therefore its first creative act of liberation is matricide."[40]

Although the emergence of ego consciousness is a necessary step in the evolution of culture and consciousness, in Jungian terms, it is a "Luciferian deed" ("There is a deep doctrine in the legend of the fall: it is that expression of a dim presentiment that the emancipation of ego-consciousness was a Luciferian deed").[41] There is a price to be paid, in other words, for liberation from the realm of preconsciousness. Prometheus, for example, the god who brings fire to the Greeks and thus initiates the dawn of civilization—the evolution from preconsciousness to consciousness—is punished by the gods and chained to the rocks of Caucasus.[42] In the modern era of consciousness, when the age of great heroes has passed, the gods of rationality and science—the saviors of the previous age—become the demons and monsters that must either be overcome or better integrated into our collective psyche. The ego, no longer the hero, is now the villain to be defeated. This is because science, technology, and rationality, which represent the ego phase of development, separate us from the irrational, the mythical, and the spiritual—the realm with which we must be reunited in order to advance to the next phase of teleological development.

Jung believed that in order for the current era of consciousness to achieve the next level of transconsciousness (individuation) we must reunite ourselves with the Great Mother and the collective unconscious. Ascent (teleological evolution) must be preceded by descent, once again, into the collective unconsciousness. To explain this idea Jung related the Gnostic tale of the son sent by his father "to seek the pearl that fell from the King's crown":

> It lies at the bottom of a deep well, guarded by a dragon, in the land of the Egyptians—the land of fleshpots and drunkenness with all its material and spiritual riches. The son and heir sets out to fetch the jewel, but forgets himself and his task in the orgies of Egyptian worldliness, until a letter from his father reminds him what his duty is. He then sets out for the water and plunges into the dark depths of the well, where he finds the pearl on the bottom, and in the end offers it to the highest divinity.

The moral of the story? "We must surely go the way of the waters, which always tend downward, if we would raise up the treasure, the precious heritage of the father."[43] Such a return to the realm of the unconscious, however, is not regressive, because, as Jung explained, the unconscious has a "Janus-face": "on the one side its contents point back to a preconscious, prehistoric world of instinct, while on the other side it potentially anticipates the future—precisely because of the instinctive readiness for action of the factors that determine man's fate."[44]

In the process of plumbing the depths of our collective unconsciousness "the meeting with oneself is, at first, the meeting with one's own shadow." The shadow, coincidental with the personal unconscious, "personifies everything that the subject refuses to acknowledge about himself and yet is always thrusting itself upon him directly or indirectly—for instance, inferior traits of character and other incompatible tendencies."[45] Like the collective unconscious, the shadow is "a living part of the personality," which "cannot be argued out of existence or rationalized into harmlessness."[46] Exploration of our own shadow is unpleasant—if not terrifying—for many, since, as Jung noted, "nothing is more disillusioning than the discovery of our own inadequacy."[47] The shadow must be faced, however, since it is the guardian at the gate of the unconscious. The shadow represents, in Jung's words,

> a tight passage, a narrow door, whose painful constriction no one is spared who goes down to the deep well. But one must learn to know oneself in order to know who one is. For what comes after the door is, surprisingly enough, a boundless expanse full of unprecedented uncertainty, with apparently no inside and no outside, no above and no below, no here and no there, no mine and no thine, no good and no bad. It is the world of water, where all life floats in suspension; where the realm of the sympathetic system, the soul of everything lives, begins; where I am indivisibly this *and* that; where I experience the other in myself and the other-than-myself experiences me.[48]

To enter into the collective unconscious the individual must first pass through the door of the shadow.

In mythology, entering the shadow and into the unconscious realm that lies beyond is represented by the hero's "night sea journey," his descent into a cave, an underworld, or a state of sleep, silence, or passivity.[49] He must pass some time in this place before emerging newly born and prepared for the battles that lie ahead. Joseph Campbell explained it this way:

> The first work of the hero is to retreat from the world scene of secondary effects to those causal zones of the psyche where the difficulties really reside, and there to clarify the difficulties, eradicate them in his own case (i.e., give battle to the nursery demons of his local culture) and break through to the undistorted, direct experience and assimilations of what C. G. Jung has called "the archetypal images."[50]

This passage is often "symbolized in the worldwide womb image of the belly of the whale."[51]

In order to advance his development and the development of the culture for which he is primary champion, the hero must learn that external battles with enemies of the flesh, although sometimes necessary, are secondary to internal battles with the soul. The hero's central conflict, in other words, is the dynamic dialectic between the conscious and unconscious. The hero's quest is to descend into the unconscious, to pass the gate of his shadow, and to spend some time in the womb of sleep, silence, or passivity in order to achieve a great pearl of wisdom. The boon, the precious gift the hero shares with the culture, is this: We have the ability to explore our own shadow, to plumb the depths of our collective unconscious without dwelling there indefinitely, so that we can achieve transconsciousness.

The paradox of this journey is that it is, in Campbell's words,

> a labor not of attainment but of reattainment, not discovery but rediscovery. The godly powers sought and dangerously won are revealed to have been within the heart of the hero all the time. . . . From this point of view the hero is symbolical of that divine creative and redemptive image which is hidden within all of us, only waiting to be known and rendered into life.[52]

The archetypal hero's journey, in other words—whether to Oz, Ithaca, or Nirvana—is to go "home," back to the place s/he has always been.

The angst and felt fragmentation of the modern era, according to Jung, is our failure to explore the archetypal realm of the unconscious. It is our inability, in other words, to "go home." As a result, we find ourselves imprisoned in a meaningless world. As Jung explained, "whether he understands them or not, man must remain conscious of the world of the archetypes. . . . A view of the world or a social order that cuts him off from the primordial images of life not only is no culture at all but, in increasing degree, is a prison or a stable."[53] Jung elaborated on this warning by noting that if the "link-up" with the unconscious "does not take place, a kind of rootless consciousness comes into being no longer oriented to the past, a consciousness which succumbs helplessly to all manner of suggestions and, in practice, is susceptible to psychic epidemics."[54] Modern cultures, according to Jung, have failed to tap into the transcendent possibilities of the collective unconscious. We have made science our god and reduced art to mere entertainment. Although "our intellect had achieved the most tremendous things," "in the meantime our spiritual dwelling had fallen into disrepair."[55] We find ourselves "uprooted and alienated in a de-souled world."[56] We live in an age where "heaven has become for us the cosmic space of physicists, and the divine empyrean a fair memory of things that once were. But 'the heart glows,' and a secret unrest gnaws at the root of our being."[57]

According to perennial philosophy, our failure to achieve transcendence is a result of our inability to give up ego identity. Although the individual or the culture may desire transcendence, this transcendence implies the "death" of the isolated self. Although our individual and collective goal is "to be delivered out of separate selfhood in time and into eternity as realized in the unitive knowledge of the divine Ground,"[58] this unitive knowledge "can come only to those who are prepared to '*die to self*' and so make room, as it were, for God" (emphasis mine).[59] This involves the "realization of the Self as within and yet transcendentally other than the individual ego."[60]

Although we experience ourselves as bodies separated in space and time, according to perennial philosophy, this is an illusion insofar as we are all connected with each other and with the universe. Rushing noted that "Einstein called this separate self-sense 'an optical delusion of . . . consciousness . . . a kind of prison for us, restricting us to our personal desires and to affection for a few persons nearest us. Our task must be to free ourselves from that prison.'"[61] Right Belief, the first step in Buddha's Eightfold Path, as explained by Aldous Huxley, is "the all too obvious truth that the cause of pain and evil is craving for separative, ego-centered existence, with its corollary that there can be no deliverance from evil, whether personal or collective, except by getting rid of such craving and the obsession of 'I,' 'me,' 'mine.'"[62]

Instead of attempting evolution, in the age of ego consciousness we repress or sublimate our awareness of transconsciousness to ego identity by finding ways to leave our mark, build bigger buildings, or claim our fifteen minutes of fame. The ego worship of the modern era, in other words, invites us to make over gods in our own image and to envision the world as a playground for our own selfish desires. In the end we paradoxically race against the clock that is death in an effort to make death meaningful, despite having lost the ability to move to the next level of consciousness out of fear of death itself. Unable to let go of its focus on ego/mind, modern society is stuck at the level of consciousness.

Although yearned for, transcendence to the next level of consciousness is also not a given. Rushing explained "that the reaching of this telos is not absolutely predetermined. Rather humans, individually and collectively may choose whether or not to transform themselves to the next stage of consciousness."[63] Open to "human choice and praxis," transcendent potential "creates both the responsibility and the necessity for rhetorical discourse."[64] The contemporary "exigence of felt fragmentation," to use Rushing's words, invites cultures to search for stories or myths that offer transcendence and a way free from the fear of ego death.

In Jung's interpretation, culture's role is to "*dream the myth outward* and give it a modern dress" (emphasis mine). This is because archetypes are never explained away or discarded, since "even the best attempts at explanation are only more or less successful translations into another metaphorical language."[65] As a result, "we are confronted, at every new stage in the differentiation of consciousness to which civilization attains, with the task of finding a new *interpretation* appropriate to this stage."[66] The problem with the contemporary age, however, is that we are separated from our archetypes and we do not "dream the myth outward"—we have failed to find "new interpretations" of the myths in the current era. As a result, "our concern with the unconscious has become a vital question for us—a question of spiritual being or non-being."[67]

Oliver Stone's films, collectively and individually, "dream the myth outward"; they offer a vision of the next stage of teleological development.

Stone's protagonists, with greater and lesser success, are willing to face their shadow, plumb the depths of the unconscious, and search for the next phase of teleological development. This requires them to slay the monsters of modern rationality, which often means slaying themselves in either an ego death or a messianic sacrifice. Attempting to move culture to the next level of consciousness, Stone's protagonists seek transconsciousness and, in effect, speak to us as time travelers through the void. Beckoning like prophetic visionaries of the dormant possibilities of the human spirit, they are the prototypical seeds from which the next generation of heroes might emerge.

Despite these heroes' teleological mission, however, or perhaps even because of it, they remain flawed moralists, confronting, as does their audience, the postmodern condition. Stone's heroes, in this interpretation, are like the lesser heroes of the Iron Age after the great heroes of the Golden Age have disappeared—lamenting the loss of the unconscious and the death of the Great Mother. Wailing and gnashing their teeth in an effort to get us back to the Garden, or in an effort to move beyond the level of consciousness to transconsciousness—the new Garden—as we will see, many of these heroes find themselves hung up on the sharp edge of the postmodern world.

Mythmaking in a Postmodern World

Scholars have long recognized the power and impact of mass media on political attitudes, values, and conceptions of history. This impact has increased with the dawn of the telepolitical age. We now live in a time when the political media consultant is a permanent fixture of senatorial and presidential staffs, when "a 30-second political spot can make or break a candidate,"[68] and when the epitome of political "discourse" is often the "photo opportunity" or the political film.[69] We now also know that few people learn about politics directly and that for most of us our "political realities" are mediated through the mass media.[70] In short, "the mass media have become the 'central nervous system' for our society and the major source of public information about politics."[71]

Popular films are often significant sources of political and cultural knowledge of the world. This is because films, "parasocial vehicles [that reveal] the very parameters of human society," often act as "iconographic shorthand for political communication."[72] In analyzing the power of films, scholars have claimed, among other things, that films project "collective images, fantasies, and values of the culture in which [they are] created."[73] Able to inform, persuade, and reinforce existing attitudes and beliefs, films are a "potent vehicle for symbolizing sociopolitical change" and for expressing cultural archetypes.[74]

Along with television, popular films have become the modern American storyteller. But how well they function in this role depends on their success at tapping into the fears, fantasies, and desires of millions of American filmgoers.[75] Scholars who have explored American films' portrayals of political issues and events argue that popular films often help audiences assimilate experiences by providing a "mechanism that allows us to make sense retrospectively by storytelling in the present, drawing on events in the past."[76] Or, more specifically, films provide "images and narratives that permit a political and social coding of the meaning of the past and the present."[77] Popular films, cinematic shorthand for the past, often function to shape that past and make it usable.[78] Films that depict or reconstruct specific historic events and personae are often particularly compelling simply because these films—representations of an era removed from actual events of that time—offer stories that may become the "textbooks" for an entire generation.

Throughout time we retain images of the bards of old telling stories to audiences gathered around hearth fires. Ideally these bards helped audiences make sense of the vague, quirky, and mysterious universe in which they lived. Stories from the mythological past, if they "rang true," served to explain everything from the workings of the human heart to the mysteries of the movements of the stars. These myths, neither false nor true, were social stories conceived and shaped over time. They possessed specific rhetorical functions, were told in mythic language, and evolved and changed as they were passed down.

This conception of the oral storyteller of antiquity is very different from literate modernity's conception of the historian. Although the ostensible function of history in modernity is the same as in premodernity—to make sense of the past for those living in the present in order to conceive of a future—Western society's understanding of the historian's role has changed. In modernity, the historian's job is to bring some objective knowable past to life, to reanimate it through symbolic expression. In Martin Medhurst's words, this involves the discovery of "facts, documents, statistics, and other forms of data which then are assimilated into a coherent whole—an interpretation—that comes as close as possible to approximating 'the way it was' or 'what actually happened.'"[79]

In contrast to modernity's historian, the historian in postmodernity, like the Homeric bards, sees the task much differently. It involves, as Medhurst explained, the creation of reality "through critical engagement with the various symbolic constructions of the past. . . . These constructions are then brought into dialogue with other 'histories' in an ever-swelling chorus of voices."[80] In postmodernity, then, history, like mythology in primary orality, is rhetorical by necessity, by design, and in effect.

Stone himself challenges contemporary understanding of the role of history, noting, "I do not believe in the collective version of history."[81] When questioned about his interpretation of the events surrounding Kennedy's assassination, for example, he declared: "What is history? Some people say it's a bunch of gossip made up by soldiers who passed it around a campfire. They say such and such happened. They create, they make it bigger, they make it better. I knew guys in combat who made up shit. I'm sure the cowboys did the same. The nature of human beings is that they exaggerate. So, what is history? Who the fuck knows?"[82] Implicit in Stone's words is a commentary on the rhetorical nature of history and the role of storytelling in shaping that history.

Paradoxically, however, despite Stone's acknowledgment that postmodern history may represent a dialogue among many truths, he seems to search in his films for *the* truth. Stone himself, as storyteller, is caught on the cusp between modernity and postmodernity. "'I have truth in the eyeball,' the director who's been called the Wagner of Hollywood has said of his style. 'If you guys don't see it because you have to be further back because it's punching you in the face, it's your problem. I can't change the way I see the world.'"[83] An old college friend of Stone's once said of him that "you had the sense that he was obsessed about getting to what he thought was the truth of things. He gave you the impression that he would do anything—take drugs, commit murder, *anything*—in order to get to the truth."[84] It is Stone's search for *the* truth in his films that hints at a seemingly paradoxical Platonic stance in the face of postmodernity.

The paradox is that the Platonist, as perennial philosopher king, must know the truth, must believe that he or she knows the truth, and must be certain that the knowledge of this truth is absolute and unequivocal. This position is revealed to many as arrogance in a postmodern world. Stone, a crusader for his version of the truth, like all perennial prophets, may be absolutely convinced of the veracity of his message. His films, however, fall prey to the same dilemma that Stone himself faces. As rhetorical history, as symbolic expressions of one man's truth, they are often labeled by critics as representations, not the embodiments of Platonic ideals that Stone asserts them to be. In other words, Stone's "shadow plays"—his filmic allegories projected on the wall—are arguments based upon the plausible and the possible that are necessarily undermined by their own claims to immutable veracities. Stone is left, then, like his characters, with the need to accept his own definition of history as rhetorical. As a result, Stone's films are often viewed as brilliant, but sometimes "flawed," postmodern morality plays.

Stone implicitly seems to acknowledge this quality in his work, as for example, in this comment: "More and more I feel that movies are not reality, but an approximation of reality, and in some cases, a wish fulfillment. It's an eternal human quality: the need to believe in something better. Life doesn't often work out that way, but movies do."[85] *Time* magazine's Richard Corliss, noting the rhetorical historicity of Stone's film *JFK*, explained:

Superficially, movies are a persuasive medium because they exist in the present tense, not the conditional. Each picture is happening before our eyes, each Stone film fantasy is, for the moment it is on the screen, the moviegoer's reality. But because films are fictions—because even a naive viewer knows Kevin Costner is an actor playing a moviemaker's interpretation of a man named Jim Garrison—the events they portray need not be factual, or even probable; they must only be plausible. Through his art and passion, Stone makes *JFK* plausible, and turns his thesis of a coup d'état into fodder for renewed debate. The movie recognizes that history is not only what we are told to believe; often it is gossip that becomes gospel.[86]

Stone's film *JFK,* like all of his films that either allude to or represent historical figures and events, enters the debate about truth, adds to the fodder from which historicity is forged, and ultimately makes its bid for the "gossip that becomes gospel"—the "way it was" or may be for the next generation of students of history.

Stone, like the prophets of old, teaches his audience through allegory and myth. According to one critic, there is a "powerful gothic strain in his work, which had reemerged in the Melville-cum-Faustian fables of *Platoon,* and *Wall Street* and the concentrated craziness of *Talk Radio.*"[87] The same charge can also be made, I will argue later, about *JFK, Born on the Fourth of July, Salvador, The Doors, Heaven and Earth,* and *Natural Born Killers.* Christina Appy has noted that "Stone is constantly basting [his films] with a mythic sauce." Stone's films are allegories, morality tales filled with stock characters who represent all of the various virtues and vices found in Pandora's box. Stone's characters are often like Greek gods, railing against human injustice, folly, and vice to provide mere mortals with lessons on how to live and work.

However, because of the mythic and allegorical qualities of Stone's films, critics have often claimed that his characters are two-dimensional icons that do not come to life for audiences. Said one critic: "Stone breezes past the richer complexities of 'mere' realism in his furious pursuit of grandiose, movie-derived iconography . . . his method of either mangling or shrinking the issues to fit the faceless, mythic demands of his own sensibility seems meretricious."[88] Speaking of the character Jim Morrison in *The Doors,* another critic noted that "where Morrison is concerned, Stone never met a metaphor he didn't want to cast in bronze and bounce off your skull."[89] Still another observed that although Val Kilmer's portrayal of Morrison "is physically convincing" it can only be an impersonation since "what the script . . . gives him to play is the icon, not the man."[90] Some of the same criticisms were raised about Stone's *Wall Street.* James Lardner, for example, asserted that "Stone and his cowriter, Stanley Weiser, appear to have approached their subject with their eyes on the big picture—on Wall Street itself—rather than on characters, relationships, scenes, etc."[91] Another called *Wall Street* "an old-fashioned liberal morality play that could have been written and directed by one of the Hollywood Ten in the late 1940s."[92] Yet another critic levied a similar charge against *Born on the Fourth of July*, claiming, "What makes *Born on the Fourth of July* so remarkable is the way it inflates Kovic's testimony to epic proportions. For the price of your ticket, you get a grand-scale re-recreation of the Vietnam War; a drama about Everyvet."[93]

The iconic, two-dimensional qualities of Stone's characters are not surprising insofar as parables are vehicles to reveal a "truth" through stories made intelligible to the people. Allegorical figures, designed to represent various traits such as greed, innocence, and deceit, are often two-dimensional. However, when constructing allegorical characters filled with all of the vices and virtues found in Pandora's box, Stone encounters a problem: When he gets to the bottom of the box, Stone, like his audience, often finds that even hope has fled as well. So instead of hope, a teleological vision for the future, Stone often presents us with nothing more than impotent rage. David Denby, speaking of Tom Cruise as Ron Kovic in *Born on the Fourth of July*, says that "the movie takes [Cruise/Kovic] down to the depths of degradation, and then part of the way back. And through it all, he wails and howls, like a figure in a Greek tragedy crying out to the gods."[94] Stone's films themselves seem to howl at the viewer in all their powerless rage at a corrupt system, a lost Eden, or some tarnished Camelot. His films pose the perennial question: Are we, like Sisyphus, doomed to roll the same rock up the same hill for an eternity? Is there no hope for change? No possibility for teleological evolution to the next stage of consciousness?

Oliver Stone, like the philosopher king in Plato's allegory of the cave, offers an interpretation of the shadow play upon the wall. Stone, like Christ, speaks to his audience with parables "because seeing they do not see, and hearing they do not hear, nor do they understand."[95] Stone, contemporary society's new bard, tells tales around the mass-mediated campfire in order to make sense of our collective mythological past. On the one hand, Stone, the Platonist, is a proclaimer of the truth, the philosopher king whose job it is to enlighten the masses about the "way it was" in the Garden before the Fall. On the other hand, Stone, the relativist or postmodern philosopher, acknowledges that the "Garden" before the Fall is an idealistic myth and that reality is in the eye of the beholder. It is this dilemma, or paradox, however, with which Stone's films and Stone's characters do battle, often resulting in their own destruction or immolation in the flames of impotent rage.

Film critic Robin Wood made a similar argument about Stone's films but from a slightly different perspective. Wood has argued that although films such as *Wall Street* and *Platoon* do not represent Stone at his best, they present the "quandary" of the American left-wing intellectual: "What does one fight for within a system one perceives as totally corrupt but in which the only alternative to capitulation is impotence?" He added that Stone's work so far is structured on the absence of an available political alternative, which could only be a commitment to what is most deeply and hysterically tabu in American culture, a form of Marxist socialism. . . . In both *Salvador* and *Born on the Fourth of July* the protagonist declares, at a key point in the development, "I am an American, I love America," and we must assume he is speaking for Stone. But we must ask, *which* America does he love, since the American actuality is presented in both films as unambiguously and uniformly hateful? What is being appealed to here is clearly a *myth* of America, but the films seem, implicitly and with profound unease, to recognize that the myth cannot possibly be realized, that capitalism *must* take the forms it has historically taken. Hence the sense one takes from the films of a just but impotent rage: without the availability of the alternative there is no way out.[96]

Basing his argument on this perception, Wood considered Stone's film *Talk Radio* "central to his work, to the point of being confessional." Wood explained that the rage of the main character, Barry Champlain, "toppling over into hysteria, parallels the tone of much of Stone's work and identifies one of its sources, the frustration of grasping that no one really listens, no one understands, no one *wants* to understand; the sense of addressing a people kept in a state of mystification so complete, by a system so powerful and pervasive, that no form of brainwashing could improve on it."[97] So it is not surprising then that "to ask Stone's heroes to shut up a little is to carve away at the very prickly vitality that makes them worthy of being placed at the eyes of Stone's hurricanes. These men talk, with the knowledge that, as Barry Champlain puts it, 'Sticks and stones may break my bones, but words cause permanent damage.'"[98]

Speaking of people of his generation, Stone noted:

For us, it starts with the Kennedy stuff, that's where the betrayal begins. Our lifetime is about betrayal as Americans. We all grew up believing in Howdy Doody. Ron (Kovic) did, I did. You have value systems you were taught to believe in, and our parents were not really practicing those values, they were practicing adultery and lying and cheating and all the things that make life *human*, in the Balzacian sense of the word. So we are caught in that internal struggle between (that and) our idealism for an era that may never have existed—Dwight Eisenhower maybe and early Ronald Reagan. Idealism versus real life, the absolutist strain versus the relativist strain. And the absolute man generally goes nuts, as Nietzsche said. You have to learn to swing.[99]

Yet Stone seems to be torn in the middle between these two strains—the absolutist and the relativist. On the one hand, he is a proclaimer of the truth, the philosopher king whose job it is to enlighten the masses about the "way it was," in Vietnam in the 1960s and 1970s, in Central America, and America, during the 1980s and 1990s. Yet, on the other hand, as a relativist, he acknowledges that the Garden before the Fall may be an idealistic myth and that reality is in the eye of the beholder. When thinking back to the 1960s and what that era meant to him, Stone said, "the Eros of that era shows—such an incredible sense of color. And it's nice to remind people that such a thing happened, that for this brief moment in time, there would be a Camelot. That's a wonderful dream to hold on to and to look back on. You have to pass the torch."[100]

Conclusion

Popular films are significant sources of political and cultural knowledge of the world. Along with television, they have become the modern American mythmakers, telling stories that draw on our collective past to make sense of the present so that we can conceive of a future.

Oliver Stone is a contemporary and controversial filmmaker: a perennial mythmaker for our times. Like the prophets of old, Stone teaches his audience with allegory and myth—urging us forward on the path of cultural and teleological development. His films' success, as well as the controversies surrounding them, is due, in part, to their refraction of political events and personae through a mythological lens. His films are often controversial because of the clash between modern and postmodern conceptions of history's function and long-standing beliefs about the role of fiction film in American society. Stone's films are successful, however, because individually and collectively they are underpinned by mythological frameworks that tap into the collective psyche of the modern age. His films tell an all too well-known tale of America's fall from grace with the deaths of Martin Luther King, Jr. and John F. Kennedy in the 1960s, our descent into the hell that became Vietnam in the 1970s, and our search, even now, for alternative visions, for new Camelots for the 1990s and into the next millennium. This American story is effectively framed in Stone's films within a universal story—or rather, a perennial story—of the evolution of human consciousness: We have moved from a premodern Paradise to a modernity marked by the devils and demons of rationality, science, and technology, and even now, despite the complex challenges of postmodernity, we move on to fashion a new Garden that will usher in humanity's reunion with the cosmos.

The central "flaw" in Stone's morality plays, however, is that Stone's protagonists/heroes—perennial philosophers searching desperately for the next stage of teleological consciousness in a post-Kennedy Camelot—rail against the imperfect but perfectible nature of humanity, only to find themselves hung up on the sharp edge of the postmodern world. Because so many of Stone's films are either constructed around historical personae, such as lead singer Jim Morrison of The Doors or President John F. Kennedy, or allude to historic events, such as the U.S. support for the Nicaraguan Contras, critics often attack their historical accuracy. As we have seen, numerous popular debates have raged around Stone's treatment of history and truth.

Stone, however, claims to be a dramatist before he is a political film-maker: "I think what links all my films—from *Midnight Express* to *Scarface, Salvador, Platoon,* and *Wall Street*—is the story of an individual in a struggle with his identity, his integrity, and his soul. In many of these movies, the character's soul is stolen from him, lost, and in some cases he gets it back in the end."[101] Whether disillusioned heroes of the Iron Age or perennial time travelers through the void, Stone's heroes seek the Garden carrying only whatever hope might be found at the bottom of Pandora's box—and in the face of postmodernity, we, like these heroes, remain unsure if any hope is really there.

Notes

1. Gary Crowdus, "Personal Struggles and Political Issues," *Cineaste* 16 (1988):21.

2. Joseph Campbell, *The Hero with a Thousand Faces,* Bollingen Series 17 (Princeton: Princeton University Press, 1973), 25.

3. Campbell, *Hero,* 104.

4. Janice Hocker Rushing, "*E.T.* as Rhetorical Transcendence," *Quarterly Journal of Speech* 71 (1985):188–203.

5. Stone commented, "I was never a religious person—I was raised Protestant, the great compromise" (Oliver Stone, interview by Richard Corliss, *Time,* 23 December 1991, 61).

6. Oliver Stone, as quoted by Alexander Cockburn, "Oliver Stone Takes Stock," *American Film* 13 (December 1987):22.

7. Stone, interview, 61.

8. Cockburn, "Oliver Stone Takes Stock," 25.

9. Pat McGilligan, "Point Man," *Film Comment* 23 (February 1987):13.

10. McGilligan, "Point Man," 12.

11. "Stone's Throw from an Oscar," *Economist,* 21 March 1987, 106.

12. "Unorthodox Behavior," *Economist,* 16 March 1991, 91.

13. Ibid., 91.

14. Stone, interview, 61.

15. Robin Wood, *International Dictionary of Films and Filmmakers,* ed. Nicholas Thomas (Chicago: St. James Press, 1991), 809.

16. *The Motion Picture Guide: The Films of 1987,* ed. Jay Nash and Stanley Ross (Evanston, IL: Cine Books, 1988), 320.

17. Stuart Klawans, review of "*Born on the Fourth of July,*" *Nation,* 1 January 1990, 28.

18. Stanley Kauffman, speaking specifically of *The Doors* ("Stanley Kauffman on Films," *New Republic,* 1 April 1991, 26).

19. Stephen Prince, *Visions of Empire: Political Imagery in Contemporary American Film* (New York: Praeger, 1992).

20. Richard Maltby, "Made for Each Other: The Melodrama of Hollywood and the House Committee on Un-American Activities, 1947," in *Cinema, Politics, and*

Society in America, ed. Philip Davies and Brian Neve (New York: St. Martin's Press, 1981), 77.

21. Terry Christensen, *Reel Politics* (New York: Basil Blackwell, 1987), 213.

22. Prince, *Visions of Empire,* 3.

23. Ibid.

24. Robert Sklar, *Movie-Made America* (New York: Random House, 1975), 316.

25. Prince, *Visions of Empire,* 197.

26. Prince, *Visions of Empire,* 88.

27. Andrew Kopkind, *"JFK:* The Myth," *Nation,* 20 January 1992, 40.

28. Rushing, *"E.T.* as Rhetorical Transcendence," 190.

29. Carl Jung, *The Archetypes and the Collective Unconscious,* trans. R. F. Hull (Princeton: Princeton University Press, 1990), 275.

30. Jung, *Archetypes,* 5. Archetypes, according to Jung, have never been in consciousness, are not individually acquired, and instead "owe their existence exclusively to heredity" (42).

31. Jung, *Archetypes,* 3–4.

32. According to Jung, archetypes are often expressed in cultural "forms that have received a specific stamp and have been handed down through long periods of time" (*Archetypes,* 5).

33. Ibid., 79.

34. Ibid., 8.

35. Ibid., 289.

36. Ibid., 22.

37. Ibid., 167.

38. Ibid., 169.

39. Ibid., 167.

40. Ibid., 96.

41. Ibid., 230.

42. Jung noted that "the spirit that dared all heights and all depths must, as Synesius says, suffer the divine punishment, enchainment on the rocks of Caucasus" (*Archetypes,* 96).

43. Ibid., 18.

44. Ibid., 279.

45. Ibid., 284–285.

46. Ibid., 20.

47. Ibid., 23.

48. Ibid., 21–22.

49. See, for example, Campbell, *Hero,* and Jung, *Archetypes.*

50. Campbell, *Hero,* 17–18.

51. Ibid., 90.

52. Ibid., 39.

53. Jung, *Archetypes,* 93.

54. Ibid., 157.

55. Ibid., 16.

56. Ibid., 109.

57. Ibid., 24.

58. Aldous Huxley, *The Perennial Philosophy* (New York: Harper and Row, 1970), 207.

59. Ibid., 21.

60. Ibid., 207.

61. Rushing, "*E.T.* as Rhetorical Transcendence," 190.

62. Huxley, *Perennial Philosophy,* 202.

63. Rushing, "*E.T.* as Rhetorical Transcendence," 191.

64. Ibid.

65. Jung, *Archetypes,* 160.

66. Ibid., 157.

67. Ibid., 24.

68. Some recent examples of this are the "Willy Horton" and the "revolving prison door" political advertisements produced by Roger Ailes for George Bush's successful 1988 campaign against Michael Dukakis.

69. See, for example, Susan Mackey-Kallis, "Spectator Desire and Narrative Closure: The Reagan 18-Minute Political Film," *Southern Journal of Communication* 39 (1991):1–17.

70. Dan Nimmo and James E. Coombs, *Mediated Political Realities* (New York: Longman, 1983).

71. Robert Denton, foreword in Prince's *Visions of Empire*; Robert Denton and Gary Woodward have argued for three ways in which mass media influence American politics. The media determine the agenda for topics of discussion, debate, and action; they give substance and shape to world events by constructing the political realities to which we respond; and they reduce abstract ideological principles to human and personal visions of politics. *Political Communication in America* (New York: Praeger, 1990).

72. Robert Savage, "The Stuff of Politics Through Cinematic Imagery: An Eiconic Perspective," in *Politics in Familiar Contexts*, ed. Robert Savage and Dan Nimmo (Norwood, NJ: Ablex, 1990), 119–120.

73. Janice Hocker Rushing and Thomas Frentz, "The Rhetoric of *Rocky*: A Social Value Model of Criticism," *Western Journal of Speech Communication* 42 (1978):64–65.

74. Ibid., 64; see also Janice Hocker Rushing and Thomas Frentz, "*The Deer Hunter*: Rhetoric of the Warrior," *Quarterly Journal of Speech* 66 (1980):392–406.

75. Nimmo and Coombs, *Mediated Political Realities,* 105.

76. Prince, for example, has provided a book-length treatment of four definitive cycles in contemporary Hollywood film production in relation to prominent political agendas in the 1980s. He analyzes American popular films as they responded to and shaped America's understanding of, for example, U.S. policies and activities in Central and South America, visions of the Cold War and communism, America's involvement in Vietnam, the crisis in confidence in American business, and the increase in societal alienation, fragmentation, and rage in American society during the 1980s (*Visions of Empire*).

77. Ibid., 151.

78. George Dionisopoulos, "Images of the Warrior Returned: Vietnam Veterans in Popular American Films," in *Cultural Legacy of Vietnam: Uses of the Past in the Present,* ed. Richard Morris and Peter Ehrenhaus (Norwood, NJ: Ablex, 1990), 83.

79. Martin Medhurst, "The Rhetorical Structure of Oliver Stone's *JFK*," *Critical Studies in Mass Communication* 10 (1993):129. Film is merely the most recent ruler of mythic language. It is also, perhaps, the most effective storyteller and transmitter of myth. Thomas Benson explained that in an audience's experience of any film "eventually visual images become not primarily iconic (resemblances) or indexical (evidences) but symbolic—visual shorthand for a variety of social myths" ("Joe: An Essay in the Rhetorical Criticism of Film," *Journal of Popular Culture* [1974]:611). Film as narrative argument takes on the role of providing stories that "ring true" with audiences' experiences in the world. See, for example, Walter Fisher's treatment of narrative as rhetorical argument in "Narration as a Human Communication Paradigm: The Case of Public Moral Argument," *Communication Monographs* 51 (1984):1–22.

80. Medhurst, "Rhetorical Structure," 129.

81. Crowdus, "Personal Struggles and Political Issues," 21.

82. Quoted in Robert Sam Anson, "The Shooting of JFK," *Esquire,* November 1991, 93.

83. Quoted in ibid., 94.

84. Quoted in ibid., 96.

85. Quoted in Cockburn, "Oliver Stone Takes Stock," 23.

86. Richard Corliss, "Who Killed J.F.K.?" *Time,* 23 December 1991, 68.

87. Kim Newman, *International Dictionary of Films and Filmmakers,* ed. Nicholas Thomas (Chicago: St. James Press, 1990), 786.

88. Devin McKinney, review of *"Born on the Fourth of July," Film Quarterly* 44 (fall 1990):46.

89. Richard Combs, review of *"The Doors," Sight and Sound* 1, 1 (1991):7.

90. Terrence Rafferty, "The Current Cinema," *New Yorker,* 11 March 1991, 82.

91. James Lardner, review of *"Wall Street," Nation,* 23 January 1988, 97.

92. *Motion Picture Guide: The Films of 1987,* 319.

93. Stuart Klawans, review of *"Born on the Fourth of July," Nation,* 1 January 1990, 29.

94. David Denby, "Days of Rage," *New York,* 18 December 1989, 101.

95. After Christ tells his disciples the parable of the sower, he concludes, "He who has ears, let him hear." In those who do not listen, Christ continues, is fulfilled the prophecy of Isaiah: "You will be ever hearing but never understanding; you will be ever seeing but never perceiving. For this people's heart has become calloused; they hardly hear with their ears, and they have closed their eyes. Otherwise they might see with their eyes, hear with their ears, understand with their hearts and turn, and I would heal them" (Matt. 13:13, Standard American Version); see also Medhurst, "Rhetorical Structure."

96. Wood, *International Dictionary of Films and Filmmakers,* 810.

97. Ibid.

98. Robert Horton, "Riders on the Storm," *Film Comment* 27 (March 1991): 58.

99. Mark Rowland, "Stone Unturned," *American Film* 16 (1991):43.

100. Ibid., 43.

101. Crowdus, "Personal Struggles and Political Issues," 21.

two

Betrayal in the Garden and Death of the Dream

We're through-the-looking-glass people here. White is black and black is white.

—Jim Garrison, *JFK*

For we know in part, and we prophesy in part. But when that which is perfect is come then that which is in part shall be done away. . . . For now we see through a glass, darkly; but then face to face: now I know in part; but then shall I know even as also I am known.

—Paul, 1 Cor.

The defeats are also battles.

—Pancho Villa (as quoted by Oliver Stone)

JFK, released in 1991, represents Oliver Stone's argument regarding America's betrayal by its leaders and the consequent expulsion of Americans from the Garden that was Camelot. Stone, in various interviews, has asserted that President John F. Kennedy's death was a seminal event for himself and for millions of others. He has claimed, "It changed the course of history. It was a crushing blow to our country and to millions of people around the world. It put an abrupt end to a period of innocence and great idealism."[1] Stone asserted that if Kennedy had lived it would have been a very different world:

> It would have been a much healthier place. The massacre in Southeast Asia would not have occurred. The cycles of poverty and recession were fueled by

Oliver Stone directing Kevin Costner (Jim Garrison) in *JFK*. Copyright © 1991
Warner Bros. Inc., Regency Enterprises V.O.F. and Le Studio Canal+.

the war economy of Johnson. Inflation resulted on a massive scale. The whole
economic world shifted as a result of the Vietnam War. . . . The forces that
killed Kennedy did not operate in a vacuum. That parallel covert government
has existed through the last 28 years. Lawrence Walsh couldn't bring Oliver
North and that bunch to justice. It's a mentality that won't go away.[2]

JFK, by Stone's own admission, is an attempt to wake the American people
up to the downward slide in society and government following Kennedy's
assassination. What is truly at stake in Kennedy's assassination and its subsequent cover-up, according to Stone, is democracy itself:

The issue of our times—as the media keep repeating—is democracy. Real
democracy is not some illusion and must be based on truth told to the people. . . . If Kennedy was killed by a political conspiracy of his opponents and it
has been covered up, then our so-called democratic system has betrayed us.
The real issue is trusting the people with their real history. . . . Only then can
we start to have a real democracy. *JFK* strikes a blow for that open debate.[3]

According to *Esquire*'s Robert Anson, "Stone decided by the time he was
writing his award-winning script for *Midnight Express* that the Kennedy
assassination had turned the American universe upside down. Before the
killing, he believed, all had been right; after it, all wrong."[4] Alexander
Cockburn, in discussing *JFK,* said, "The core notion here is that something
good (the presidency, JFK's secret agenda for peace, the aims of the Found-
ing Fathers) has been betrayed."[5] According to *Time* magazine, Stone puts

the trial of Oliver North and the entire Iran-Contra affair in the same category as the assassinations of King, John F. Kennedy, and Robert Kennedy, all of which are portrayed as part of a "parallel government catering to various worldwide military and industrial interests."[6]

Kennedy's death, in other words, represents America's "fall from grace" and the "descent into hell" that was to become Vietnam. *JFK* is Stone's wake-up call to the American people about the slippery-slope ethics that have guided the United States since the assassination of the Kennedys, the beginning of the Vietnam War, the rise of the military-industrial complex, the rampant excesses of unchecked capitalism, and the political liability of misguided American foreign policy in places like Chile, Nicaragua, El Salvador, and Panama.

But *JFK* is about more than the attempt to restore Camelot—the particularly American version of the myth. The film, like many of Stone's films, is best viewed in the larger framework of Judeo-Christian mythology. It tells the story of an obsessed crusader for the truth, New Orleans District Attorney Jim Garrison (Kevin Costner), the only figure in history to bring a defendant to trial for conspiracy to kill President John F. Kennedy. Garrison is the clearest incarnation of a messianic figure in any of Stone's films. As Jim Morrison in *The Doors* says, "the shaman has a vision and then the whole tribe is healed." President John F. Kennedy, according to *JFK*, possessed such a vision, a vision that if he had lived to carry out would have healed the American tribe. *JFK*, for example, expresses the oft-quoted hypothesis that Kennedy planned to gradually withdraw American troops from Vietnam, effectively ending our involvement in Southeast Asia before it truly began. Near the end of the film, Garrison says to the jury empaneled to try Clay Shaw for conspiracy to murder J.F.K., "What took place on November 22nd, 1963 was a coup d'état. Its most direct and tragic result was the reversal of President Kennedy's commitment to withdraw from Vietnam." Kennedy's assassination, according to *JFK*, ended this plan. Although Kennedy failed, his spirit is reincarnated in the form of Jim Garrison, a second hero following in the footsteps of the first.

Jim Garrison, in Stone's estimation, is "a lonely but determined crusader battling overwhelming odds in the interest of truth and the American way."[7] Like Richard Boyle in *Salvador,* Barry Champlain in *Talk Radio,* and Jim Morrison in *The Doors,* Garrison challenges the complacency of the American public and its tendency to passively accept the lies of the government and mass media. As Corliss has claimed, "The film is a call for a kind of informed innocence. Stone says: Open your eyes wide, like a child's. Look around. See what fits."[8] And like Boyle in *Salvador,* Bud Fox in *Wall Street,* and Ron Kovic in *Born on the Fourth of July,* Garrison, over the course of the film, learns to see and through seeing is enlightened about the corruption of the American political system.

Garrison, however, like all messianic heroes, needs to suffer a rite of passage, or "die to his self," to be worthy of his role. Just as Christ spends three days in the tomb after his earthly death and before his resurrection, Garrison, in *JFK*, suffers for three years in the dark before awakening to the "truth" of Kennedy's assassination. Garrison, like the classic hero of mythology, needs to descend into the darkness, or pass some time in a place of sleep, silence, or passivity, before he can be reborn. Once he emerges from this darkness, however, he truly sees, possessing a vision, like Kennedy's, that will guide and heal the American people. No longer duped by appearances—the cover-up of the Kennedy assassination conspiracy—Garrison, the second hero, can carry on the crusade of the first. However painful the journey might be, Garrison, Kennedy's "son," is able to ascend from Plato's "cave of darkness," where the people are entertained by the mere shadow play of appearances upon the wall, into the blinding light of the truth. Garrison, after waking from three years of sleep, is able to see things as they truly are instead of "through a glass darkly." Although "white is black and black is white," he is now able to invert the logic and make sense of what David Ferrie calls the "mystery wrapped in a riddle, inside an enigma" that is Kennedy's assassination.

Stone, like Garrison, is also Kennedy's son, continuing the search for the truth regarding Kennedy's murder that Garrison, and many others like him, began. According to Corliss, Stone "sees himself as a modern movie Garrison, a brave man vilified for unearthing the sordid cleansing truth."[9] Stone seemed to imply this role for Garrison and himself when he said, "One hopes [*JFK*] would make people want to strip away the lies and covert operations. A couple of lunatics like Jim Garrison keep saying, hey, wake up, something happened. People like me, sons of Jim Garrison, promulgate the theory."[10]

We, the audience, are also Kennedy's and Garrison's sons and daughters, called upon by Stone to continue the search for the truth. *JFK,* for example, ends with the epitaph, "The past is prologue. Dedicated to the young—in whose spirit the quest for truth marches on." Stone's *JFK* urges all Americans, and particularly young Americans, to carry on the crusade that Garrison began, the crusade that Stone continues with his films, despite persecution or ridicule: to search out not only the truth regarding Kennedy's assassination, but also the truth behind the lies told to us by our government, our media, and our corporate institutions. Only then, Stone implies, can we heal the festering wound that is, in Garrison's words, "the secret murder at the heart of the American Dream" and restore Camelot to its former glory.

Medhurst, in his analysis of *JFK,* draws a similar conclusion regarding Garrison's and our role. He has argued that the film is "an extended metaphor" for "the loss of innocence and humankind's capacity to restore it." It is about a world "plunged into darkness" by Kennedy's assassination. But it is a world in which hope still exists, "a hope embodied in the second Kennedy, a man who also believes in truth and justice and who, through his investigation of the assassination, will resurrect the spirit that was stolen from the American people on November 22, 1963."[11] Medhurst has drawn on the "Adam Myth," the story of humanity's fall from grace, to argue that Garrison is the "second Adam" who will restore the world "to its original state of innocence through a spiritual rebirth."[12]

Garrison is an atypical Stone "savior," however, because even though Garrison, the man, earned a reputation as a less than squeaky-clean public servant—numerous accusations of underworld connections and bribing of witnesses emerged during Clay Shaw's conspiracy trial—Kevin Costner portrays Garrison as a noble, if somewhat obsessed, protector of the people's right to know. This is atypical insofar as Stone's saviors are usually seedy characters, physically or psychologically unappealing in some way. James Woods as Boyle in *Salvador*, for example, with his pockmarked face, his lean and hungry body type, and his protruding eyes, represents a "naturally" unappealing Stone protagonist. Eric Bogosian, as Barry Champlain in *Talk Radio,* is rendered grotesque by Stone's use of extreme close-ups to highlight his sweaty, blemish-filled face. Even Tom Cruise, cast against type as Ron Kovic in Stone's *Born on the Fourth of July*, manages to look physically unattractive with lank, unwashed long hair, a drooping moustache, and a sagging beer belly. Woody Harrelson's Mickey, Stone's over-the-top muscle-bound serial killer in *Natural Born Killers,* is perhaps the best example of an unappealing Stone protagonist. Costner's portrayal of Garrison, however, was often compared to James Stewart's portrayal of Mr. Smith in the Frank Capra classic *Mr. Smith Goes to Washington.* According to one critic, Stone also made such a comparison: "The D.A., Stone said, was somewhat like a Jimmy Stewart character in an old Capra movie— someone who undertakes to investigate something that had been covered up. He makes many mistakes. He has many frustrations. He has few successes. He is reviled, ridiculed, and the case he brings to trial crashes."[13] Corliss claimed that "Costner's summation is right out of an old Frank Capra movie in its declaration of principles in the face of murderous odds. Lost causes, as Capra's Mr. Smith said, are the only causes worth fighting for."[14] Thus, according to Frank Beaver, "*JFK* resulted in a different kind of Stone film—one with more bathos than edge, a cause movie rather than a caustic one."[15]

Possibly because of Stone's squeaky-clean rendition of him, Garrison is also a less complex figure than many of Stone's heroes. On a teleological level he is not as advanced as other Stone protagonists such as Mickey and Mallory in *Natural Born Killers*, Jim Morrison in *The Doors,* or Le Ly Hayslip in *Heaven and Earth*. This is because his actions are always external

In a setting reminiscent of a Frank Capra film, New Orleans District Attorney Jim Garrison (Kevin Costner) fights "City Hall" and media opinion in a contentious battle for truth regarding President Kennedy's assassination in *JFK*. Copyright © 1991 Warner Bros. Inc., Regency Enterprises V.O.F. and Le Studio Canal+.

to him and because good and evil are always portrayed as distinct entities in his battle to uncover the truth beneath the dissimulations of the American government and the mass media. Unlike other Stone protagonists, he has yet to turn inward and confront the lessons of the unconscious and his shadow self. As a result, on a teleological level, as we will see, Garrison is best seen as a bridge hero between modern and transmodern consciousness.

Although *JFK* was not the first film to adopt a conspiracy perspective regarding the assassination of President John F. Kennedy, it has certainly been the most popular and most widely criticized conspiracy film. As previously noted, *JFK* also has the distinction of being one of only a few films in U.S. history that has prompted political action as a result of its release. In many ways, it is also the most sophisticated and complicated of Stone's films, taking as its theoretical polemic the search for the "truth" with the realization that there is no single, ultimately knowable truth about the Kennedy assassination. As such, *JFK* warrants considering at some length the circumstances surrounding the film's production, its critical and popular response, and the political actions resulting from its release. In particular, the debate surrounding *JFK*'s portrayal of the Kennedy assassination provides an unusual opportunity to explore the issues of filmic representation, historical accuracy, journalistic integrity, and artistic license played out against the background of this controversial film.

The *JFK* Debate

Critics' and journalists' response to *JFK* was immediate, passionate, and primarily negative. It soon became fashionable to engage in "*JFK* bashing." According to one *Los Angeles Times* article, the "'*JFK* knocking business has thus far consumed 1.2 million words.' It had filled 27 columns in the *New York Times* alone. It has produced a Big Brother cover on *Newsweek* warning the world 'not to trust this movie.'"[16] One critic went so far as to argue that "shaping up in the news media has been something close to a 'Stop Oliver Stone' campaign."[17]

Time magazine quickly became one of Stone's central detractors, claiming that by connecting himself with "the far-out fringe of conspiracy theorists, filmdom's most flamboyant interpreter of the 1960s . . . may wind up doing more harm than homage to the memory of the fallen president."[18] "His history is bogus and his aesthetics questionable," averred Alexander Cockburn.[19] Conservative columnist George Will particularly hated the film, charging: "In his three-hour lie, Stone falsifies so much that he may be an intellectual sociopath, indifferent to truth. Or perhaps he is just another propagandist frozen in the 1960s like a fly in amber, combining moral arrogance with historical ignorance . . . *JFK* is an act of execrable history and contemptible citizenship by a man of technical skill, scant education and negligible conscience."[20]

Despite the wealth of passionate arguments against *JFK* by its detractors, a significant number of critics applauded Stone's efforts. Andrew Kopkind, writing for the *Nation*, called *JFK* a "historic achievement." *New Statesman and Society* writer John Pilger labeled the film "an American version of *Repentance*," concluding that "like Costa Gavras' *Missing* and Oliver Stone's earlier *Salvador*, *JFK* got through the gates and the guardians—and those who adopt their language—understandably are disappointed and incensed."[21] Exclaimed another sympathetic critic, "It does strike me that if the Vietnam War is fair game for revisionism, so is the Kennedy assassination."[22] *Newsweek*'s David Ansen also applauded Stone, noting, "Real political discourse has all but vanished from Hollywood filmmaking; above and beyond whether Stone's take on the assassination is right his film is a powerful, radical vision of America's drift toward covert government. What other filmmaker is even thinking about the uses and abuses of power?"[23]

The central criticisms of Stone's film had to do with its depiction of U.S. history, its threat to traditional interpretations of events and characters in the Kennedy assassination, Stone's use of dramatic license in depicting events, and the film's potential impact on a generation of youth too young to remember the actual events surrounding Kennedy's assassination.

One of the major concerns of liberal and conservative journalists and film critics alike was *JFK*'s potential effect on a generation of young people for whom television and film are the textbooks for lessons in U.S. history and politics: "'We live in a media age,' says film critic Leonard Maltin. 'If a television or theatrical movie can paint a vivid enough picture for young people, they'll believe that's the way it was.' That's clearly what Oliver Stone is hoping will happen. 'JFK' is not just an entertainment. It's a work of propaganda."[24]

Other journalists seemed to challenge this argument and implicitly support Stone's right to his version of the Kennedy assassination. One writer, presumably speaking for the twenty-something generation, whose minds grownups were afraid *JFK* would pollute, challenged this type of patronizing argument, claiming:

> One objection to *JFK* that keeps cropping up is this: Grownups with $40 million budgets should not "rewrite" history because this is Very Bad For Our Nation's Youth who will suddenly and irrevocably Lose Faith in America's Great Institutions. What's more, it's disrespectful of a National Tragedy that should politely have faded away by now. I maintain that Stone's pot-pourri of sometimes sickening, often didactic, sometimes hilarious discrepancies is Good For Young People because it gives them a splendid opportunity to sharpen their Critical Thinking.[25]

Nora Ephron, a filmmaker who has herself been accused of taking liberties with historical "facts" in films such as *Silkwood*, echoed this sentiment, saying, "Older people are worried younger people will get the notion that the Joint Chiefs of Staff killed JFK—so what if they do? I don't know why they think this anymore than I do—and who cares? Eventually they will grow up and figure it out for themselves. Or else they won't. It's not the filmmaker's responsibility."[26]

Why the swift and predominantly negative response to Stone's *JFK*? Many journalists felt that Stone's film was attacked because it threatened traditional interpretations of events and characters in the Kennedy assassination and challenged the credibility of those "interpreters." Danny Schechter, a radio journalist who was in the process of making a documentary about *JFK*'s production, believed that "journalism's response is coming out of an institutional guilt complex of not having done the kind of investigative job it could have into the Kennedy assassination. . . . Journalists collectively feel like Oliver Stone is treading on their turf."[27] Seeming to concur with this explanation for journalists' attack on his film, Stone implicated the mass media's handling of the Kennedy assassination by arguing that although the media are not entirely conscious of it, "there is such a form of informational equilibrium that preserves the status quo . . . you can virtually call it silent consent."[28] In an angrier mood, Stone charged that the "media establishment" gets nervous "when art gets political," particularly when they disagree with the politics of the artist's viewpoint. He also asserted, "When this priesthood is challenged as the sole or privileged interpreters of *our* history they bludgeon newcomers, wielding heavy clubs like 'objectivity' and charging high crimes like 'rewriting history.'"[29]

It seemed to Stone that the "Stop Oliver Stone" campaign was almost a sinister example of the same type of conspiracy in government and the mass media that he was criticizing in *JFK*. As he explained, "There's an agenda here. They're controlled in certain ways. . . . Let's not be naive. . . . This controversy is meant to kill off the film, precensor it and maximize negative advanced impact . . . What this indicates is that they are scared. When it comes to President Kennedy's murder, they [the media] don't want to open the doors. They don't want the first inch of inquiry to go on."[30]

Some journalists seemed to agree with Stone's conspiracy explanation for the media's attack on *JFK*. Pilger, for example, told the story of a fellow journalist who wrote "one laudatory paragraph" about Stone's film and "ended up having to resign after her editor killed it 'on principle.'" "'My job,' said the principled editor, 'is to protect the [*Washingtonian*] magazine's reputation.' These are the words that threatened his magazine's reputation: 'If you didn't already doubt the Warren Commission report, you will after seeing Oliver Stone's brilliantly crafted indictment of history as an official story. Is it the truth? Stone says you be the judge.'"[31]

Another criticism of *JFK* had to do with its depiction of historical events. Journalists, for example, raised a host of questions about filmmakers' responsibility to historicity. When asked in an interview with *Time* magazine if he felt filmmakers "had a responsibility to historical fact," Stone replied, "Whenever you start to dictate to an artist his 'social responsibility' you get into an area of censorship. I think the artist has the right to interpret and reinterpret history and the events of his time. It's up to the artist himself to determine his own ethics by his own conscience."[32] Other critics pointed out that Stone's frequent defense of *JFK* was that although the film contained speculations, individual facts were thoroughly researched. Whenever a particularly speculative claim was made in the film, Stone would present the scene in sepia-tone to set it off from others. Stone concluded about his choices in *JFK*, "I feel I've behaved responsibly. I've done all my homework."[33]

In response to Stone's commitment to historical accuracy, Stone's defenders claimed that "Stone has every right to do what he does."[34] Stone himself consistently denied one of the central claims of his critics—that his version of the Kennedy assassination was the definitive truth. As he said, "Our movie is a metaphor for all those doubts, suspicions, and unanswered questions. The movie is not, as Lardner [of the *Washington Post*] suggested, the

'Jim Garrison story.' It does use the Garrison investigation as the vehicle to explore the various credible assassination theories, and incorporates everything that has been discovered in the 20 years since Garrison's efforts."[35] "I'm not interested in pinning the murder on specific individuals," claimed Stone. "I'm interested in the whydunit as opposed to the whodunit."[36] And Stone explained in another interview, "In making *JFK*, my point was not to indict individuals, but to understand history. . . . The Clay Shaw trial is over, but the larger question—who killed Kennedy and why?—still persists."[37] Further, "If the movie is cut the way I think it is going to be cut . . . I think you will leave the theater ready to think about things and, I hope, rethink them, and begin to wonder about some of the givens, some of the sacred cows, some of the official story. Because that's what I think the Warren Commission is. It is America's official story."[38]

In response to the journalists' attack on *JFK*, Stone frequently asserted that the filmmaker is allowed to interpret and reinterpret history as seems fitting: "Filmmakers make myths. They take the true meanings of events and shape them. D. W. Griffith did it in *Birth of a Nation*. In *Reds*, Warren Beatty probably made John Reed better than he was [but] was truthful in a mythic sense. I made Garrison better than he is for a larger purpose."[39]

In another interview with *Time*, Stone made a similar argument about *JFK*'s mythic, or "counter-mythic" status. Admitted Stone: "So I'm giving you a detailed outlaw history or counter-myth. A myth represents the true inner spiritual meaning of an event. I think the Warren Commission was a myth, and I think this movie, hopefully, if it's accepted by the public, will at least move people away from the Warren Commission and consider the possibility that there was a coup d'état that removed President Kennedy."[40]

Stone was aided in his claim of dramatic license to create countermyths by such liberal critics as Andrew Kopkind, who claimed that Stone's method in *JFK* "is to substitute another myth . . . for the 'official' one that seems to have been a comfort for so long but is so shot full of holes by now that it can barely float."[41] Kopkind went on to compare what Stone did in *JFK* with what John Ford did in *December 7th*, a film about the bombing of Pearl Harbor in World War II that mixes historical reconstructions and documentary footage, while offering historical speculations and mythic interpretations of everyday individuals.

Some critics, however, would not let Stone get away with his "mythic" explanation to avoid criticism of his film's lack of historical accuracy. According to one, the central problem with Stone's claim to *JFK*'s mythic status was that "Stone tries to have it both ways. He maintains that *JFK* is all true, until someone insists forcefully that it isn't. Then he tacks the other way and says he is trying to construct an alternative 'myth.'"[42]

Other critics, by contrast, seemed to concur with Stone's assessment of the filmmaker's job and the constraints operating on anyone working in the docudrama genre. As one critic remarked:

The problem with *JFK* . . . is the problem of the docudrama. A movie or a television show that re-creates history inevitably distorts history. It has to compress things into a short span; it has to extract clarity out of the essential messiness of life; it has to abide by certain dramatic conventions: major scenes, major characters, major speeches. All this makes for exaggeration. "It's like writing history with lightning," explained Woodrow Wilson when he saw the first docudrama, "Birth of a Nation," in 1915.[43]

Another critic added: "Movies are, almost by definition, a demagogic art form: they can emotionally persuade you of just about anything, which is precisely why Stone's movie will be dissected with vehemence. An entire generation of filmgoers is hereafter going to look at these events through Stone's prism. If history is a battlefield, 'JFK' has to be seen as a bold attempt to seize the turf for future debate."[44]

Stone acknowledged the larger rhetorical purpose of *JFK*, and at times, seemed to shift the debate away from *JFK*'s role as history to focus on the film as a catalyst for further critical exploration into the Kennedy assassination and for political action regarding the push for declassification of the remaining Warren Commission files. He urged:

The American public should demand access to the files of the House Select Committee (sealed until 2029). And a public inquiry should get underway about the CIA [Central Intelligence Agency]. They should be reined in. They were supposed to gather intelligence originally, not practice covert operations and destabilize governments. As an intelligence-gathering apparatus, they have been sorely remiss recently on the Soviet Union as well as in Iraq and Iran. Maybe the movie can contribute to a climate for reform.[45]

Stone's film did indeed contribute "to a climate for reform" by stirring up the still-muddy waters surrounding the Warren Commission's single-assassin, single-bullet conclusion regarding Kennedy's murder. The January 13, 1992, issue of *Newsweek,* for example, reported that the majority of letters to the editor about *Newsweek*'s December interview with Stone supported Stone's challenge to the Warren Commission. Many letter writers felt that "Stone had performed a 'wake-up' service that should have been provided by the nation's press."[46]

Nine months later, on October 26 of that same year, President George Bush signed into law the President John F. Kennedy Assassination Records Collection Act of 1992. The bill provided for the establishment of an independent commission charged with releasing all government records related to Kennedy's assassination except those that clearly jeopardized personal privacy or national security. President Bush remarked upon the occasion of the bill's passage, "I sign the bill in the hope that it will assist in healing the wounds inflicted on our Nation almost three decades ago."[47] Despite all of the controversy that surrounded *JFK*, Stone seemed to have gotten his wish. The unstated irony of such a moment was, for some, the realization that

George Bush, the United States' first ex-CIA president, presided over the declassification of documents that Stone's *JFK* implied were repressed by the CIA in the first place; furthermore, the "wounds inflicted on our Nation almost three decades ago" of which Bush speaks, were wounds, according to Stone's version of events, inflicted by the CIA and the military-industrial complex to begin with. Bush, in other words, was only helping to clean up his own agency's mess.

In summary, journalists' response to *JFK* was swift and predominantly negative, as "*JFK* bashing" rapidly became journalists' favorite sport. Their central criticisms had to do with *JFK*'s depiction of U.S. history, its threat to traditional interpretations of the assassination events, Stone's use of dramatic license in depicting events, and the film's potential impact on Americans too young to remember Kennedy's assassination. Never shy about entering the media fray, Stone quickly responded to his critics by defending his right to offer a countermyth to what he considered the official myth of the Warren Commission Report. Stone and other critics claimed that the "Stop Oliver Stone" campaign was either coming out of journalists' institutional guilt for failing to cover the assassination thoroughly or it was a media conspiracy to destroy Stone's credibility. Despite the film's numerous detractors, however, many film critics lavished *JFK* with praise, often excusing the liberties Stone took with historical events by pointing out the inherent difficulties with docudrama as a genre. Regardless of whether he was flattered or angered by the responses to his film, however, Stone's larger purpose seemed to be to shift the debate regarding Kennedy's assassination away from the "who" to the "why" and, more important, to the release of then classified files regarding Kennedy's assassination. With the release of many of these files by Congress in 1992, Stone got his wish. Although more and more information regarding Kennedy's murder becomes available to the public on a regular basis, questions about who shot Kennedy and why still remain unanswered for millions of Americans today.

Perhaps what is most fascinating about the debate that erupted around Stone's *JFK* is not the various arguments put forward but that the debate occurred at all. That a Hollywood filmmaker's interpretation of a historic event could cause such strong reactions in journalists and film critics alike points to film as a powerful cultural voice and to the filmmaker as the new bard of the mass-mediated campfire. The debate also highlights the problematic nature of historical interpretation and the realization that modernist definitions of historicity, like modernist definitions of reality, are quickly being challenged in a postmodern world.

JFK: The Analysis

JFK provided Stone with his greatest technical, logistical, and emotional challenge. With a running time of three hours and eight minutes and composed of over one hundred scenes and two hundred speaking roles, the film rates as Stone's longest and most complicated film to date. Stone's initial attraction to the project stemmed from his interest in former New Orleans District Attorney Jim Garrison's 1988 book *On the Trail of the Assassins.* Wanting to broaden the appeal and political context of the film, however, Stone eventually drew on various assassination theories and books, such as Jim Marrs's *Crossfire: The Plot That Killed Kennedy.* Stone and Zachary Sklar, Jim Garrison's editor for *On the Trail of the Assassins,* wrote the script together.

Shooting began in April 1991. Shot in Dallas, Washington, D.C., and New Orleans over a period of eighty days at a cost of $40 million, the film required the restoration of four square blocks of downtown Dallas to achieve period accuracy. At first denied the opportunity to shoot in the Texas School Book Depository by Dallas officials, Stone fought and eventually won access. The film was released by Warner Brothers in December 1991.

Although many fiction films and documentaries have been made about John F. Kennedy's assassination, *JFK's* precursor, in many ways, is a 1973 film called *Executive Action,* which also hypothesizes that the conspiracy to kill Kennedy involved high-ranking members of the so-called military-industrial complex.

Stone establishes his thesis regarding Kennedy's assassination from the film's beginning. The film opens with historical footage of President Dwight D. Eisenhower's now famous farewell speech, in which he coins the phrase "military-industrial complex" and cautions against its growing power in the United States:

> Now this conjunction of an immense military establishment and a large arms industry is new in the American experience. The total influence—economic, political, spiritual—is felt in every city, every statehouse, every office of the federal government. We must guard against the acquisition of unwarranted influence—whether sought or unsought—by the military-industrial complex. We must never let the weight of this combination endanger our liberties or democratic processes.

Eisenhower's speech is interspersed with a montage of images from the 1960s—historical footage of such things as the Vietnam War, J.F.K.'s election, clips of John F. Kennedy's speeches, Martin Luther King, Jr., Malcolm X, and Fidel Castro. These clips provide a background for the development of Stone's explanation of the "who" and "why" of Kennedy's murder. In the style of a newsreel commentary, we hear in voice-over:

> November 1960, JFK wins one of the narrowest election victories in history over Nixon. He inherits a secret war against the communist Castro dictatorship in Cuba, a war run by the CIA and angry Cuban exiles. Castro is a successful revolutionary frightening to American business interests in Latin America. This

war culminates in the Bay of Pigs invasion in April 1961 when Kennedy refuses to provide air cover for the exiled Cuban brigade. Kennedy, taking public responsibility for the failure, privately claims the CIA lied to him and tried to manipulate him into ordering an all-out American invasion of Cuba.

In October 1962 the world comes to the brink of nuclear war when Kennedy quarantines Cuba after announcing the presence of offensive Soviet nuclear missiles ninety miles off American shores. Soviet ships with more missiles sail towards the island but at the last moment they turn back. The world breathes with relief. In Washington, rumors abound that JFK had cut a secret deal with Russian Premier Khrushchev not to invade Cuba in return for Russian withdrawal of missiles. Suspicions abound that Kennedy is soft on communism.

During this commentary, we see historical footage of Kennedy's 1963 speech at American University in Washington. This address is interspersed with black-and-white and color photos and home movies of the Kennedy family, of John Kennedy as a boy and as a young man. Over these images, we hear President Kennedy explain: "What kind of a peace do I mean and what kind of a peace do I seek? Not a Pax Americana, enforced in the world by American weapons of war. We must examine our own attitudes towards the Soviet Union. Our most basic common link is that we all inhabit this small planet. We all breathe the same air. We all cherish our children's futures, and we are all mortal." This address is followed by a scene, also in black-and-white, of a woman being unceremoniously dumped from a moving car onto a country road, intercut with historical footage of President Kennedy's fateful arrival at the San Antonio airport. We see shots of this mysterious woman in a hospital bed on the edge of delirium, moaning repeatedly to the attendant doctors, "They're going to kill Kennedy. Call somebody. Let's stop 'em. These are serious fucking guys." Finally, we witness historical re-creations of Dealey Plaza mixed with clips from the now famous Magruder film of Kennedy's ride through the plaza. Shots ring out as we once again experience the murder of President John F. Kennedy on that fateful day in downtown Dallas, Texas, on November 22, 1963.

Seven minutes into the film, Stone has established his thesis regarding why Kennedy was killed, who did the shooting, and the significance of his assassination for America. Kennedy, according to Stone, had angered the confluence of interests that were labeled the military-industrial complex by his predecessor, Dwight D. Eisenhower. He had failed to call the all-out air strike against Cuba that would have protected American business interests and appeased the hawks in Congress and the military, whose main foreign policy goal was combating communism around the world while making money doing so. By negotiating with Khrushchev, Kennedy further angered the CIA and provoked charges that if he was not a communist sympathizer, he was at least a communist patsy. Kennedy implies in his address at American University that he would pursue a policy of détente rather than using military force to solve problems with the Soviet Union and in Vietnam. The CIA, possibly in conjunction with the mob, needed to eliminate him as the central stumbling block to their political, economic, and military interests around the world. Kennedy's assassination in Dealey Plaza was a fait accompli, according to Stone, as far back as his November 1960 election as president. As a result of Kennedy's murder and its successful cover-up by all parties involved, Americans, in Eisenhower's prophetic words, continue to let "the weight of this combination [the military-industrial complex] endanger our liberties [and] democratic processes." Kennedy, a prophet with a vision of humanity that rose above the merely national ("Our most basic common link is that we all inhabit this small planet. We all breathe the same air. We all cherish our children's futures, and we are all mortal"), was gunned down before he could enact the policies to achieve this vision. The dream was slain before it had a chance to take root in the hearts of the American people. Ego consciousness—protecting our interests and ensuring the triumph of American capitalism around the world despite the costs—replaced the glimmer of hope, the new way of conceiving humanity's evolution, which was to have been the dream of Camelot.

We should be ashamed to be Americans, as Stone quickly reminds us in the scene that follows. It is here that we are introduced to New Orleans District Attorney Jim Garrison, interrupted in his office by his assistant, Bill, with the news of Kennedy's shooting. Both hurry down to a local bar to watch the unfolding events on television. Garrison, Bill, and the bar patrons watch as the television plays what we recognize as historical footage of a CBS news bulletin about Kennedy's assassination. The news anchor is Walter Cronkite, a giant of modern television journalism. Visibly shaken, Cronkite removes his glasses and announces, "From Dallas Texas, apparently official, President Kennedy died at 1:00 P.M. Central Standard Time, two o'clock Eastern Standard Time, some thirty-eight minutes ago." Through Cronkite's emotions we, the audience, experience or possibly re-experience our own emotions that surround this event. Garrison, also shaken by Cronkite's pronouncement, echoes words that are meant to apply to every American then and now when he exclaims, "God, I'm ashamed to be an American today."

By passively accepting the death of the Kennedy spirit, we allow the continued triumphs of individuals like Guy Bannister (Edward Asner)—also watching the news of Kennedy's assassination from another New Orleans bar—who proclaims with joy upon the announcement of Kennedy's death, "That's what happens when you let the niggers vote. They get together with the Jews and the Catholics, they elect an Irish bleeding heart. Here's to the new frontier, Camelot in smithereens!" The "new frontier," our hope of teleological evolution, has been reduced to turf protection, immigrant hate, and an us-versus-them mentality. The Guy Bannisters of the world, backed by the mob, the CIA, and members of the military-industrial complex, will continue to win, the film tells us, if we allow them to destroy the dream that was just beginning to emerge in John F. Kennedy's vision of the "new frontier."

As the plot of *JFK* develops, Garrison is alerted to the possibility of a local connection regarding Lee Harvey Oswald. Accordingly, Garrison sets up a meeting with his senior investigators for the next day. This meeting, called for Sunday morning, is the first of a number of Sunday meetings that will take place between Garrison and his investigative team—Sunday meetings that culminate in the early morning Easter Sunday meeting between Garrison and New Orleans businessman, and suspected conspirator, Clay Shaw.

Stone's choice of Sunday for the meeting days in the developing investigation is far from coincidental. Each of the three Sunday meetings—this one; a 7:30 A.M. "walking tour" through the French Quarter with Garrison's investigation team later in the film; and the final Easter meeting with Clay Shaw—invites a messianic framework of interpretation. Sunday, and particularly Easter Sunday—the day Christians celebrate Christ's resurrection from the tomb, his triumph over death, and, metaphorically, their own triumph over death and their resurrection in Christ—connotes Garrison's own pending messianic status. He will take on the role of "savior" of the American Dream, first played by Kennedy, in order to "resurrect the spirit that was stolen from the American people on November 22, 1963."[48]

Garrison's messianic status as savior of the American Dream, however, is only achieved after his having been asleep to the truth regarding Kennedy's assassination for three years.[49] His sleeping, on a messianic or mythological level, refers to the "death" or submersion of the hero/savior into darkness before his ascent, or "waking," into light and enlightenment. Like Jonah's three days in the belly of the whale, like Christ's three days in the tomb before his resurrection, Garrison's three years must be spent stumbling in the darkness of lies, deceit, and confusion before he discovers the truth regarding Kennedy's death.

Our first glimmer of Garrison's awakening begins as we witness him burning the midnight oil and endlessly scanning one of the volumes of the Warren Commission Report in growing disbelief. The scene begins with a close-up of a mantel clock. The time reads three o'clock in the morning. As the camera pans from the clock to Garrison, we hear the clock chime the third hour. We then see a montage of rapidly edited images; a close-up shot of the words in the book Garrison is reading slowly overexposed to a blinding white light, a close-up of a microphone, an ashtray with a lit cigarette and a man's pair of glasses, a shot of a man (Mr. Bowers) wearing glasses that reflect a strong glare, a close-up of a Dallas police officer wearing a Dallas Police Department insignia on his lapel (as he moves slightly the gold initials throw a blinding white glare), a shot of a freight car filled with

transients backlit with the harsh light of the sun, another shot of Mr. Bowers with light reflecting off his glasses, shots of the embankment at Dealey
Plaza, a shot of a shattered car windshield with Mr. Bowers slumped dead
over the wheel, a shot of white glare through trees, and a close-up of one
lens of a pair of eyeglasses.

The "reflected glare off glass" motif implies that the truth regarding
Kennedy's assassination is hard to see. We, like Garrison, have been
"blind" to the truth. Numerous shots of eyeglasses in this montage sequence also imply a blindness, yet a desire to see more clearly; people who
are visually impaired need glasses just as wearing glasses improves vision.
Garrison wears eyeglasses and yet even they are not enough to see the
truth. His vision was "weak" in the past but now is becoming "stronger"
as the conspiracy to kill J.F.K. "comes into focus." This montage, and its
accompanying voice-over of Mr. Bowers testifying to the Warren Commission about what he saw on the embankment at Dealey Plaza, raise a number of questions for Garrison and for us: Were the reported hoboes walking
in the area behind the embankment just that? or were they CIA agents sent
either to do the shooting or ensure its success? Was Mr. Bowers, the man
seen dead behind the wheel of his car, killed by accident in a car crash? Or
was he murdered for testifying to the Warren Commission about four sus-
picious men standing behind a picket fence on the grassy knoll in Dealey
Plaza?

This montage of images acts as a segue to Garrison's dreams about the
assassination. Suddenly we are in his bedroom as he abruptly wakes and
sits straight up in bed. His movements disturb his wife, Liz (Sissy Spacek),
who also wakes and tries to get him to go back to sleep. Unwilling to do so,
Garrison exclaims, "Do I have to spell it out for you? Lee Oswald was no
ordinary soldier. He was probably in military intelligence. That's why he
was trained in Russian." Trying to quiet him, Liz replies, "Go back to
sleep." Garrison, shaking off her encouragement to close his eyes to the
truth, rebuts, "There's no accident he's in Russia. Goddamnit! I've been
sleeping for three years!"

Garrison, after three years in darkness, like Christ after three days in a
pitch-black tomb, has been awakened to the truth. As the hour strikes three
on Good Friday and Christ gives up the ghost by dying to his unresurrected
self, so Garrison, at the third chime of the clock, also "dies" to his old self
and is resurrected with an enlightened vision. Now it is time for Garrison
to wake up his "disciples" and the American people about the truth regarding Kennedy's assassination.

Two days later, on Sunday morning—the day of Garrison's resurrection
to the truth—he takes his two assistants, Bill and Lou, on a "walking tour"
of the French Quarter. It is here that Garrison demonstrates how "blind"
they have all been to the truth and how deceptive appearances can be. As
they walk through the quarter, Garrison points out that buildings that seem

innocuous from their facade actually house such operations as the Office of Naval Intelligence, the Federal Bureau of Investigation (FBI), the CIA, and the Secret Service. Garrison also demonstrates that Guy Bannister, a former FBI operator, shared an office with Lee Harvey Oswald. Although Bannister's office address was 531 Lafayette Street and Oswald's, 544 Camp Street, they actually were one and the same building. Oswald, in other words, knew and probably worked with Bannister; Bannister was a former FBI man, and, in Garrison's words, both lived in "the heart of the U.S. intelligence community in New Orleans." Garrison abruptly announces to his men, "We're going back into the case, Lou—murder of the president." In disbelief, Bill responds, "Good lord, wake me up, I must be dreaming." Garrison replies, "No, you're awake Bill, and I'm deadly serious." Bill and Lou, like Garrison, have been sleeping for three years; they have let themselves be deceived by appearances. They have been fooled, in other words, by the shadow play upon the wall, mere semblances of the truth rather than the truth itself.[50]

"Waking" is tied to "seeing" in *JFK*. As Medhurst points out, sight/vision, like waking/sleeping, is a central metaphor in the film.[51] Numerous characters, for example, smoke throughout the film, "blowing smoke" and putting up "smoke screens" to hide behind. The truth, in other words, is not only hidden by blinding glare off glass, but it is often shrouded in a haze of smoke. Even the judge at Clay Shaw's trial smokes heavily throughout the proceedings, leading us to conclude even before the trial begins, as Medhurst notes, that justice will not be served.

Sight/vision is a central metaphor in many of Stone's films. In *The Doors,* for example, Jim Morrison explains to fellow band member Ray Manzarek that he wants to call the group "The Doors" in a tribute to William Blake's statement, "When the doors of perception are cleansed then we will see things as they truly are." Barry Champlain, in *Talk Radio,* at one point exclaims in despair to his listening audience, "I'm not afraid to see. I come in here every night. . . . I tell you what you are. I have to, I have no choice. You frighten me." In *Salvador,* the "camera eye" of photographer Robert Cassady is also a lens focused on the truth. Aware of how dangerous it is to see clearly, Cassady ultimately sacrifices his life to capture the truth on film regarding CIA support for the death squads in El Salvador.

Clear sight, the ability to see through the trail of cover-up smoke left by Kennedy's assassins, is also dangerous. When Guy Bannister's unwitting assistant in the plot to kill Kennedy tells his boss, "I've seen enough here this summer already to write a book. . . . I've seen a lot of strange things, strange people," Bannister promptly bashes his head with a pistol and proclaims, "You haven't seen a goddamn thing. You didn't see a goddamn thing, you hear me, you little weasel. You didn't see a goddamn thing." In this film, as Medhurst points out, "to see—to open one's eyes and look at the evidence—is immediately established as a dangerous thing to do."[52]

It takes some time, however, for Garrison to open his eyes to the true meaning of events surrounding Kennedy's murder. Only after his meeting with the mysterious Mr. X in Washington, D.C., does he finally fit all of the pieces of the puzzle together in order to see things in a way he had not before. Upon his return from Washington, his wife is quick to notice this, charging, "You've changed!" Retorts Garrison, "Of course I've changed. My eyes have opened and once they're open, believe me, what used to look normal seems insane. . . . Can't you see, goddamnit!" Liz responds in despair, "I don't want to see, goddamnit. I'm tired. I've had enough." Garrison has figured things out and now "sees," when before he was blind. Liz Garrison is unwilling to share her husband's insight, however, perhaps because she realizes how dangerous such a vision might be.

JFK reminds us again and again of how the truth can be dangerous and frightening but ultimately uncompromising. We, like Garrison, must learn how to see things as they truly are, despite the sacrifices that may entail. When Jim Garrison's son, Jasper, played by Oliver Stone's son, Sean Stone, tells his father that he is scared because maybe the same people that shot Kennedy are going to shoot him, Garrison reassures Jasper that this will not happen. He adds, however, that "there's nothin' wrong with feeling a little scared. Tellin' the truth can be a scary thing sometimes. It scared President Kennedy, and he was a brave man. But if you let yourself be too scared, then you let the bad guys take over the country. Then everybody gets scared." Garrison's message to his son in the film echoes what Oliver Stone, as Garrison's "son," would perhaps say to his own son, Sean. It is a message that we, the mythical sons and daughters of Kennedy, Garrison, and even Oliver Stone, would do well to heed also.

Garrison, however, like Christ in his ministry and, ironically, like Oliver Stone in his making of *JFK*, suffers ridicule for his newfound vision of the truth. Late in the film as Garrison is preparing conspiracy charges against Clay Shaw, he and his wife watch a television "special report" entitled "The JFK Conspiracy: The Case of Jim Garrison." The commentator intones:

> After several weeks of investigating in New Orleans, a team of reporters has learned that District Attorney Jim Garrison and his staff have intimidated, bribed, and even drugged witnesses in their attempt to prove a conspiracy involving New Orleans businessman Clay Shaw in the murder of John F. Kennedy. Is Mr. Garrison dodging the oft-repeated charges that he is ignoring mafia connections to the conspiracy because in some way Mr. Garrison is indebted and tied to the mob? The more one looks at Jim Garrison the more one finds he has destroyed reputations, spread fear and suspicion, and worst of all, exploited this nation's sorrow and doubt. Mr. Garrison has said, "Let justice be done though the heavens fall." He seeks the truth. So do we.

In one of his few moments of relative inaction, New Orleans District Attorney Jim Garrison (Kevin Costner) gains strength from his children (Sean Stone and Kathy Bibb) and what they represent in his one-man quest for truth. Copyright © Warner Bros. Inc., Regency Enterprises V.O.F. and Le Studio Canal+.

In a case of art imitating life, these words, supposedly spoken by a broadcast journalist over thirty years ago, could have been said in 1991 about Oliver Stone's attempts to reopen speculation surrounding Kennedy's assassination. Oliver Stone, like Garrison, was accused by journalists of ignoring or downplaying potential mafia connections in *his* version of Kennedy's murder. Stone, like Garrison, was also accused of sullying the memory of many individuals, including that of Pennsylvania Senator Arlen Specter, the member of the Warren Commission who first advanced the one-bullet theory of Kennedy's assassination. The path that leads to the truth, as both *JFK*'s Garrison and Oliver Stone see it, is often not an easy road to walk.

Garrison not only suffers persecution at the hands of the press, but he is also ridiculed and ultimately betrayed by his own men. In a classic Last Supper motif, Garrison is joined around a long table by his "disciples," his various assistant investigators on the case. As they proceed to discuss fine points of the developing case against Clay Shaw, Garrison asserts to his staff, "This was a coup d'état with President Lyndon B. Johnson waiting in the wings." With this statement, Garrison's assistant Bill finally comprehends Garrison's claim that the assassination conspiracy reaches all the way to President Lyndon B. Johnson. Unnerved, Bill jumps up to counter this coup d'état theory with a mafia theory instead. Garrison's rebuttal to Bill invites a messianic reading of this scene: "You ever read your Shakespeare, Bill? Julius Caesar? Brutus and Cassius, they too are honorable men. Who killed Caesar? Ten, twelve Senators. All's it takes is one Judas. CIA, Bill, a few people on the inside." Bill, like Judas, is unable to accept a direct attack on the government by his leader. The game has gotten much too dangerous. Just as Christ's campaign against the Jewish authorities became too distasteful for Judas, the stakes have gotten much too high for Bill. In a final angry explosion, Bill, like Judas, walks out, never to return to the case.

However, Garrison, like a forgiving Christ, does not disown Bill; rather, he asserts to the remaining gathered "disciples" that, if possible, he wants Bill back. This creates a temporary rift between Garrison and Lou, Garrison's other right-hand man in the case. Lou, like Bill before him, also jumps up and exclaims that he cannot work on the case if Bill, the betrayer, returns. This is a rift that Garrison will not allow. In the Garden of Gethsemane when Judas betrays Christ with a kiss, one of his disciples draws a sword and strikes the high priest's servant. "Put your sword back in its place," exclaimed Jesus, "for all who live by the sword will die by the sword."[53] Like Christ, Garrison will not allow infighting by members of his team. Lou must toe the line or leave. It is also in the Garden of Gethsemane after the sword incident that Christ's disciple Simon Peter asked him where he was going. Jesus replied, "'Where I am going, you cannot follow now, but you will follow later.' Peter asked, 'Lord, why can't I follow you now? I will lay down my life for you.' Then Jesus answered, 'Will you really lay down your life for me? I tell you the truth, before the rooster crows, you will disown me three times!'"[54] Prophetically, Lou, like Simon Peter, also betrays his leader by walking out on the investigation in anger, although like Simon Peter, Lou will later return to support Garrison in his trial against Shaw.

JFK's climax comes with Garrison's ultimately unsuccessful trial against Clay Shaw. Although Shaw is the defendant in the case, we implicitly realize that it is the American people who are on trial. In Garrison's dramatic courtroom summation, his words directly charge the American people with Hamlet-like complacency, not only in Kennedy's death but also in the ensuing death of the American Dream. We, not Clay Shaw, are on trial here. Explains Garrison to the jury:

> We've all become Hamlets in our country, children of a slain father leader whose killers still possess the throne. The ghost of John F. Kennedy confronts us with the secret murder at the heart of the American Dream. He forces on us the appalling question: Of what is our constitution made? What is our citizenship, and more, our lives worth? What is the future of a democracy where a president can be assassinated under conspicuously suspicious circumstances while the machine of legal action scarcely trembles. . . . You, the people—the jury system sitting in judgment on Clay Shaw—represent the hope of humanity against government power. In discharging your duty, in bringing the first conviction in this house of cards against Clay Shaw, ask not what your country can do for you, but what you can do for your country. Do not forget your dying king. Show this world that there is still a government "of the people, for the people, and by the people." Nothing as long as you live will ever be more important.

Echoing the words of President Abraham Lincoln, Garrison warns the audience that nothing less than the future of democracy is at stake. Echoing the words of John F. Kennedy, Garrison asks of us the same sacrifices that Kennedy did—sacrifices demanded of the generation of the 1960s, asked again of the generation of the 1990s. What are we being asked to do? Not to engage in knee-jerk patriotism, not to hate whatever enemy the government tells us to vilify, not to believe whatever explanation of events the government provides, but rather to ask our own questions, to challenge official versions of the truth wherever they may appear. As Mr. X says to Garrison in Washington, D.C., "Don't take my word for it. Don't believe me, do your own work, your own thinking." Garrison is the reincarnation of the Kennedy spirit. Stone's *JFK* urges us to carry on the crusade that Garrison began, that Stone continues in his films, despite persecution or ridicule—to search out not only the truth regarding Kennedy's assassination, but the truth behind the lies told to us by our government, our media, and our corporate institutions. Only then, Stone implies, can we heal the festering wound at the heart of the American Dream and restore Camelot to its former glory.

In a courtroom of the American judicial system, where there will be no justice, Jim Garrison (Kevin Costner) approaches the judge's (John Finnegan) bench in *JFK*. Copyright © Warner Bros. Inc., Regency Enterprises V.O.F. and Le Studio Canal+.

Although the film ends shortly after the conclusion of Clay Shaw's trial, *JFK* could as easily have ended in Washington, D.C., when Garrison, after meeting with Mr. X, visits Kennedy's tomb. As Garrison stands in front of the eternal flame that burns on Kennedy's grave, we watch a father explain to his son the meaning of the place on which they stand. The boy clearly represents the next generation, those who will carry on the search for truth. Kennedy's torch, the legacy passed down to Garrison and to Stone, is passed down to the young—to those individuals, in *JFK*'s final words, "in whose spirit the quest for truth marches on."

There is no doubting that this is a difficult quest. After a long editing session on *JFK*, Stone reflected in an interview with Robert Anson, "When you make a movie like this and you get attacked from all sides, sometimes you don't win. Sometimes you fail. But it is well worth it if you lost in an honorable cause. Pancho Villa, I always think of what he said, 'The defeats are also battles.'"[55] Stone's words about the famous Mexican defender of civil rights, Pancho Villa, could also apply to Stone's interpretation of America's slain father/leader John F. Kennedy and one of his staunchest supporters, former New Orleans District Attorney Jim Garrison: Their defeats were also battles waged in the name of an "honorable cause."

Notes

1. Frank Beaver, *Oliver Stone: Wakeup Cinema* (New York: Twayne Publishers, 1994), 199.

2. David Ansen, "What Does Oliver Stone Owe History?" *Newsweek,* 23 December 1991, 49.

3. Oliver Stone, "Who Is Rewriting History?" *New York Times,* 20 December 1991, A35.

4. Robert Sam Anson, "The Shooting of JFK," *Esquire,* November 1991, 96.

5. Alexander Cockburn, "The Kooks Have It," *New Statesman and Society,* 17 January 1992, 14.

6. Lance Morrow and Martha Smilgis, "Plunging into the Labyrinth," *Time,* 23 December 1991, 74.

7. Anson, "Shooting of JFK," 97.

8. Richard Corliss, "Who Killed J.F.K.?" *Time,* 23 December 1991, 70.

9. Ibid.

10. Ansen, "What Does Oliver Stone Owe History?" 49.

11. Martin Medhurst, "The Rhetorical Structure of Oliver Stone's *JFK,*" *Critical Studies in Mass Communication* 10 (1993):129–130.

12. Ibid., 130.

13. Quoted in Anson, "Shooting of JFK," 97.

14. Corliss, "Who Killed J.F.K.?" 70.

15. Beaver, *Oliver Stone: Wakeup Cinema,* 172.

16. John Pilger, "Shaming the System," *New Statesman and Society,* 7 February 1992, 10. For a complete review of the debate about *JFK,* see "The *JFK* Debate," in Oliver Stone and Zachary Sklar, *JFK: The Book of the Film* (New York: Applause Books, 1992), 187–529.

17. Tom Bethell, "Conspiracy to End Conspiracies," *National Review,* 16 December 1991, 48.

18. Cited in Anson, "Shooting of JFK," 102.

19. Cockburn, "Kooks Have It," 14.

20. George Will, "*JFK:* Paranoid History," *Washington Post,* 26 December 1991, A23.

21. Pilger, "Shaming the System," 11.

22. Bethell, "Conspiracy to End Conspiracies," 48.

23. Ansen, "What Does Oliver Stone Owe History?" 50.

24. Kenneth Auchincloss, "Twisted History," *Newsweek,* 23 December 1991, 47.

25. Lisa Nesselson, "*JFK:* Everybody Must Get Stoned . . . ," *Paris Free Voice,* 15 February 1992, 7.

26. Nora Ephron, "The Tie That Binds," *Nation,* 6 April 1992, 453.

27. Renee Loth, "Oliver Stone's *JFK* Reopens Old Wounds," *Boston Globe,* 22 December 1991, A19.

28. Morrow and Smilgis, "Plunging into the Labyrinth," 75.

29. Stone, "Who Is Rewriting History?" A35.

30. Stone as quoted in Anson, "Shooting of JFK," 94.

31. Pilger, "Shaming the System," 10.

32. Morrow and Smilgis, "Plunging into the Labyrinth," 74.

33. Anson, "Shooting of JFK," 98.

34. Andrew Kopkind, "*JFK:* The Myth," *Nation*, 20 January 1992, 41.

35. Oliver Stone, "Stone's *JFK:* A Higher Truth?" *Washington Post*, 2 June 1991, D3.

36. Anson, "Shooting of JFK," 98.

37. Quoted in ibid, 42.

38. Ibid., 98.

39. Ansen, "What Does Oliver Stone Owe History?" 49.

40. Morrow and Smilgis, "Plunging into the Labyrinth," 74.

41. Kopkind, "*JFK:* The Myth," 41.

42. Cockburn, "Kooks Have It," 14.

43. Auchincloss, "Twisted History," 47.

44. Ansen, "What Does Oliver Stone Owe History?" 50.

45. Ibid., 49.

46. Beaver, *Oliver Stone: Wakeup Cinema*, 179.

47. George Bush, "Statement on Signing the President John F. Kennedy Assassination Records Collection Act of 1992," *Weekly Compilation of Presidential Documents*, 28, 27 October 1992, 2135.

48. Medhurst, "Rhetorical Structure," 129–130.

49. Medhurst ("Rhetorical Structure") considers sleeping/waking one of a number of "dialectical pairs" or opposing motifs that inform *JFK*. Others include sight/blindness, appearance/truth, and past/present.

50. Medhurst made the same observation when he noted about this scene and others like it in *JFK*, "The Platonic overtones are unmistakable. We live in a world of reflections where only shadows of the truth are known. Reflections, if accepted as true knowledge, will never lead to the truth" ("Rhetorical Structure," 135).

51. Medhurst, "Rhetorical Structure."

52. Ibid., 132.

53. Matt. 26:51–52, New International Version.

54. John 14:36–38 New International Version.

55. Anson, "Shooting of JFK," 176.

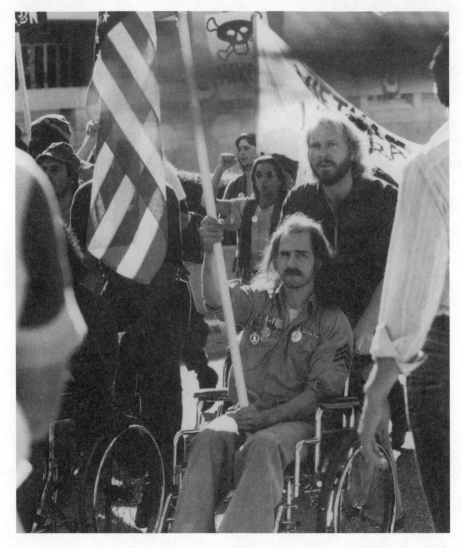

Tom Cruise as disabled vet Ron Kovic in Oliver Stone's 1989 release *Born on the Fourth of July,* a film Stone produced, cowrote (with Ron Kovic), and directed. Copyright © 1989 Universal City Studios Inc. Courtesy of MCA Publishing Rights, a Division of MCA Inc. All rights reserved. Photo by Roland Neveu.

three

Descent into Hell:
The Vietnam Nightmare

I think now, looking back, we did not fight the enemy; we fought ourselves and the enemy was in us.

—Chris Taylor, *Platoon*

Just lately I've felt like I'm home. You know, like maybe we're home.

—Ron Kovic, *Born on the Fourth of July*

Lasting victories are won in the heart, not in this land or that.

—Le Ly, *Heaven and Earth*

In this chapter, which continues the application of a sociomythological framework, partial readings are given of Oliver Stone's *Platoon, Born on the Fourth of July,* and *Heaven and Earth.* These films invite audiences to explore America's loss of innocence after the assassination of John F. Kennedy. Taken as a whole, this Vietnam trilogy constitutes Stone's perspective on America's most disputed war.

Platoon, Oliver Stone's first film about Vietnam, takes Chris Taylor, a young recruit filled with good intentions and patriotic beliefs, and deposits him in a "hell," where many of his illusions about bravery, the army, and the U.S. cause in Vietnam are badly shaken, if not destroyed. *Born on the Fourth of July,* Stone's second Vietnam film, covers a greater time span than *Platoon.* It begins by capturing the youthful innocence and optimism that supposedly marked American society before Kennedy's death and continues beyond *Platoon*'s conclusion, describing Vietnam's effects on a country torn apart by civil unrest and racism. *Heaven and Earth*, Stone's most recent contribution to the genre of Vietnam films, begins before the French and American invasions in Vietnam and follows the experiences of a Vietnamese woman, Le Ly Hayslip, who is the film's protagonist, up until the late 1970s. Through Le Ly's personal and political journey from Vietnam to America and back again, Stone explores American involvement in Vietnam and the war's effect on her native country, on Southeast Asia, and on the United States.

Platoon invites the audience into an arena where battles are fought between archetypal fathers (Sergeants Barnes and Elias) for an individual's soul. The film's protagonist, Chris Taylor, must learn over the course of the film how to construct himself not simply by rejecting one of these fathers and accepting the other, but rather by integrating both in a balancing act that acknowledges Chris's own ability to be both good and evil. In the same manner that Chris confronts his internal Barnes—his shadow—in order to realize his Elias potential, so *Platoon* asserts that we Americans must also face the collective shadow that is Vietnam in order to suffer our own rite of passage. Vietnam becomes our heart of darkness, our passage from a pre-Edenic innocence to a post-Armageddon knowledge. Even though Taylor's battle for self-knowledge begins in a leech-infested swamp in Vietnam, the film's conclusion hints that the future direction for Stone's heroes is internal and that our most significant battles are those of the soul.

This odyssey of the soul is further explored in both *Born on the Fourth of July* and *Heaven and Earth*. Ron Kovic, in *Born on the Fourth of July*, like Taylor, comes to realize that Vietnam and its lasting effects on his body represent an internal battle to uncover the truth about himself and about Vietnam. His boon is to share such knowledge with the American people. *Heaven and Earth*, the third film in Stone's Vietnam trilogy, also asserts an increasing sense of the hero's journey as spiritual and inward rather than rational and outward. Le Ly Hayslip invites us to see that the true battlefield was not in Vietnam but in the hearts and minds of the people who survived that war.

In order to best appreciate Stone's vision of the Vietnam War in *Platoon*, *Born on the Fourth of July*, and *Heaven and Earth*, it is helpful to first place these films in the context of Hollywood war films, and more specifically, within the genre of the American Vietnam film.

The Hollywood Vietnam War Film

Although a survey of political filmmaking in Hollywood reveals a relatively centrist landscape, two notable exceptions emerge—the World War II combat films and the Vietnam War films that followed some thirty years later. The major difference between these two types of films is that World War II combat films, appearing at the beginning of the conflict and enduring throughout the war, overtly exhibited prowar sentiment,[1] whereas Vietnam films, with few exceptions, did not begin appearing until eight years after the American involvement in Southeast Asia had ceased, and these films were primarily antiwar. Essentially absent from the screen for almost a decade after the war's conclusion, Vietnam usually served as no more than a backdrop for the "war is hell" or "war is the heart of darkness" message of most Vietnam films. Portrayed as the realm of brave individual heroes, the Vietnam War and its effect on Americans at home provided a canvas for exploring a soldier's or veteran's growth and self-discovery. Vietnam films, in other words, rarely criticized or condemned U.S. policy and its effects in Southeast Asia.

During the Vietnam War, the war itself was noticeably absent from the Hollywood screen. John Wayne's film *The Green Berets,* released in 1968, offered the only exception. Patterned after World War II commitment films and financially supported by the U.S. government, it provided a conservative Cold War analysis of the political situation in Southeast Asia and was designed to encourage American support for the conflict. Despite considerable political controversy, however, the film made money and was one of the most popular films of 1968. Although it was a commercial success, it was considered a public relations fiasco. As one critic commented, the film "was just as stupid—ideologically speaking—as you were afraid it would be and far worse—as an action film—than you suspected it could be."[2] Other than *The Green Berets,* however, which was a pet project for John Wayne, Hollywood maintained its conventional position regarding explicitly partisan politics and steered clear of overt discussion of the controversial Vietnam War and its implications for almost a decade after *The Green Berets'* release.

Although Vietnam remained a seemingly untouchable topic during the conflict, many films, particularly Westerns, used the war as a subtext, just as film noir had done with communism a decade earlier. This technique appeared in such films as *The Wild Bunch* (1969), *Little Big Man* (1970), and *Two Mules for Sister Sara* (1970). Other films of the early and mid-1970s, such as *Billy Jack* (1971), *Black Sunday* (1976), *Taxi Driver* (1976), and *Heroes* (1977), although not specifically about the conflict in Southeast Asia, used Vietnam as a pretext to explain a character's bizarre or dysfunctional behavior. The veteran in these films was usually portrayed as either having been driven to violence as a result of the war or having been taught violence as part of his training. The vet as "human frag bomb" who could not "turn it off" when he came stateside, however, was very different from World War II films' portrayal of soldiers going "over there" to fight fascism so that they could come back home to the applause and affection of friends and sweethearts.

No films that focused directly on the Vietnam War were released for almost a decade after *The Green Berets,* but with the 1977 release of *Coming
Home* there appeared to be some evidence that Hollywood was ready to
abandon its self-imposed restriction on making films about Vietnam. Possibly due to the topicality and marketability of assessing the Vietnam experience, by 1980 eight films about Vietnam had been released. A veritable
Vietnam genre had been born. Unlike the prowar combat films of the
1940s, however, these films were primarily antiwar and viewed the war itself (rather than the Vietnam vet of earlier films) as the villain. The central
characters in films of this era had problems, as did the vets in earlier films,
but now their problems were portrayed as society's problems.

Despite their political relevance, Vietnam films of the late 1970s and
1980s, with few exceptions, preferred a generic "war is hell" critique to an
explicit condemnation of U.S. policy and its effects in Southeast Asia.[3] Topicality provided no more than a backdrop for the "war as the heart of darkness" message of most Vietnam films of the decade.[4] Leo Cawley, for example, claimed that "a census of the whole Vietnam film library, from right to
left, or from militarist to anti-militarist, would show a lopsided count with
the right-wing, militarist end badly overcrowded."[5] Cawley maintained
that in films with even a slight promilitarist slant the primary message was
still that "war is hell or war is insane." Films on the far right of the Vietnam film spectrum took this message and interpreted it as "war is hell but
also a lot of fun." Nowhere, Cawley pointed out, did we find films that explicitly argued that the Vietnam War was wrong and should not have been
fought. He went so far as to say that most Vietnam films, even if they did
not explicitly use the conventions of the World War II films, at least supported the ideology of those films.[6]

The typical Hollywood Vietnam film not only portrayed war "as the
heart of darkness," according to Cawley, it also painted war as the realm of
brave individual heroes. These films asserted that wars are fought and won
by personal bravery and that survival is a matter of fitness rather than
luck.[7] Examples of this were the Chuck Norris *Missing in Action* films and
the Sylvester Stallone *Rambo* series. The heroes in both films, for example,
"go it alone" to complete missions that seemingly change the course of
events in Vietnam. The theme of individual bravery, seen even in films with
a more centrist or liberal critique such as *The Deer Hunter* and *Apocalypse
Now,* persisted despite the more realistic assessment that wars are not cru-
sades led by individual heroes but group efforts where success depends as
much, if not more, on luck as on bravery.

Since Vietnam films often portrayed the war as the realm of individual
actions by brave soldiers, it is not surprising that most of these films also
painted war, according to Cawley, as a rite of passage for young American
males. War as a rite of passage implies that combat situations teach truths

impossible to learn elsewhere.[8] We see this, for example, in Michael's "one shot" theory of the hunt in *The Deer Hunter*. It emerges as central to Willard's transcendent experiences with Colonel Kurtz in *Apocalypse Now*. It is prevalent in such seemingly diverse films as *The Green Berets* and *The Deer Hunter*. John Wayne's question in *The Green Berets* to the skeptical reporter Beckwith—"Have you been over there?"—seems to be echoed in the comment made by a discharged Green Beret to Michael, Stevie, and Nick in *The Deer Hunter* in a bar at Stevie's wedding. When asked by Michael what serving in Vietnam was like, the veteran's only reply, repeated again and again, is: "Fuck it." The message? You cannot possibly understand the heart of darkness and the trials and tribulations that were Vietnam unless you were there.

Platoon (1986)

Platoon, released in 1986, fits the mold of the typical Vietnam film in its view of war as a rite of passage for young men and its sacrifice of a politically specific statement against U.S. involvement in Vietnam for the more generic "war is hell" critique. *Platoon* differs from many Vietnam films in its argument that war is a group rather than an individual effort and that luck can be as important as brains in surviving combat situations. The film's most notable difference, however, is its "you were there" feeling, coupled with the sensation that some larger spiritual truth, some transcendent experience, is waiting to be discerned.

The strikingly realistic film style used in *Platoon* gives the film, as Richard Coombs noted, the feel of an Ernest Hemingway or Norman Mailer war novel.[9] Thanks to Stone's handheld camera style, for example, our awareness of the grime, sweat, and pain of the young recruits as they hump through the jungles of Southeast Asia is almost visceral. We smell their fear, taste their dry-mouthed exhaustion, and sense their confusion and despair. Indeed, the film was hailed by many as the first Hollywood production to show Vietnam "the way it really was."[10] *New York Times* Vietnam reporter, David Halberstam, called *Platoon* "the first real Vietnam film . . . and one of the great war movies of all time. The other Hollywood Vietnam films have been a rape of history. But *Platoon* is historically and politically accurate."[11] Numerous Vietnam vets also pronounced *Platoon* the most movingly realistic of all Vietnam films. John Wheeler, president of the Center for the Study of the Vietnam Generation in Washington, D.C., and chair of the Vietnam Veterans' Memorial Fund, explained that "before, we [vets] were either objects of pity or objects that had to be defused to keep us at a distance. *Platoon* makes us real. The Vietnam Memorial was one gate our country had to pass through; *Platoon* is another. It is part of the healing process. It speaks to our generation. Those guys are us."[12]

The film's perceived realism may be due, in part, not only to Stone's reliance on his own combat experience in Vietnam but also to the way Stone constructed the filming environment. Stone took his cast and crew to the Philippines, where he shot the film in a fast-paced fifty-four days. Prior to shooting, Stone enlisted the help of a Vietnam vet and twenty-year marine, Captain Dale Dye, who put the actors through fourteen days of boot camp in the Philippine jungles, forcing them to live under the conditions experienced by soldiers fighting in Vietnam. Carrying rifles and sixty-pound backpacks, the actors found themselves humping through leech-swollen streams and insect-ridden jungles. Eating cold army rations, rappelling down fifty-foot cliffs, and sleeping in two-man foxholes, the actors quickly gained off-camera experience for their on-camera roles. Captain Dye not only trained the actors in jungle warfare, however, he also served as the film's consultant, ensuring the historical accuracy of everything from props and set pieces to costumes, even teaching the actors "gruntspeak"—the four-letter-word language of the Vietnam foot soldier.[13]

The film's emphasis on "documentary" realism, as we will see, also evokes the sensation that some larger spiritual truth, some enlightening experience, is just around the corner. Equating *Platoon* with Herman Melville's *Moby Dick*, Coombs called the film "a factual tale as spiritual odyssey" in which "Vietnam is either a swamp of thrusting, devouring life or a pattern of light through trees, either a jungle primeval or an overarching temple." Coombs went on to argue that it is "this split, between 'how it was' reportage and blinding spiritual truth that has made *Platoon* so appealing."[14]

Platoon was greatly anticipated, since it represented the first Vietnam film written and directed by a Vietnam vet. It was praised by critics and filmmakers alike. Filmmaker Woody Allen called it a "fine movie, an excellent movie."[15] Brian De Palma, for whom Stone wrote the screenplay for *Scarface*, said of Stone's growing maturity as a filmmaker: "He has now channeled his feeling and energy into a cohesive dramatic work. He's an auteur making a movie about what he experienced and understands. Seeing *Platoon* get through the system makes the soul feel good."[16] *Time*'s Richard Corliss claimed that "with craft, cackle, a little bombast and plenty of residual rage [Stone] has created a time-capsule movie that explodes like a frag bomb in the consciousness of America."[17] Noted *Newsweek*'s David Ansen, "After nine years of waiting, Stone has made one of the rare Hollywood movies that matter."[18] *Platoon* is special, according to critic Pat McGillis, because it "charts the dead logic of the 'morally repulsive' war; it may be the benchmark of Vietnam movies (from the U.S. point of view), the one by which all films about combat are measured."[19]

Although few critics denied the film's impact, many of them, from both the Left and the Right, took exception to the film's politics. Not surprisingly, conservative critics reacted strongly. For example, *Washington Times* magazine writer John Podhoretz called *Platoon* "one of the most repellent movies ever made in this country." The film, claimed Podhoretz, "blackens the name and belittles the sacrifice of every man and woman who served the United States in the Vietnam War (including Stone)."[20] More surprising was the response of some critics from the Left who found the film too conservative. As one averred, "*Platoon* is a right-wing wringing of hands. It springs from the heart of the Eighties—an ignorant heart, a black heart, the dangerous heart of this Age of Reagan."[21] Other critics charged that the film successfully managed to please both hawks and doves: "Most war films come in one of two flavors—pugnacious, like *Rambo* or pacifist, like *All Quiet on the Western Front. Platoon* manages to be something in between: a lament about the brutality of war that nevertheless depicts it graphically."[22] Others complained that because of the film's focus on the psychology of jungle warfare, like most Vietnam films, it never goes beyond the traditional "war is hell" critique to say something more meaningful about our involvement in Southeast Asia.[23]

Although Stone wrote the script for *Platoon* in the mid-1970s, he met with little success in his attempts to find backing for the project. Said Stone of the film's screenplay, "I wrote it as straight as I could remember it. But nobody wanted to make it because it was 'hard, depressing, grim.'"[24] The film's producer, Mark Bregman, met with a similarly negative response from Hollywood. Bregman remembered, "For two years in the late '70s I banged on every door in California to get it done . . . but at that time Viet Nam was still a no-no."[25] It was ten years before Stone could arrange financing for the film. Hemdale, the progressive British film company that had financed *Salvador,* eventually came through once again for *Platoon.* Hemdale chairman John Daly felt confident about Hemdale's investment since Stone's *Salvador* had "crystallized the reality of war with pathos and passion and was a good indication of what Stone was capable of achieving."[26] *Platoon* "was a picture we wanted to support," noted Daly. "We respect Oliver's passions. Besides, he spent only $6 million on *Platoon,*" less than one-half the average Hollywood film budget.[27]

Despite its modest $6.5 million budget, *Platoon* went on to become Stone's most critically acclaimed film to date, taking Academy Awards for Best Picture, Best Director, Best Editing, and Best Sound. Stone also won the Directors' Guild of America Award and the Golden Globe Award for Best Director. In addition, both Willem Dafoe and Tom Berenger received Best Supporting Actor nominations for their roles in the film. *Platoon* eventually grossed over $250 million in box-office receipts and video sales.

During the opening shot of *Platoon*, a graphic depicting a quote from Ecclesiastes reads "Rejoice, O young man in thy youth," which establishes a mythopoetic framework. As the air fills with the deafening buzz of a busy military air base and a hazy yellow dust rises from the heat-swollen tarmac, we see a platoon of fresh recruits emerge from the gaping maw of a troop transport plane. "Like Jonah disgorged from the belly of the whale,"[28] these soldiers emerge as children about to begin their initiation into manhood. Like Jonah, they must submit to this initiation if they are to grow, to become men. In a medium shot, we see Chris Taylor (Charlie Sheen) blink and rub his eyes, stinging from the dust and haze, in a gesture that possibly indicates his bewilderment at the confusing blur of sights that greet his eyes. Taylor and other new recruits watch as their places on the plane are taken by a seemingly endless line of body bags and battle-weary troops that files past, the dead on carts, the living on stretchers, crutches, and their own two feet. In a series of shot-and-reverse-angle shots, Taylor locks eyes with a seasoned soldier of about the same age and height, weary and downtrodden but alive and heading home. As Taylor gazes at his counterpart, our shock of recognition is tangible. Taylor and the rest of these "cherries" are the "fresh meat" that will satiate the war god for a few more weeks or months—depending upon the voraciousness of its appetite—until they also return home, either on a stretcher or in a body bag.

The significance of this moment is heightened by Stone's use of a mystical and meditative musical refrain from Samuel Barber's *Adagio for Strings* that accompanies many moments throughout the film. It is a technique used to similar effect in *Salvador* and, as Beaver noted, "depending on one's critical preferences," it either adds "a tragic tone to the presentation of men at war" or it "distance[s] the viewer from the immediacy of war's fury."[29] It may, in fact do both, placing the viewer in the midst of a tragic moment while also painting an individual incident onto humanity's vast canvas, the testament to man's immeasurable virtuosity in showing both inhumane stupidity and compassionate understanding.

The next shot is a graphic that reads "September 1967—Bravo Company—25th Infantry—somewhere near the Cambodian border." This is followed by an extremely low-angle shot looking up through a jungle canopy looming hundreds of feet above. Blazing-white "heavenly" light filters down. We then see this same jungle in close-up from the ground level—from the "grunts'" perspective as they use machetes to hack and slash their way through this devouring monster. Every inch of ground is won by sheer willpower. Taylor, in voice-over, recites lines from a letter he has written home: "Somebody once wrote, 'Hell is the impossibility of reason.' That's what this place feels like—hell." The jungle with which these recruits do battle is both a heaven, a place of transcendent beauty, and a hell, a leech-infested swamp that seeks to rot their very souls. It is both the Garden of Eden and its antithesis. It is a trial and a tribulation. The evening after a particularly brutal firefight, for example, Taylor and Elias, one of the platoon's two sergeants, gaze up at a panoply of stars that glisten in a blue-black velvety sky. Sergeant Elias comments, "I love this place at night. The stars—there's no right or wrong in 'em. They're just there." Despite the moral ambiguities that rage around these men in their daily battles to understand the hell that is Vietnam, Elias, possibly at peace with himself and the world, is able to attain a glimpse of the transcendent. He is able, in William Blake's words, "to see the world in a grain of sand, and a heaven in a wildflower; hold infinity in the palm of [his] hand, and eternity in an hour."[30]

War as the heart of darkness, a traditional critique in many war films, is an important element in *Platoon*. But it is more than a motif for its own sake: The external living hell with which the recruits struggle is also a manifestation of an internal battle for their souls. As many critics have noted, Chris Taylor is initiated into a complex manhood in Vietnam by two archetypal "fathers," his platoon's two sergeants, Elias and Barnes. Both men hold different philosophies about life and about how to fight and stay alive in Vietnam. Sergeant Barnes is the archetypal embodiment of evil, whereas Sergeant Elias, a "crusader" and "water walker," in Barnes's words, is an archetypal messiah. As hero, Chris Taylor's plight is to construct himself, not simply by rejecting the evil that is Barnes and accepting the goodness that is Elias but rather by integrating both in a precarious balancing act that acknowledges his capacity for both good and evil. Chris, in other words, must confront his own shadow, his internal Barnes in order to realize his Elias potential.

Speaking of *Platoon*'s two very different sergeants, Stone has said that they were "two gods" who represented:

> two different views of the war, the angry Achilles versus the conscience-stricken Hector fighting for a lost cause on the dusty plains of Troy. . . . And I would act as Ishmael, the observer, caught between those two giant forces. At first a watcher. Then *forced* to act—to take responsibility and a moral stand. And in the process grow to a manhood I'd never dreamed I'd have to grow to. To a place where in order to go on existing I'd have to shed the innocence and accept the evil the Homeric gods had thrown into the world. To be both good and evil.[31]

Platoon, like *Wall Street*, invites the audience into a mythic arena where battles between archetypal heroes are waged in a struggle for the individual's soul. Vietnam is the Manichaean landscape against which Taylor, perhaps like Stone, works out his personal salvation and accepts both the good and evil in the world and in himself by negotiating his relationships with these two men.

Such "shedding of innocence" on a personal level also marks for Stone what happened when we Americans "broke our cherry" on the hard and unfathomable reality that was the war in Vietnam. Vietnam became our heart of darkness, our rite of passage from a pre-Edenic innocence to a post-Armageddon knowledge. The question for Stone is whether we will learn from this knowledge or be doomed to repeat the mistakes again.

The first half of *Platoon* is primarily concerned with Vietnam as Taylor's personal rite of passage. Early in the film, Taylor explains in voice-over: "It's scary cause nobody tells me how to do anything 'cause I'm new. Nobody cares about the new guys. They don't even want to know your name. The unwritten rule is a new guy's life isn't worth enough because he hasn't put his time in yet and they say if you're gonna get killed in the 'Nam it's better to get it in the first few weeks, the logic being you don't suffer that much." It is implied here, however, that if you do make it through your first few weeks, you gain an experience invaluable for shaping the rest of your life. If you pass the trial by fire that is "'Nam," only then can you die to your old self and be resurrected as something new.

Although Taylor will get this chance, his fellow recruit, Private Gardener, will not. Almost from the beginning of the film, the two new recruits Taylor and Gardener are associated with each other. When Taylor vomits and passes out at the sight of his first dead body, it is Gardener who is called upon to give him water and help him up. Barnes shouts at Taylor, "What the hell's the matter with you Taylor, you are one simple son of a bitch. Get that other cherry up here. Gardener!" Although Taylor makes it home alive, Gardener is killed in the platoon's first firefight. Gardener's death is made into a lesson by Barnes, who assures his troops that going home in a body bag like Gardener is what will happen to them if they fail to embrace the challenge that is 'Nam.

Taylor seems conscious both of the "opportunity" that this heaven-hell offers him and of its role as his rite of passage when he explains in another letter he sends home: "Maybe I'll finally find it—down here in the mud. Maybe from down here I can start up again and be something I can be proud of without having to fake it, be a fake human being. Maybe I can see something I don't yet see or learn something I don't yet know." This is followed by a brief glimpse of a vine-covered statue of a towering Buddha—an ominous jungle god keeping brooding watch over all he sees.

Vision—the clear sight that is so central to Jim Garrison in *JFK*, to Jim Morrison in *The Doors*, and to the photographer Robert Cassady in *Salvador*—is often gained from ground level, from the muck and mud of human existence; or it is glimpsed, in Taylor's case, in the face of a jungle Buddha. To walk the razor edge of consciousness—like Jim Morrison's building ledges—to live life in the extreme, as in Vietnam, is to truly live. It matters, however, what you do with this knowledge.

Unlike Gardener, Taylor survives his "trial by fire" to be resurrected into a "new life." This resurrection occurs later in the film when he is accepted as a seasoned recruit, someone whose name was now worth knowing. After receiving his first bloodying in battle—his badge of honor—Taylor is assigned light duty at a military outpost. It is here that he enters into his new life, and as is common in Stone's films, his initiation is through drugs. Taylor is invited into a below-ground bunker populated by the "heads." As he enters this smoky underground haven, however, a soldier from his platoon challenges his right to be there, saying, "What you doin' in the underworld, Taylor?" The soldier that brought Taylor replies, "Oh this here ain't Taylor, Taylor been shot, this man here is Chris, he been resurrected." Chris (Christ) has literally passed through trial by (gun)fire; he has died, shed his old life, and been newly "baptized" (renamed) and resurrected into a new consciousness.

It is not surprising that this new life is found underground—in an "underworld," a cave. In *The Doors,* Jim Morrison first sees visions of his music ministry and his impending death inside a cave in a desert in the Southwest, where he has gone to do peyote with his newfound followers— the band members of "The Doors." Likewise Mickey and Mallory, in *Natural Born Killers,* also come as close to enlightenment as they will ever get in the cave or womblike ceremonial house-hogan of their spiritual mentor, the Navajo Indian. According to Jung, "the cave is the place of rebirth," a "secret cavity in which one is shut up in order to be incubated and renewed."[32] Jung explained the cave's meaning, noting:

> Anyone who gets into that cave, that is to say into the cave which everyone has in himself, or into the darkness that lies behind consciousness, will find himself involved in an, at first, unconscious process of transformation. By penetrating into the unconscious he makes a connection with his unconscious contents. This may result in a momentous change of personality in the positive or negative sense. The transformation is often interpreted as a prolongation of the natural span of life or as an earnest of immortality.[33]

The rebirth meaning of the cave is also echoed in the story of Jonah and the whale and in Christ's death and resurrection. According to Campbell, in his initiation the hero frequently must descend into a cave, an underworld, or a place of darkness. This passage is often "symbolized in the worldwide womb image of the belly of the whale."[34] The Bible text reads, "For as Jonah was three days and three nights in the belly of a huge fish, so the Son of man will be three days in the heart of the earth."[35] Chris Taylor, in other words, by entering this bunker, this underworld (the place where he will later confront his own shadow in the form of his counterpart, Sergeant Barnes), is about to undergo a transformation. He has arrived at the threshold of the unconscious and, that being so, is about to begin his journey inward.

This underworld is also a house of healing, because it is here that the soldiers, both black and white, forget the pain of their existence, mingle, embrace, and dance to music. As we hear the strains of Jefferson Airplane's

"White Rabbit"—a song about drugs and altered consciousness—Taylor takes a long drag from a proffered hash pipe and coughs. Sergeant Elias, also in the bunker, asks if this is his first time in the underworld doing drugs. Taylor says yes as Elias continues, "Then the worm has definitely turned for you man, feel good?" Chris nods and Elias adds, "Feeling good's good enough." Chris responds, "Yeah, it feels good; I've got no pain in my neck now." In this cave of altered consciousness—aided by drugs—Chris has found relief from both the physical and psychological pain of the war. It is also significant that Chris receives his healing from his spiritual guide and mentor, Sergeant Elias. As Campbell has noted, the hero is often aided in his quest for enlightenment by a spiritual or supernatural guide or helper.[36] Although Chris will have other teachers in Vietnam, Elias quickly becomes a central role model as Chris struggles to maintain a sense of human worth and dignity and an understanding of right and wrong.

In the same scene, Elias then turns, cocks his rifle, and points it at Taylor. Taylor is momentarily startled by what seems like an act of aggression in this supposed house of healing. Elias commands him: "Put your mouth on this." As Taylor hesitantly takes the barrel of Elias's gun into his mouth, Elias blows Chris a "shotgun," a long stream of secondhand smoke from his joint, in this case blown down the barrel of the gun and into Chris's opened mouth.

This is a multilayered image for a number of reasons. First it is erotic and phallic, a homosexual reference seemingly out of place in this realm of "macho men." In Jungian terms we are witnessing these soldiers' anima, the release of their feminine unconscious, usually so well-guarded by the masculine persona or mask. As Jung also noted, however, usually the most masculine male persona has the most feminine anima. Elias's gesture is also not surprising in this most feminine of archetypal places. The cave, or underworld, as Jung and Campbell explained, is a mother symbol, a womb: "The place of magical transformation and rebirth, together with the underworld and its inhabitants, [is] presided over by the mother."[37] In this sense, Elias's gesture toward Chris speaks to the yin/yang of human existence, in which even sexuality is a balancing of opposites combined into a whole. Here, in the womblike underworld of the unconscious, even these war-hardened veterans can be soft, affectionate, and playful with each other.

Elias's proffered "toke" from the barrel of his gun is also a seemingly incongruent image because relief and possibly healing are found at the "business end" of a weapon of destruction. The gesture reads similarly to the now-famous 1960s image of a riot control police officer photographed with a Vietnam War protester's daisy sticking out of his rifle barrel. For a brief moment, it is as if both the meaning of the war and its agency have been renegotiated. As such, the scene is also reminiscent of the Buddhist idea that good and evil—like male and female sexuality—are one. In Vietnam, as

Stone described it, "in order to go on existing I'd have to shed the innocence and accept the evil the Homeric gods had thrown into the world. To be both good and evil."[38] Taylor, in the underworld, is learning this lesson well.

In *Platoon,* as in many of Stone's films, Stone also distinguishes between "good" and "bad" drugs. In *The Doors,* for example, drugs, particularly acid (LSD), are "good" when they transport Morrison and The Doors band into altered and more spiritual states of consciousness, which is most apparent in the group's pilgrimage to the desert. In contrast, drugs, particularly alcohol, are "bad" when they help destroy Morrison's significant relationships and hasten his inevitable demise, which is most obvious toward the end of *The Doors* when we see Morrison getting fat and sloppy as he guzzles Jack Daniels from the bottle.

In *Platoon* we find evidence for a similar statement regarding the difference between good and bad drugs. The "good soldiers" with whom Chris Taylor hangs out smoke pot. The "bad soldiers" led by Barnes drink beer and chug whiskey. Good drugs like marijuana, hash, and various hallucinogens bring enlightenment and healing, whereas bad drugs, usually alcohol, bring destruction. The scene in the underworld, for example, is immediately juxtaposed with an above-ground scene in the barracks, where the beer and whiskey crew are partying. The feeling of gentle and healing camaraderie found in the underworld is noticeably absent here. The lights are bright, no one is laughing, embracing, or dancing, and the music—country rather than soul or rock—sets a very different tone. The dichotomy between the two worlds is not only established by Sergeant Barnes's presence here, but by the first song lyric we hear, a plaintive country voice singing, "We don't smoke marijuana."

The film's split view on drugs is later reinforced near the end of the film when a menacing Barnes enters the underworld to condemn the potheads he finds there, saying: "Why do you smoke this shit? So you can escape from reality? Me, I don't need this shit. I am reality. There's the way it ought to be and there's the way it is. Elias was full of shit and was a crusader. Now I got no fight with any man who do what he's told. But when he don't, the machine breaks down and when the machine breaks down, we break down." Barnes is the reality of unredeemed evil, and escaping this "reality," or rather transcending this "machine-age" view of humanity, is what crusaders like Elias are all about. Barnes, consumed by his shadow, will never know elevated states of consciousness and therefore cannot pursue or even dream of a more integrated path for human enlightenment. Elias may be too good for this world, and thus must be martyred, but Barnes, the film asserts, is hardly a laudable alternative.

Platoon is the most blatant of Stone's films in its use of Christian iconography. And, as in many of Stone's films, betrayal is at the heart of *Platoon*'s messianic allegory. Elias (Elijah) is a Christ figure who, by the end of the film, is betrayed by Barnes, his Judas and his evil counterpart. As mentioned, Barnes not only calls Elias a "crusader"; he also refers to him as a "water walker." And when Barnes betrays Elias, shooting him in cold blood and leaving him for dead in the jungle, Barnes fulfills his Judas contract. It remains for the Vietcong to finish off the wounded Elias in his final, dramatic attempt at escape. Taylor, airlifted out with the remaining members of his platoon after a firefight, looks down in horror and sees Elias, running full tilt across an open field, gunned down in slow motion by seemingly hundreds of pursuing Vietcong. As he dies, Elias throws up his arms in a sacrificial Christ posture as the music swells.

The film's messianic references were not lost on critics, many of whom found them heavy handed. As one noted: "Barnes as a symbol of evil and Elias as a rough-hewn Christ-image become artificial stick figures. Barnes apparently kills Elias, as though Oliver Stone is offering the cynical message that only the ruthless can expect to win a war. Elias apparently rises from the dead, only to die once more, arms outstretched, as a crucified witness to the ultimate triumph of holiness."[39] This critic, however, failed to see the more interesting ramifications of the film's resolution. Although it is true that Elias's murder by Barnes reads like the betrayal of a martyred messiah, we must remember that the film concludes with Taylor murdering Barnes. Although the execution is seemingly justified, we cannot forget that by taking Barnes's life, Taylor engages in the same type of vigilantism practiced by Barnes against Elias. What are the implications? Earlier in the film, when the surviving platoon members are discussing what to do about Barnes's murder of Elias, Taylor suggests that they murder Barnes. One of the soldiers notes that Barnes has been shot seven times and is still alive, adding, "Nothing can kill Barnes but Barnes." It is not much of a leap to argue that when Chris succeeds in killing Barnes at the end of the film it is actually the "Barnes" in him that kills Barnes. Or, the reasoning can be inverted: By killing Barnes, Taylor is killing the Barnes in himself. Chris, in other words, is confronting/slaying his own shadow/ego.

As Campbell has explained, although the hero quest often appears as external to the hero, for example, when he must slay a dragon or the personification of evil in some other form, it is ultimately internal because the "enemy" the hero must slay is often himself, or in other words, it is his own ego. To be born again, the hero must die to self in order to transcend to something greater than self.[40]

Taylor's murder of Barnes also acknowledges the heart of darkness that exists in all of us, that is, our capacity to be both good and evil, or in Jungian terms, the shadow side of our psyche and our need to confront our own shadows if we are to grow. This is the lesson—albeit won at a high price— that Chris Taylor must learn to become a man.[41]

The film's conclusion reinforces the idea that the individual's most significant battles are internal, often involving a Manichaean struggle between the conscious and the unconscious, the self and the shadow. Taylor, in a final voice-over as he is being airlifted out of Vietnam, says, "I think now looking back, we did not fight the enemy; we fought ourselves, and the enemy was in us. A war is over for me now, but it will always be there for the rest of my days, as I'm sure Elias will be fighting with Barnes for what Rhah called 'the possession of my soul.'" The landscape for any future battles, for Taylor—and for all future archetypal heroes—is internal.

Taylor continues in voice-over to explain what this inward journey involves: "Those of us who did make it have an obligation to build again, to teach to others what we know and to try with what's left of our lives to find a goodness and meaning to this life." And so, like Chris Taylor, Stone invites us to continue to seek salvation from the sins of our fathers, from Vietnam, from godless and heartless technology in the age of reason. And if salvation is not possible, we, like Taylor, must continue to look for an explanation that will render life, and perhaps death, meaningful once more.

Born on the Fourth of July (1989)

Born on the Fourth of July tells the story of Ron Kovic, a Vietnam vet who came back from Vietnam paralyzed from the mid-chest down. The film is one in a long list of films about disabled Vietnam vets making sense of their lives and their experiences in Vietnam. The image of the Vietnam vet reconstructing his life stateside, such as Stevie in *The Deer Hunter*, Luke in *Coming Home*, Alex Cutter in *Cutter's Way*, and Ron Kovic in *Born on the Fourth of July*, also became metaphoric for the American public's attempt to do likewise. Based on Kovic's autobiography, the film is about his journey of self-discovery and his sharing of this discovery with the American people. Kovic's quest, like Chris Taylor's before him, although beginning as an outward journey (he also goes to Vietnam to find himself), eventually turns inward. Like Kennedy, Kovic is an archetypal hero searching for the truth, no matter how painful that truth might prove to be and regardless of the sacrifices that must be made in its pursuit. Kennedy loses his life and Garrison loses his reputation, whereas Kovic loses his biological manhood and the use of his legs. But like Kennedy and Garrison, what Kovic gains is an audience for his message and the assurance that his quest for truth and meaning will be carried on by those who come after him. We, the American public, to use Campbell's term, are offered Kovic's "boon."[42] We are charged with the responsibility of carrying the torch that Kennedy passed to the next generation of Ron Kovics and Jim Garrisons.

Ron Kovic, employed by Stone as technical adviser for the film, seemed to embrace this burden when he asserted that film, like literature,

has a responsibility to instruct, to teach, to portray the truth so effectively that those who read it or watch it on the screen are not the same again and are so deeply moved that when choices are to be made, correct choices are made, and when decisions are to be made, correct decisions are made. Our acts of creativity—when we write, when we make films—should give direction, should be a map of the soul to betterment, a *good* map that gets people to their destination intact.[43]

Nominated for eight Academy Awards, *Born on the Fourth of July* won Stone an Oscar for Best Director, the Directors' Guild of America Award, and a Golden Globe Award for Best Director. *Born on the Fourth of July,* like *Platoon,* was a film that Stone had been wanting to make for a long time. Scheduled for filming twelve years before its actual release (with Al Pacino as star, Stone as writer, and William Friedkin as director), the picture was canceled four days before principal photography was to begin. At that time, Stone promised Ron Kovic that once he was in a position to call the shots in Hollywood, which he clearly was after *Platoon,* he would make Kovic's story into a film.

Despite *Born on the Fourth of July*'s box-office success and numerous awards, it was less well-received than *Platoon*. Critics who did not care for the mythic qualities in *Platoon* liked them even less in *Born on the Fourth of July*. One of them noted: "Stone cannot resist grandiloquence. Individual

Ron Kovic (Tom Cruise) in *Born on the Fourth of July* finds his political voice as he becomes an active protester of American involvement in Vietnam. Copyright © 1989 Universal City Studios Inc. Courtesy of MCA Publishing Rights, a Division of MCA, Inc. All rights reserved. Photo by Roland Neveu.

pieces may seem on the mark—'the way it really was'—but Stone is constantly basting them with a mythic sauce. And so what comes out this time is not a searching examination of Ron Kovic's life, but a symbolic life, the effort to make Kovic's experience represent the history of an entire nation."[44] Comparing *Born on the Fourth of July* to *Glory,* a film about a black battalion in the Civil War, another critic claimed that "although 'Born' deals with more recent times, it feels more distant, more rhetorical."[45] David Ansen chided, the film "is trying so hard to be archetypal it ends up feeling unreal. You can't connect to the characters because they've been deprived of personality; they're simply white-bread symbols of deluded American patriotism."[46]

As in previous films, Stone's use of Christian iconography in *Born on the Fourth of July* was also dismissed by the critics. Pauline Kael observed, "The movie is constructed as a series of blackout episodes that suggest the Stations of the Cross; rising strings alert you to the heavy stuff. Then the finale—Resurrection—takes Ron into white light, and John Williams lays on the trumpets."[47] *Commonweal* critic Christina Appy asserted that if "Oliver Stone is on hand to direct the Second Coming don't expect grainy documentary. The face of the Lord will be made to shine down upon us—in super tight focus—and the throbbing violin swells of a John Williams score will roll in from the sun-streaked horizon."[48]

Whether they picked it or panned it, critics of the film often commented on its emotional pyrotechnics. David Ansen called it "a primal scream of a movie," "the cinematic equivalent of heavy metal," adding "fueled by rage, pain, self-pity and political outrage, this long, relentless movie tries for a knockout in almost every scene. . . . [The] movie offers you two choices; you can be overwhelmed by it, or do battle with it. Either way it leaves you drained."[49]

Those who admired the film, however, were adamant in their praise. Klawans, for example, asserted that *Born on the Fourth of July* "probably tells you more about American society and politics than all previous Vietnam movies combined. . . . It gives you more of one man's reality than you can easily handle, combined with more political honesty than anyone could expect from Hollywood."[50] Even Ansen admitted that "the movie is a tirade against the authoritarian macho mentality that led us into Vietnam. . . . Stone is conversant in the politics of emotionalism. . . . There's no denying that Oliver Stone has a vision; his conviction, his anger and his talent are for real.[51]

From the opening shot of *Born on the Fourth of July,* Stone establishes the innocence of pre-Vietnam America. A graphic that reads "Massapequa, Long Island, 1956" is followed by a brief sequence of Ron Kovic as a child innocently "playing war" with friends in a wooded lot. This brief scene presages the not-so-innocent war games Kovic will later play in Vietnam as a youth and the internal war that will rage in his heart as an adult.

As the scene changes to a Fourth of July parade down Main Street in Massapequa, we realize that this could be anyone's town, anyone's past. Stone emphasizes this by shooting the entire sequence in sepia-tone with red, white, and blue highlights. To the tune "It's a Grand Old Flag," we see shots of the high-school band, led by drum majorettes and baton twirlers. We hear crowds cheering and waving and see numerous images of American flags carried by parade marchers and onlookers. We may even remember the words of the song as we sing to ourselves: "It's a grand old flag/It's a high-flying flag/And forever in peace may it wave/It's the emblem of the land I love/The home of the free and the brave." We are witnessing Hometown, U.S.A., at a time before Americans began questioning their government or the promises of the American Dream, a place, in Stone's eyes, without cynicism, despair, or doubt, an era when being American was something to proclaim with assurance and optimism to the rest of the world.

The tone changes to a minor key, both musically and visually, however, as the Veterans of Foreign Wars go past, some in cars and some in wheelchairs, and some with missing arms and legs. A round of firecrackers explodes. Some of the vets flinch as if reexperiencing gunfire from their own private war.

In a series of shot-and-reverse-angle shots little Ronnie Kovic, sitting on his father's shoulders, locks eyes with one of the armless vets marching by. Reminiscent of the opening scene of *Platoon,* it is as if Ron Kovic, like Chris Taylor, witnesses his own fate and his own battle-scarred return mirrored in the faces of the vets passing before him. As in *Platoon,* the shot is also accompanied by elevated music to reinforce its poignancy. Ron Kovic, born on the fourth of July, is the typical all-American boy—not just patriotic but superpatriotic. "Ain't he a little Fourth of July firecracker," intones his mother. Rubbing Ron's head affectionately, Ron's father replies, "Yeah, he's my little Yankee Doodle boy." Being born on the fourth of July means something to Ron Kovic as a young boy, but what it will mean to Ron as a young man changes drastically over the course of the film.

Although all of Stone's films view contemporary American history through the lens of the Kennedy presidency, *Born on the Fourth of July* overtly frames our experiences in Vietnam and beyond within a Camelot context. The next scene, for example, begins with strains of President John F. Kennedy's first Inaugural Address. As the Kovic family gathers around their television set, Kennedy addresses the audience:

> . . . young Americans, to answer the call to service around the globe. Now the trumpets summon us again. Now is no call to bear arms 'though arms we need, but a call to bear the burden of a long twilight struggle, a struggle against the common enemies of man; tyranny, poverty, disease, and war itself. In the long history of the world only a few generations have been granted the role of defending freedom in its hour of maximum danger. I do not shrink

from this responsibility, I welcome it. Let the word go forth from this time and place that the torch has been passed to a new generation of Americans, born in this century. Let every nation know that we shall pay any price, bear any burden, support any friend, oppose any foe to assure the survival and the success of liberty. And so, my fellow Americans, ask not what your country can do for you but what you can do for your country.

Ron's mother turns to him and says, "I had a dream Ronnie—you were standing in front of a big crowd and you were saying great things. Just like him, just like him."

The film establishes a parallel between Kennedy's and Kovic's quests for the truth. The irony of the moment is that although Ron's mother most likely envisions her son standing proudly in front of an audience to proclaim the justness of America's defense of liberty around the globe, when asked to do so in front of another crowd of Fourth of July revelers, Ron, the returned Vietnam vet, is mute. His moment of greatness, his revelation of the truth—the hero's "boon" that he will share with the people—will instead come some twenty years after his mother's proclamation, at the 1976 Democratic National Convention in New York City. Although we do not witness the actual speech, we sense that its message will be quite different from the speech he would have made even a few years before.

But now, at the film's beginning, Ron seems to heed the president's words regarding the need for sacrifice. We see shots of Ronnie training with his high-school team. As the team members scale walls, climb ropes, and run endless laps in the gym, we hear the couch intone, "You wanna win? You gotta suffer. You wanna be the best, you gotta pay the price for victory and the price is sacrifice, sacrifice, people." The message of sacrifice at the price of success is later reinforced by Ron's mother, who explains to Ron's brother, "Your brother's a hard worker, Tony, 'cause he wants to be the best. Win or lose, in school, sports, in life, as long as you do your best that's what matters to God." Ron later echoes this message when he explains his reasons for enlisting for service in Vietnam to his skeptical father, saying, "Don't you remember what President Kennedy said? There's not gonna be an America anymore unless there are people who are willing to sacrifice. I love my country." Ron Kovic, like Chris Taylor in *Platoon,* joins the service because it is the honorable thing to do. Just as Taylor, a white middle-class American, enlists so that the war would not be fought only by minorities and the working class, Kovic also joins out of a sense of duty as an able-bodied American to defend "freedom in its hour of maximum danger."

Kovic, however, confronts a very different Vietnam than did Chris Taylor in *Platoon*. Whereas Taylor's Vietnam is a rotting slug-infested swamp, Kovic's is a hazy and arid desert, a barren wilderness of oblivion. At one point a fellow soldier proclaims, "So hot out this must be hell or purgatory."

But more important, whereas Taylor's Vietnam represents the beginning of his transformation, Kovic's quest for manhood and meaning only occurs after he returns from Vietnam. It is not long before Kovic, in his second tour of duty, is seriously wounded, like Chris Taylor, in a firefight. Unlike Taylor, however, Kovic's injuries are serious enough to send him stateside, where his real battle, an internal one, begins.

We witness the beginning of Kovic's unraveling patriotism in the Bronx Veterans' Administration Hospital, where he is sent for rehabilitation. As numerous critics have pointed out, these scenes of a rat-infested, broken-down, and understaffed hospital—where not only supplies but sympathy are in short supply—are the most poignant and startling of the film. It is here that Kovic begins to realize that the easiest way for many Americans to deal with their guilt over a war many felt should not have been fought was to ignore the most visceral and unpleasant reminders of it, the broken bodies and minds of the soldiers sent into battle. The Vietnam War, as Stone asserts in *Born on the Fourth of July* and *Platoon,* was an internal one—a conflict that tore public opinion apart, set family members against each other, and divided the minds of men and women. As a black nurse reminds Kovic in the hospital, "You don't know shit about what's goin' on over here in this country. . . . It ain't about burning the flag in Vietnam, man. . . . It's about Detroit and Newark. It's about racism."

Despite inklings of his pending transformation in the hospital, however, Kovic remains a staunch supporter of American ideals to the fellow vets and hospital staff members he encounters there. From the perspective of Campbell's monomyth, Kovic refuses to accept the "call to adventure." He fails, in other words, to truly understand the lessons that Vietnam should have taught him.[52]

It is only when he returns home to his mother's uncomfortable reception that Kovic begins to question his assumptions about what it means to be an American and what it meant to sacrifice his body in Vietnam. In one scene in particular, Kovic returns home after a long night of drunkenness only to enrage his mother, embarrass his father, and awaken the entire neighborhood with his anger and despair. This scene, also notable because it frames Kovic's experiences in Vietnam in the context of Kennedy's assassination and Christ's crucifixion, is a classic Stone "wake-up call." The protagonist, suddenly awakened to the truth, attempts to literally wake up those around him with his newfound knowledge:

> *Ron.* This is what you believe in, isn't it, Mom? [Ron waves a cross with a cru-
> cified Christ on it.] This is what you believe, but I don't. I don't believe in
> him anymore. He only had to spend three days up there. Me, I gotta spend
> the rest of my life. I wish I were dead like him.
> *Mother.* You don't know what you're saying.

Ron. That's the problem, Mom. I'm not dead. I gotta live. I gotta live and I gotta roll around. I gotta remind you of Vietnam, and you don't know. You don't wanna see us. You want to hide us. You want to hide us 'cause it is a can of shit and I am a fucking dummy. I believed everything they told us. "Go fight, go kill." Sergeant Man, Marine Corps . . . It's all a lie. We went to fight communism—

Mother. You're gonna wake up the whole neighborhood!

Ron. Wake 'em up, tell them. Cuzaks, Cappalanies, Walshes, you tell them. Tell them all what they did to me. What they did to this whole block, this whole country. We went to Vietnam to stop communism. We shot women and children.

Mom. You didn't shoot women and children. What are you saying?

Ron. Blessed the war. Communism, the insidious evil. They told us to go.

Mom. Yes, that's what they told us.

Ron. Thou shalt not kill, Mom, thou shalt not kill women and children. Thou shalt not kill, remember? Isn't that what you taught us?

Mother. I didn't force you to go.

Ron. Yes, you did; yes, you did, and it's all falling apart. King, Kennedy, Kent State . . . fucking communism won. It's all for nothing. Tell her, Dad, tell her. It's a fucking lie. There's no God—God is dead as my legs. There's no God. There's no country.

Kovic, by brandishing a crucifix and comparing Christ's death on the cross to the "death" of his own body, asserts his own crippled messianic status. He is the classic Stone hero—maimed and disillusioned in a seemingly senseless sacrifice and railing against the injustices of meaningless life. Lost in a universe where God is dead, Kovic is ill at ease in a postmodern world of broken promises with no hope of teleological advancement.

Christ's death on the cross and the demise of God as a transcendent possibility are echoed in *Born on the Fourth of July*'s portrayal of the eclipse of the American Dream. In the series of short clips that follow this scene, we see the 1968 presidential election, the fateful 1968 Democratic National Convention in Chicago, footage of the antiwar protests outside the convention hall, and the deadly response of Mayor Daly's riot police. As we see shots of a burning American flag, we hear strains of Don MacLean's song "American Pie": "Bye, bye, Miss American Pie/Drove my Chevy to the levee but the levee was dry/And good 'ol boys were drinking whiskey and rye/Singing this will be the day that I die/This will be the day that I die." The death of the transcendent dream is echoed in the death of the American Dream, coincidental with the loss of so many American soldiers in Vietnam.

Kovic's personal awakening—his hero's resurrection from desperate self-loathing to a purposeful plan of action—occurs sometime later, however, in a desert in southwestern Mexico. As in *The Doors* and *Natural Born Killers,* the desert is a place of transformations. Jim Morrison in *The*

Doors, for example, like Christ, witnesses his life's "mission" and pending death in a desert, and Mickey and Mallory in *Natural Born Killers* also meet their spiritual guide, the Navajo Indian, there. In *Born on the Fourth of July* what begins as a scene from an absurdist play ends as a similarly transforming experience for Kovic. It is here that Kovic, in Campbell's words, after finally accepting the hero's "call to adventure," crosses the first threshold of the quest.[53]

Kovic, along with other disabled Vietnam vets, heads for Mexican seaside towns to drown the pain of their existence in drugs, cheap sex, and all-night carousing. The climax of this senseless journey of self-destruction occurs when he and another disabled vet named Charlie (Willem Dafoe), on their way to the next Mexican watering hole, are dumped in the desert by a cab driver grown tired of their endless anger and verbal abuse. Wheeling around in the vast emptiness of space, these two men hurl epithets at each other in a bizarre competition over who killed the most babies in Vietnam:

> *Charlie.* Did you ever have to kill a baby, a little gook baby?
> *Ron.* How do you know what I did?
> *Charlie.* I didn't think so, you're full of shit. You never killed a baby, you never had to kill a baby because you never put your soul into that war—you never put your soul on the line, man.
> *Ron.* How do you know; how the fuck do you know? Maybe I killed babies, maybe I killed more babies than you did, you fuck. Maybe I killed a whole bunch of babies, but I don't talk about it. I don't have to talk about it.
> *Charlie.* Why not? Why the fuck not? What are you hiding? What? Are you better than anybody else? You a hero maybe? You've got a whole bunch of medals, but deep down you're full of shit.

With this last line the two disabled vets begin spitting at each other. They then wrestle and fall from their wheelchairs to the ground as they continue to fight. Although the majority of the scene is shot in medium shots and close-ups, adding to its intensity, an occasional extreme long shot is used to emphasize the absurdity of the two pathetically small figures fighting over who killed the most babies in this endless and barren vista. We are truly on "the dusty plain of Troy," a landscape against which the stakes of the battle between these reduced heroes seem both pitifully small and enormously large at the same time.

Inklings of Ron Kovic's transformation occur at the end of this scene. Just before these two wounded heroes are rescued by a passing Mexican peasant, Kovic leans over the prostrate Charlie to say: "You don't get it. We had a town once, Charlie, and a mother and father and things that made sense—remember things that made sense? That you could count on before we all got so lost? What are we going to do, Charlie? What the fuck am I gonna do?" In sum, before Kennedy's death all had felt right; after it, nothing did. These lines spoken by Kovic capture the essence of the despair often felt by Stone's ill-at-ease protagonists as they "rage against the dying of the light"[54] and mourn for the loss of a home in a universe that once made sense.

Although no answer to Kovic's question immediately presents itself, the very next scene finds him at the grave of a fellow soldier, Private Wilson, whom Kovic shot and killed by accident during a firefight in Vietnam. According to Campbell, the third step in the hero journey, after he has answered the call to adventure (to self-discovery) and has crossed the first threshold, is a series of trials designed to test his resolve.[55] Kovic's new willingness to admit to himself and to Private Wilson's family that he killed their son in Vietnam is the first trial in his journey of transformation. In Jungian terms, this trial is Kovic's confrontation with his shadow. Kovic, in other words, is about to begin the healing process by confronting his demons and acknowledging to himself and to others his shame over shooting a fellow soldier in battle.

Prepared to be ridiculed and rejected by Wilson's family, he instead finds himself embraced, reassured, and sent on his way with a newfound resolve to declare the truth about America's involvement in Vietnam. For the remainder of the film, Kovic becomes a central voice in the antiwar protests (similar to Richard Boyle in *Salvador*), demonstrating at numerous rallies and at the 1972 and 1976 Democratic and Republican National Conventions. Although thrown out of the 1972 Republican convention in Miami, Kovic is invited to speak at the 1976 Democratic convention in New York City. It is here that Kovic, the enlightened hero, is finally able to share his boon with the American people, the precious gift he obtained only by descending into the depths of his own despair and betrayal and facing his own shadow.

Surrounded by supporters and well-wishers, the triumphant and smiling Kovic waits in the wings of the hall where he will address the gathered conventioneers and the American people via national television. Asked by a reporter how it feels "to be addressing the entire country," Kovic replies, "Overwhelming, an honor; it's been a long ways for us vets. Just lately, I've felt like I'm home, you know, like maybe we're home." As Kovic is wheeled to the podium, the film ends with the song with which it began—"It's a Grand Old Flag."

Kovic, like so many able-bodied and disabled vets, is finally feeling accepted by a country that denied his very existence. His hero quest is about to end, the Homeric odyssey has come full circle as he delivers his "boon" to the American people. Now the song "It's a Grand Old Flag" has new meaning: Americans should love their country, with judgment rather than innocence, not out of blind patriotism but with the knowledge that its actions are sometimes wrong. Further, perhaps the greatest act of love is to honor that for which America stands—the ability, paradoxically, to continually challenge that for which it stands. As Americans, we have gone through trial by fire and must not forget the mistakes we have made or the lessons learned in Vietnam. If we truly want to be at home in the universe we need to accept who we are; we should not seek a return to the innocence of the Garden—no longer possible in a post-Vietnam world—but rather fashion a world built upon our mistakes. Just as Kovic, by facing his shame, finds a home in a universe that seemed to reject him, America also needs to face the shame of Vietnam—to construct our home by starting with "the stone the builders rejected" (Psalms 118:22) and acknowledge who we are in our quest to discover what we can become.

Heaven and Earth (1993)

Despite the numerous differences that mark many of the films of the Vietnam era, all of the films, with few exceptions, portray the Vietnam War as primarily an American and a male experience. Although the war is often depicted as affecting women, particularly in their relationships with men, for example, as in *Coming Home* and *Cutter's Way*, the driving narrative force is always male and the primary tragedy is always that of the male soldier or veteran. And although the Vietnamese culture figures to greater and lesser extent in most Vietnam films, until recently American cinema audiences have not been treated to sympathetic or complex portraits of either the North or South Vietnamese people. *Heaven and Earth* is a startling exception to both rules, using as it does a Vietnamese woman's point of view to explore American involvement in Vietnam and the war's effect on her country, on Southeast Asia, and on the United States.

Heaven and Earth, despite its lack of critical or popular success, is also an important part of the Stone Vietnam trilogy because it chronologically completes the story that begins with *Platoon* and continues through *Born on the Fourth of July*. Although *Heaven and Earth* begins during the war in Southeast Asia, like *Born on the Fourth of July* it continues beyond its conclusion to bring us almost up to the 1990s. *Heaven and Earth* also portrays the most advanced progress on the path of spiritual enlightenment taken by any of Stone's Vietnam heroes. Although Chris Taylor in *Platoon* is witness to the struggle for his soul waged by two messianic figures, the spiritual effect of that battle on him has only just begun by the film's conclusion. By comparison, Ron Kovic in *Born on the Fourth of July* is an active participant in the Homeric odyssey for meaning and significance in life. Both Kovic and Taylor, however, pale by comparison with Le Ly, the young Vietnamese protagonist of *Heaven and Earth,* who seems to know from the start that the odyssey of survival in Vietnam is, and has always been, the journey toward the Self.

Heaven and Earth is based on Le Ly Hayslip's autobiographies *When Heaven and Earth Changed Places* and *Child of War, Woman of Peace.* The first book is an account of her experiences growing up in central Vietnam before, during, and after the French and American invasions. The second book recounts her experiences after the Vietnam War when she has moved to America. Stone has explained his attraction to Le Ly's story, calling it a "chance for me to step out of my own experience again to see the war from another point of view."[56]

Initially inclined to shoot the film in the Philippines because of his success with shooting *Platoon* and *Born on the Fourth of July* there, Stone and his scenic designer Victor Kempster ultimately settled on Phang-Nga in the south of Thailand. Vietnam was not a location option because of strong opposition from the current regime in Ho Chi Minh City. As Stone put it, "We ran into hard-liners—men with missing arms, missing eyes, men not particularly open to accusations [for wartime brutality]. . . . They did not encourage us to make the movie [in Vietnam] unless we changed certain aspects of it."[57]

Stone's crew re-created Le Ly's village of Ky La, planting over four hundred hectares of fallow rice paddies and building thirty-four stone and concrete village houses from the ground up. The majority of the Vietnamese roles in the film, including that of the protagonist, Le Ly, are played by

Le Ly Hayslip (Hiep Thi Le), with her father (Dr. Haing S. Ngor), contemplates the impact of the Vietnam War on her life, her family, and her country in *Heaven and Earth*. Copyright © 1993 Warner Bros. Productions Limited. Monarchy Enterprises C.V. and Le Studio Canal+. Photo by Roland Neveu.

Asian and Vietnamese nonprofessionals.[58] A monumental undertaking, the company required for the shoot consisted of 450 crew members, 100 actors, and close to 1,200 extras—ethnic Vietnamese from northeastern Thailand.[59]

Stone wrote *Heaven and Earth*'s screenplay two years before the film's November 1993 opening. Principal photography began on October 19, 1992. The Vietnam portion of the film took over sixty-four days to shoot. Additional photography was done in Bangkok and Phuket Town in Thailand, and at various locations in Vietnam. The final one-third of the film was shot during four weeks in Los Angeles.

Critics noted the significant difference between *Heaven and Earth* and almost all of Stone's previous films. Critic Jeff Yang, for example, described the problem Stone faced with *Heaven and Earth*, pointing out that "Stone's point of view was suspect. After all, over the last decade, he'd not only raised the ire of Asian Americans, but also drawn fire for his marginalization of female characters. Could he successfully bring an Asian woman's story to the screen?"[60] Le Ly Hayslip also apparently shared misgivings about Stone's ability to tell her life story. After meeting with him, however, Hayslip asserted that she had "changed her mind about Oliver Stone," noting, "Now I feel Oliver is my soulmate; he's the *only* person who could have told my story."[61] Stone readily admitted the validity of the criticism of his past portrayals of female and ethnic characters, explaining, however, that he attempted to address this in *Heaven and Earth* by "embrac[ing] the feminine principle. And in terms of the Asians, in *Heaven and Earth* I tried very hard to show that Vietnam is not this 'other' place. That the Vietnamese have families. That they care about life. And they may have a little wiser perception of the soul."[62]

Stone also acknowledged the spiritual impulse that informed his telling of Le Ly's story. Attracted to Buddhism through his acquaintance with Le Ly, Stone began to study Buddhist thought. He explained, "I'm just a novice, but I do practice it. . . . Being exposed to it through Le Ly, I've had a real chance to understand how it applies to everyday life. It's not removed or distant; it's a working path, and it's worked for 2000 years."[63]

Stone's increasing sense of his hero's journey as spiritual and inward rather than rational and outward is evidenced in the opening shots of *Heaven and Earth*. The film opens with a graphic scroll that develops the film as a docudrama with an underlying spiritual tone:

This film is based on the true-life story of Phang Thi Le Ly Hayslip from Ky La, a rice-farming village in central Vietnam. It is the early 1950s and Ky La has been under the domination of France for nearly 70 years as part of the country's vast Indochinese colonial empire. The French rulers are far away in Saigon, Hanoi, or Paris, but in Ky La life goes on as it has for a thousand years—protected by Father Heaven, Ong Troi, and Mother Earth, Me Dat. Between Heaven and Earth—Troi Va Dat—are the people, striving to bring forth the harvest and follow Lord Buddha's teachings.

The opening shot is of a Buddhist monk in saffron robes, who is seemingly deep in prayer. This is followed by an image of Le Ly, the protagonist, as a child. She stands next to her father—also bowed in prayer. A close-up of an immense golden Buddha slowly dissolves to a richly green rice paddy, where we view endless acres of rice turned into a rippling sea by the breeze. In voice-over, we hear Le Ly as an adult say, "I lived in the most beautiful place on earth. My earliest memories were working alongside mother in the fields—always working, my mother. Each grain of rice a symbol of life never wasted. While we worked she would teach me everything I had to know about life." Le Ly as a child in the field with her mother then says, "Mamma, where did I really come from? Where do babies come from?" "From my belly button," replies her mother. In voice-over, Le Ly continues, "Our rice paddies were always near the cemeteries because we believed the spirits passed through the soil into the rice so the new generation, in eating the rice, was sharing in the spirits of their ancestors."

In this opening sequence we are privy to a glimpse of the Garden before the Fall. The use of a green filter and a wide-angle lens makes the verdant rice paddies glow with a saturated fertility and an abundant endlessness. It is a lyrical, holy, and unspoiled world where life, in a grain of rice or in the seed of a babe in its mother's belly, is both reverential and matter of fact. Life, the film reminds us, is also intimately acquainted with and created from death. The souls of the dead provide grounding and possibility for the living. Life in the Garden before the Fall was maintained by a perfect balancing act between life and death and between Heaven and Earth, as the people, striving to follow the middle path, "bring forth the harvest and follow Lord Buddha's teachings."

It is not long, however, before senseless death and religious impiety enter the scene to expel these people from their Garden. Le Ly continues in voice-over, saying, "Then one day in the summer of 1955 the French came." The music changes to a minor key as the camera becomes erratic and restless and the shot darkens to grey. We see images of a big tank rolling across the once green and pristine landscape, crushing everything in its path. Le Ly continues: "They destroyed our village and the following year we went hungry and I will never forget my father's eyes as he watched our house burn to the ground, but as it had happened for so many centuries, we rebuilt our lives. Then in 1963 the peasant countryside changed forever. From my father I learned to love God and the people I could not see—my ancestors—but I would learn in time my father's words would be twisted by events." Evil has entered the Garden in the shape of the French, and later the American, invaders. We learn in *JFK* that the plague that began spreading in America after Kennedy's death and the growth of the military-industrial complex started in the black hearts of America's leaders, but in this film we find that the place where the virulent strain worked its corruption was in the lives and on the lands of the Vietnamese peasants. The technological ability to build weapons of mass destruction, first developed in World Wars I and II, was perfected in Vietnam. The cost of this terministic obsession, *Heaven and Earth* seems to imply, was the sacrifice of all that was good in our collective mythical preconsciousness—respect for life and the natural environment, a reverence for the god-essence in all, and an understanding of the spiritually evolutionary soul.

Le Ly's spiritual odyssey, like that of Stone's other Vietnam protagonists, takes her down into the depths of despair and degradation. Tortured by the South Vietnamese, raped rather than shot by the Vietcong, she eventually escapes to Saigon, where she works as a kitchen maid for a wealthy Vietnamese businessman. Seduced and impregnated by her master, she once again flees in shame. She moves in with her sister, a prostitute whose profession we sense Le Ly would have adopted if she had not met Steve, an American GI searching for love and compassion and a place to rest his weary head. They eventually marry and leave Saigon for the United States when the American presence in Vietnam begins to unravel. The demons that haunted Le Ly in Vietnam, however, continue to pursue her in America as her marriage to Steve breaks down, resulting in his suicide. The film ends with Le Ly's return to her family and her village, accompanied by her almost-grown son and daughter, who meet, possibly for the first time, Le Ly's mother and family.

As she returns to the grave of her father and the small Buddhist shrine that stands on the outskirts of her village, Le Ly, in voice-over, speaks of the lessons she has learned from her personal odyssey of the heart:

> I gave my offerings to all the dead of the village. I had come home. Yes, but home had changed and I would always be between South, North, East, West, peace, war, Vietnam, America. It is my fate to be in between Heaven and Earth. When we resist our fate, we suffer; when we accept it, we are happy. We have time in abundance—an eternity—to repeat our mistakes; but we need only once correct our mistake—and at last hear the song of enlightenment with which we can break the chain of vengeance forever. In your heart you can hear it now. It's the song your spirit has been singing to you since the moment of your birth.

We witness here the clearest proclamation of any Stone protagonist about the next step of teleological development. On the one hand, rather than "wailing and gnashing" her teeth about the injustices of the modern world and the seemingly unjust trials and tribulations she has had to endure, as most Stone protagonists do, Le Ly has, on the one hand, taken a very traditional position in Buddhism—the acceptance of fate, the belief in reincarnation, and a cause-and-effect explanation of karma and soul debt. On the other hand, however, she offers the argument that the next phase of the hero's quest must be inward rather than outward. To slay the monsters of rationality the old hardware is no longer sufficient. The tools supplied by science and technology that raised civilization out of the era of preconsciousness into the age of ego consciousness are not only rusty, they are irrelevant. We need instead to listen to "the song [our] spirit has been singing to [us] since the moment of [our] birth." The search for meaning has moved inward, since the lesson we must now learn is that in order to truly find "home," in Ron Kovic's words, we must remember, as does Chris Taylor, that "the enemy is within us," and as such, as Le Ly adds, "Lasting victories are won in the heart, not in this land or that."

Notes

1. After 1940, Hollywood films exhibited an overtly prowar agenda. In 1940, for example, such anti-Nazi films as *Foreign Correspondent*, directed by Alfred Hitchcock, and *The Great Dictator*, directed by Charlie Chaplin, were released. In 1941, as the war in Europe began heating up, an increasing number of prointervention films, such as *A Yank in the RAF*, *Man Hunt*, and *Sergeant York*, were produced. The culmination of the production of this type of commitment film, was, of course, reached with *Casablanca,* released in 1943. This prowar sentiment was due to a number of factors. First, Hollywood began witnessing the arrival of Jewish émigrés from Nazi-occupied Europe such as Billy Wilder and Fritz Lang, both of whom did a great deal to shape the anti-Fascist cinema of the 1940s. At the same time playwrights, schooled on the New York stage and in the social and radical theater groups of New York, moved to Hollywood, bringing their liberal perspectives with them. Finally, the rise of fascism in Europe pushed Hollywood to adopt an anti-Fascist agenda, thus creating a demand for these politically liberal and leftist writers (Brian Neve, *Film and Politics in America: A Social Tradition* [New York: Routledge, 1992]).

Warner Brothers, in particular, hired a number of politically conscious writers. In fact, of all the studios in the late 1930s, Warner Brothers emerged as the studio willing to show audiences that "the screen could legitimately take its place beside the printing press as a channel for the discussion of public ideas" (Richard Griffith, "The American Film: 1929–1948," in *The Film till Now*, ed. Paul Rotha and Richard Griffith [London: Vision Press, 1949], 457). Although the unionization of studio personnel, particularly writers, had begun changing Hollywood by the late 1930s, film studios, led by Warner, began to see their role as informing the American public about the threat of pro-Nazi organizations in America.

These prowar films were aided, in part, by the Office of War Information (OWI) and the Bureau of Motion Pictures, part of the OWI's domestic branch. In 1942, for example, the administration released the *Government Information Manual for the*

Motion Picture Industry, a manual that has been called "the clearest possible statement of New Deal, liberal view on how Hollywood should fight the war" (Neve, *Film and Politics,* 68).

Such prointervention films, however, did not meet with unanimous acceptance of the public or the government. Many isolationist members of Congress, for example, were incensed by what they saw as the war hysteria and prointervention propaganda coming out of Hollywood. Possibly as a result, the brief tradition of politically motivated filmmaking that marked Hollywood's wartime cinema was not carried over into postwar circumstances (Neve, *Film and Politics,* 112). The window for overtly political filmmaking all but closed during the decade after World War II and did not reemerge until after the Vietnam War had come to an end.

2. Richard Schickel, "Duke Talks Through His Green Berets," *Life,* 19 July 1968, 8.

3. The 1980s, the decade of Reagan conservatism, also brought forth a number of more conservative films geared toward reevaluating the Vietnam experience. In particular, there was a wave of conservative revisionist films such as the Sylvester Stallone *Rambo* and Chuck Norris *Missing in Action* series of movies.

4. The message comes from Joseph Conrad's *The Heart of Darkness*, adopted by Francis Ford Coppola as the predominant motif in *Apocalypse Now* (1979), and echoed in such films as *The Deer Hunter* (1979), *Platoon* (1986), and *Full Metal Jacket* (1987).

5. Leo Cawley, "The War About the War: Vietnam Films and American Myth," in *From Hanoi to Hollywood: The Vietnam War in American Film,* ed. Linda Dittmar and Gene Michaud (New Brunswick, NJ: Rutgers University Press, 1990), 69.

6. The only major difference between the ideology of Vietnam films and World War II films was that in World War II films Americans won because we played by the rules. In Vietnam films the message was often that Americans lost because we played by the rules. In other words, if only we had been tougher, slyer, and had done to the enemy what they did to us and had not held back out of some moral conviction, we would have won. This refrain, for example, was particularly loud in the Chuck Norris *Missing in Action* films and in the Sylvester Stallone *Rambo* films of the mid-1980s, where the primary message was that refraining from brutality put American forces at a significant disadvantage in Vietnam (Cawley, "War About the War," 69–80).

7. Ibid.

8. Ibid.

9. Richard Coombs, review of *"Platoon," Sight and Sound* 56 (1987):138.

10. Richard Corliss, *"Platoon*: The Way It Really Was, on Film," *Time,* 26 December 1987, 54.

11. Ibid., 57.

12. Ibid.

13. Dan Goodgame, "How the War Was Won," *Time,* 26 January 1987, 58.

14. Coombs, review of *"Platoon,"* 138.

15. Corliss, "Way It Really Was," 56.

16. Ibid.

17. Ibid., 55.

18. David Ansen, "A Ferocious Vietnam Elegy," *Newsweek,* 5 January 1987, 57.

19. Pat McGilligan, "Point Man," *Film Comment* 23 (February 1987), 12.

20. Corliss, "Way It Really Was," 56.

21. Sydelle Kramer, review of *"Platoon," Cineaste* 15 (1987):49.

22. "Stone's Throw from an Oscar," *Economist*, 21 March 1987, 106.

23. Kramer noted, "Stone's soldiers share the drugs of the counter culture, its obscurity, its messianic fervor, but not its questions, not its moral confusions. These soldiers allude to racism, the black man's draft, but never to whether they should be fighting or not" (review of *"Platoon,"* 50).

24. Oliver Stone, "One from the Heart," *American Film* (January/February 1987):17.

25. Corliss, "Way It Really Was," 56.

26. John Daly, "Haunted by Stone's Hell," *Stills* 29 (1987):18.

27. Corliss, "Way It Really Was," 56.

28. Richard Blake, "Mind and Heart," *America*, 21 February 1987, 159.

29. Frank Beaver, *Oliver Stone: Wakeup Cinema* (New York: Twayne Publishers, 1994), 95.

30. William Blake, "Auguries of Innocence," in *Bartlett's Familiar Quotations*, ed. Christopher Morley (Boston: Little Brown and Company, 1951).

31. Stone, "One from the Heart," 19.

32. Carl Jung, *The Archetypes and the Collective Unconscious*, trans. R. F. C. Hull (Princeton: Princeton University Press, 1990), 135.

33. Ibid., 135–136.

34. Joseph Campbell, *The Hero with a Thousand Faces*, Bollingen Series 17 (Princeton: Princeton University Press, 1973), 90.

35. Matt. 12:4, New International Version.

36. Campbell, *Hero*, 69–76.

37. Jung, *Archetypes*, 82.

38. Stone, "One from the Heart," 19.

39. Blake, "Mind and Heart," 159.

40. Campbell, *Hero*, 25, 149–171.

41. According to Beaver, Stone intentionally creates "soiled" heroes like Taylor in *Platoon* and Richard Boyle in *Salvador* because the "moral contradictions" of these types of characters are more realistic and stylistically complex (Beaver, *Oliver Stone: Wakeup Cinema*, 95).

42. Campbell, *Hero*, 172–192.

43. Robert Seidenberg, "Interview with Ron Kovic," *American Film* 15 (January 1990):56.

44. Christina Appy, "Vietnam According to Oliver Stone," *Commonweal*, 23 March 1990, 187.

45. Tom O'Brien, "At War with Ourselves," *Commonweal*, 9 February 1990, 86.

46. David Ansen, "Bringing It All Back Home," *Newsweek*, 25 December 1989, 74.

47. Pauline Kael, "The Current Cinema," *New Yorker*, 22 January 1990, 122–123.

48. Appy, "Vietnam According to Oliver Stone," 187.

49. Ansen, "Bringing It All Back Home," 74.

50. Stuart Klawans, review of *"Born on the Fourth of July," Nation*, 1 January 1990, 29.

51. Ansen, "Bringing It All Back Home," 74.

52. Campbell, *Hero,* 59–68.

53. Ibid., 77–89.

54. Dylan Thomas, "Do Not Go Gentle into That Good Night," in Robert C. Williams, ed., *A Concordance to the Collected Works of Dylan Thomas* (Lincoln: University of Nebraska Press, 1967).

55. Campbell, *Hero,* 77–89.

56. Michael Singer, *Oliver Stone's Heaven and Earth* (Boston: Charles E. Tuttle Co., 1993), 120.

57. Nisid Hajari, "Stone Angel," *Entertainment Weekly,* 19 November 1993, 42.

58. Singer, *Heaven and Earth,* 122.

59. Hajari, "Stone Angel," 40–45.

60. Jeff Yang, "Stone Turned," *Village Voice,* 11 January 1994, 58.

61. Ibid.

62. Ibid.

63. Ibid.

four

After the Fall: (Self-)Portraits of the Tortured Artist-Visionary

Cinema derives not from painting, literature, sculpture, theater, but from ancient popular wizardry. It is the contemporary manifestation of an evolving history of shadows, a delight in pictures that move, a belief in magic. Its lineage is entwined from the earliest beginning with priests and sorcery, a summoning of phantoms.

—Jim Morrison

You know what made photographers great, Rich? They weren't after money—they captured the nobility of human suffering. That's what Capra caught, he caught that moment of death. You got to get close, Rich, to get the truth. You get too close, you die.

—John Cassady, in *Salvador*

I'm not afraid to see. I come in here every night. I make my case. I make my point. I say what I believe in. I tell you what you are. I have to; I have to; I have no choice. You frighten me.

—Barry Champlain, in *Talk Radio*

In this chapter, various sociomythological themes and their constructions are explored in *The Doors* (1991), *Salvador* (1986), and *Talk Radio* (1988). All three films reflexively ruminate on the artist-visionary's responsibility to take a stance on issues of sociopolitical importance. At the same time, these films acknowledge the difficulty of doing so in a world where the "good guys," the "bad guys," and "the right thing to do" are often moving targets.

Oliver Stone directing Val Kilmer (Jim Morrison) in Stone's 1990 tribute to The Doors' lead singer Jim Morrison. Copyright © 1991 Tri-Star Pictures, Inc.

The artists in these films are visionaries—individuals able to see further than the rest of society and "turn the culture on" with dreams of future possibilities. Like the philosopher or religious mystic, they are the ones able to interpret the shadow play upon the wall while seeing the shadows for what they are—mere approximations of the truth rather than the truth itself. Able to leave Plato's cave of veiled sight, they ascend into the overly bright light of day to risk blindness or even death in an uncompromising search for the truth.

These protagonists, Jim Morrison in *The Doors,* Barry Champlain in *Talk Radio,* and Richard Boyle in *Salvador*—all master wordsmiths—are also "flawed" artists, because although they rail against the injustices of the American political and cultural scene, they remain uncertain (as do we living in the postmodern world) whether transcendence beyond the current era is even possible. Since models for transconsciousness do not yet exist, these heroes, crying out against the sins of modernity, can identify the problem but only hint at the solution. Ultimately, however, this uncertainty is merely a temporary roadblock, a necessary first step in bridging the gap from one era of consciousness to the other. Stone's heroes shape themselves from the existing postmodern rubble that lies about them, as we will see, because this is the only building material available to them.

The Doors (1991)

Spanning the years 1966 to 1971, *The Doors* is Oliver Stone's interpretation of the life, death, and passion of the rock group The Doors' lead singer, Jim Morrison. Carolco Company approached Stone to direct a filmed version of *The Doors* after having bought the rights to the band's story and music. Stone agreed to the project as long as he could both write and direct the film. Financed with a $30 million budget, Stone's version of *The Doors* is ostensibly Jim Morrison's story. It begins with Morrison's youth, when he was a film student at the University of California at Los Angeles (UCLA), moves through his development as a singer-songwriter, when, along with Ray Manzarek, he formed the group The Doors, covers the group's rapid rise to fame, and documents Morrison's self-destruction through drugs and alcohol until his death from an overdose in a Paris flat in 1971.

Stone's interest in the project may have stemmed from his fascination and strong identification with Morrison. Stone's second wife, Elizabeth, remarked that Jim Morrison and The Doors had played a significant role in her husband's youth: "The music of 'The Doors' gave him a contact with the outside world while he was in Vietnam, and when he came home he really got into Jim as a person and related strongly to him."[1] Stone, in his own words, considered Morrison "a shaman," explaining, "He was a god for me, a Dionysian figure, a poet, a philosopher."[2]

If *JFK, Born on the Fourth of July*, and *Platoon* represent America's fall from grace, then *The Doors* represents the time after the Fall, after Kennedy's death when the doors to Camelot had seemingly closed forever. *The Doors* begins where *JFK* ends—with America plunged into a war in which we would lose our very soul, a war that we would never have fought, Stone argues in *JFK*, if Kennedy had lived. According to Beaver, "*The Doors* and its protagonist can be viewed as the third and final entry in a triptych of films by Stone about young males whose lives become inextricably and painfully tied to the dark years of Vietnam-era America. Like Chris Taylor of *Platoon* and Ron Kovic of *Born on the Fourth of July*, Jim Morrison suffers the confusion arising from an unending war, experienced this time not from within a combat platoon but from the stage of a rebellious rock concert arena."[3] However, despite the disillusionment of the Vietnam era, according to *The Doors*, Morrison, like Jimi Hendrix, Janis Joplin, and others, represented society's continued searching—half cynically and half hopefully—for a new Eden, a restored Camelot, a cleansed vision that would allow Americans to "see things as they truly were," instead of "through a glass darkly."

As in *JFK, Born on the Fourth of July*, and *Platoon*, betrayal is at the heart of *The Doors*. Stone portrays Morrison and his generation as betrayed by promises broken in the escalating American involvement in Vietnam. In

The Doors, for example, backstage at a Doors concert in New Haven, Connecticut, Morrison's lover, Patricia Keneelly, challenges his claim that his parents were killed in a car accident. At an earlier press conference Jim had lied about his parents' whereabouts, saying they were killed "in one of those horrible car crashes in New Mexico in the 1950s. . . . My father ran right into a truckload of Navahos. They were all over the highway, bleeding. Their souls, kind of stirring in the breeze, just leapt into mine." Both Morrison's parents, Patricia reminds him, are alive and well, adding "your father's an admiral in the U.S. Navy who was at the Gulf of Tonkin when the Vietnam War broke out—deputy chief of operations." It is not surprising that Morrison lies about his father. As a key figure in the Vietnam conflict, his father represents the military mentality, charged with betraying an entire generation of Americans by sending them off to die in a war no one wanted to fight—young men, run over like "a truckload of Navahos" and left, along with the American public that mourned them, "all over the highway, bleeding." The Gulf of Tonkin incident is also one of the most controversial events in the Vietnam War, representing for many Americans a significant shift in our role in Vietnam and thus a betrayal of earlier promises made by successive U.S. administrations regarding the level of our involvement in Southeast Asia. The youth of Morrison's generation, *The Doors* implies, were sacrificed in the war of their fathers. Swept away by the bloodlust of American imperialism, these young soldiers were no more than innocent lambs led to slaughter. Their sacrifice at the altar, however, unlike Christ's death on the cross, would be meaningless. There would be no redemption for the sins of the military-industrial complex.[4]

From the perspective of perennial philosophy, *The Doors'* Jim Morrison represents the prototypical hero who will slay the monsters of rationality and ego consciousness in order to move society to the next level of awareness and unity with the universe. From the perspective of Greek mythology, however, *The Doors* tells the story of the Iron Age (the time after the Golden Age of great heroes, when heroes had simply been noble buffoons), an era marked by incessant suffering and betrayal caused by the evils released from Pandora's box. In Christian mythology, the film represents not only humanity's expulsion from the Garden but also Christ's betrayal in the Garden of Gethsemane. Like Garrison and Kennedy in *JFK,* Morrison in *The Doors* is the "second Adam,"[5] reenacting the passion, vision, and ultimately, the betrayal and death of Christ. But Morrison, like many of Stone's protagonists, represents a disillusioned and imperfect Christ in whom the new covenant—the promises made by God—have been broken. At one point in the film, Morrison complains to his girlfriend Pam Courson (played by Meg Ryan), "Who am I? Where's the feast they promised us? Where's the new wine? Dying on the vine." These lines echo the words of the Old Testament prophet Isaiah, who, speaking of the Lord's devastation of the earth due to the wantonness of his people, says, "The new wine dries up and the vine withers; all the merrymakers groan. . . . No longer do they drink wine with a song . . . In the streets they cry out for wine; all joy turns to gloom, all gaiety is banished from the earth."[6] And in another biblical passage in Joel: "Wail, all you drinkers of wine. . . . the new wine is dried up, the oil fails."[7]

Morrison, in Stone's film, seems to yearn for a transcendent spirituality—the promises of the new wine—nowhere to be found in the "godless" age of modern rationality. By the end of the film, we are left uncertain, however, whether Morrison, in death, unlike Christ, was able to achieve what he could not in life—to "break on through to the other side" of transconsciousness. As Stuart Klawans noted, "'Break on through to the other side' is Jim's creed; at first, he thinks he'll smash through the doors of perception into William Blake's promised Eden. Only later does he realize that the other side feels very much like the empty air, waiting just beyond all those building ledges he likes to walk along."[8]

The Doors' overt reliance on Christian mythology was not lost on some critics. For example, one noted: "In telling his grim tale Stone seems to be aiming for the solemnity and mystery of a High Mass—no less than a representation of Morrison's passion and sacrifice. . . . *The Doors* is essentially religious narrative."[9] Noted another: "Morrison presented himself as a combination of shaman and *poète maudit* [cursed poet], and he was a star in life and a legend in death because he made the physical, intellectual, and spiritual excesses of the counterculture sexy. He was, in a sense, the perfect pop-culture idol of a chaotic time, and his death—in a Paris flat, the ideal setting for a Romantic poet's demise—sealed his myth."[10] Stone acknowledges the mythic qualities of Morrison's music, life, and death, explaining that "a lot of the other music was great, but the depth of Jim's vision was what carried it. 'The End,' 'When the Music's Over'—they're epic stories, Homeric ballads, in a sense."[11]

As was the case with Stone's portrayals of mythic figures in *Platoon* and *Born on the Fourth of July*, critics were split in their assessment of the effectiveness of the technique in *The Doors*. In Klawans's analysis,

> *The Doors* . . . keeps turning into an invocation of the gods. Of course it's going to be bombastic. An archetype is merely a cliché, as seen by somebody who lacks a sense of humor. Just so, the shamans and symbols in *The Doors* crowd out any opportunity for laughter. In doing so, they also obscure part of the truth about the late sixties: It was a time of self-immolation but also of great, ludicrous fooling around. Yes, some of the fun ended in death; but then, some of it was just fun.[12]

And in Ansen's opinion, "*The Doors* simultaneously mythologizes and debunks Morrison, but it never dares make him lifesize. Stone is interested in the rhetorical Jim Morrison, not the real man—the rhetorical pain and anguish, not the true vulnerability of a sensitive, formerly overweight young man who wanted to be a poet but was idolized as a sex symbol."[13] These split assessments of the film, not surprisingly, as we will see, mirror the potential split in the audience's reception of the film as well.

The Doors begins in a recording studio where Jim Morrison (Val Kilmer), speaking from behind the glassed-in walls of a dimly lit recording booth, intones in a theatrical voice:

> "The movie will begin in five moments," the mindless voice announced. "All those unseated will await the next show." We filed slowly, languidly into the hall. The auditorium was vast and silent. As we seated and were darkened the voice continued, "The program for this evening is not new. You've seen this entertainment through and through. You've seen your birth, your life and death. You might recall all of the rest. Did you have a good world when you died? Enough to base a movie on? Is everybody in? Is everybody in? Is everybody in? The ceremony is about to begin."

This monologue is accompanied by the opening strains of The Doors' song "Riders on the Storm." As the image—a low-flying aerial shot of the desert—takes us out over the edge of a cliff and across a barren plain, Morrison continues in voice-over, "Let me tell you about heartache and the loss of God, wandering, wandering in hopeless night. Out here in the perimeter there are no stars. Out here we are stoned immaculate." As the music continues, the scene changes to a sepia-tone shot of a circa-1940s car crossing the desert. The caption reads "New Mexico, 1949." The music and lyrics become clearer as we hear, "Riders on the storm/Riders on the storm/Into this house we're born/Into this world we're thrown/Like a dog without a bone . . . /Riders on the storm." Another caption, "Venice Beach, California, 1965," places us at a party where a young Morrison introduces himself to Pamela Courson (Meg Ryan). A second caption, "UCLA Film School," puts us in Morrison's college classroom for a screening of his student film. As the camera cuts to a full shot of the auditorium screen, along with the rest of his classmates, we watch Morrison's film. An erotic dancer gyrates on top of a television set. Her half-naked figure is slowly revealed as the camera tilts down her body. This is followed by historical footage of a crowd at Nuremberg in Germany greeting Adolf Hitler and a shot of Hitler saluting the crowds. In voice-over, as these images are presented, we hear Morrison recite:

> Nietzsche said all great things must first wear terrifying and monstrous masks in order to inscribe themselves on the hearts of humanity. Listen, Children, to the sound of the Nuremberg night. In the seance the shaman leads, a sensuous panic. He acts like a madman of professional hysteria. Have you ever seen God? Mandala. A symmetrical angel. This world is a monster of energy. Without beginning, without end. Likewise without increase or income, disclosing nothing. This world, this world is a will to power and nothing besides.

This last line is delivered by Morrison on camera in a medium shot as he walks and reads, holding a book by Nietzsche. The camera zooms out to a full shot to reveal that what Morrison is walking along is the precarious ledge of a building.

The "shaman of sensuous panic" for an entire generation, the Dionysian "madman of professional hysteria," Morrison is negotiating the ledge of consciousness/unconsciousness and life/death. No longer wishing to wander "in hopeless night" and feeling "heartache and the loss of God" in the modern age of rationality, he wants to transcend earthly consciousness, risk the edge, and push the limits in order to see visions of future possibilities. We, the audience, watching from the students' perspective in the auditorium, are invited along on his transconscious quest. We are asked to walk the ledge with him.

Will we take up this invitation or scorn it? At its conclusion, for example, Morrison's film is critiqued by the professor (played by Oliver Stone himself) as "a little incoherent," then other students take turns bashing it as well. Morrison, deeply hurt by the response, yells, "I quit," and flees the auditorium. Thus, during this opening sequence we are asked to assume one of two positions, either that of skeptical audience member asked to assess whether all the Morrison hype and bluster is exactly that, or that of identifying audience member, compassionately understanding the struggles of the "misunderstood artist," the "persecuted visionary," who, like Barry Champlain in *Talk Radio,* is unwilling to "cast his pearls before swine."

The Doors, by beginning with Morrison's student film and his opening monologue, also offers a reflexive commentary on the artist-filmmaker's role in society.[14] In *The Doors,* Morrison's girlfriend Pam asks him, "What's a shaman?" Jim replies, "He's a medicine man. He gets deeper and deeper and then he has a vision and the whole tribe is healed. All cultures have a version of it. Greeks have theater and gods. The Indians say the first shaman invented sex. They call him 'The-One-Who-Makes-You-Crazy.'" The filmmaker, like the shaman-poet, must heal a wounded culture by dreaming visions of a new society and must then find a way to "turn the culture on" to those visions by translating them into art. Stone's artist-filmmaker, in one interpretation, like Morrison's shaman, is a spiritual guide, a philosopher-poet leading culture on a quest, a journey in search of higher awareness, new spiritual truths, and enlightened consciousness. From the other perspective, however, the guide may be a self-deluded pompous ass with no sense of humor. This is an important fork in the road for viewers of this film. Audience members who hated the film most likely took the latter route, whereas those who liked it most likely found themselves in a love-hate relationship with the film's protagonist, not unlike many filmgoers' response to Richard Boyle in *Salvador.*

This is not just any quest, however; it is Christ's ministry and passion. Early in *The Doors,* for example, Morrison takes a trip to the desert with his band members to achieve mind expansion through peyote, the traditional drug of southwestern Native Americans. Like Christ's forty days in the desert prior to the beginning of his active ministry, this scene represents the turning point in Morrison's crusade for higher consciousness, the beginning of his journey to "break on through to the other side," and his attempts to bring others through the doors of consciousness with him. (The Doors, Stone reminds us, took their name from William Blake's poem, "The Doors of Perception." Morrison quotes Blake, noting, "When the doors of perception are cleansed, things will appear as they truly are.") In the desert, Morrison not only receives his calling but also consecrates and assures his followers. Just as Christ encouraged his apostles to be strong for the trials that would await them in their active ministry, just as Christ assured them that he would be with them "until the end of time," so Morrison echoes these words, telling his band members, "We're a tribe now, a tribe of warriors. I promise you I'll be with you till the end of time. Nothing will destroy our circle."

As Morrison and his band members begin to "trip" the camera work becomes extremely subjective and impressionistic. We, the audience, are invited along on this "long, prolonged derangement of the senses." In what seems either a catatonic or prophetic state, Jim calls out to his followers:

> Ride the snake. Close your eyes, see the snake, see the serpent appear . . . long, deadly, all the history of the world is on his scales . . . It's big and it's moving, devouring consciousness, digesting power, monster of energy. It's a monster. Kiss the snake on the tongue. But if it senses fear, it'll eat us instantly. But if we kiss it without fear, it will take us through the Garden, through the gate, to the other side. Ride the snake until the end of time.

What is the audience to make of this seemingly inchoate and rambling monologue? It remains senseless unless seen from the perspective of perennial philosophy and Christian mythology. The snake, of course, is the classic Christian symbol, depending on interpretation, of wisdom or seduction/ sin. Goddess cults, as indeed the film portrays them, prefer to see the snake as a symbol of power and wisdom. As a purveyor of enlightenment, however, as the one who told Eve about the apple of knowledge, the snake is ultimately responsible for our expulsion from the Garden. In the language of perennial philosophy, then, the snake is an archetype of reason or rationality, the development of which resulted in our separation from the natural and the spiritual world of preconsciousness. To the extent that the modern era of consciousness represents a separation from all that was good in preconsciousness, the snake represents both wisdom and the "sin" of that wisdom. Therefore, in order to transcend to the next level of consciousness (transconsciousness), in order to fashion a new Garden, we must either slay the "snakes" of rationality (defeat the monsters of consciousness) or learn to better integrate them into society's collective psyche. Although it is "a monster" we may have to "kiss the snake" of knowledge, and "if we kiss it with-

Members of The Doors on a peyote-induced vision quest in a southwestern desert in *The Doors*. Left to right: Ray Manzarek (Kyle MacLachlan), Jim Morrison (Val Kilmer), Robby Krieger (Frank Whaley), and John Densmore (Kevin Dillon). Copyright © 1991 Tri-Star Pictures, Inc.

out fear, it will take us through the Garden, through the gate, to the other side." A return to the Garden of *preconsciousness,* however, is no longer possible or even desirable, since we have eaten from the apple of knowledge and have known "sin." Our salvation—our hope of transcendence—requires embracing the knowledge of who we are without fear or obsession, while continually striving to become more than we are as well. Transconsciousness, as movement forward rather than backward, paradoxically calls for a kind of informed innocence.

Just as Christ in the Garden of Gethsemane went away from his disciples to pray alone, so Morrison also leaves his circle of followers to wander off into the desert. Just as Christ sees/speaks with his Father (God) and intuits his impending crucifixion, Morrison, during his peyote-induced vision, meets an old Indian, his shaman or spiritual guide, and is shown his own death—laid out in a bathtub with his arms outstretched in the classic pose of crucified Christ. We then see an image of a naked man (Morrison?) floating in slow motion down a long, brightly lit hallway, through a door, and possibly, "to the other side" of consciousness, where in death he may receive the truth revealed by the serpent of knowledge denied him in life.

When he comes out of the desert, Morrison, then, like Christ, has seen visions of what the future holds. But again like Christ, Morrison is also afraid of his "mission" and its fated conclusion with his early death (Christ in the Garden of Gethsemane, before his arrest and trial, pleads with his Father in heaven, "Let this cup pass from me, if possible"). Earlier in the film, when asked by his girlfriend if he fears death, Jim says he does not; but here, in the desert with his disciples, he says, "I'm lying. I *am* afraid."

During this scene we hear the sound track of The Doors' song "The End": "This is the end/Beautiful friend/This is the end/My only friend/ The end/Of our elaborate plans/The end/Of everything that stands/The end/No safety or surprise/The end/I'll never look into your eyes again." It seems counterintuitive for Morrison's vision quest to *begin* with the song "The End." Still, this choice implies, on some level, that the beginning of the hero's quest is often the first step toward his "death." This is the case regardless of whether the hero is messianic and must forfeit his corporeal life in order to achieve resurrection, like Christ, or is perennial and must slay his ego in order to achieve a transcendent self. On another level, the choice of "The End" as the song to begin Morrison's vision quest may represent the hopelessness of his journey, even at the outset, and therefore implies the hopelessness of all of the "elaborate plans" of Morrison's generation. Stone's Morrison, like Stone himself, may be plagued by the postmodern possibility that Camelot after Kennedy's death, as Stone said, is nothing more than just "a wonderful dream to hold on to and to look back on."[15]

Although Morrison may be a "flawed" god in the face of postmodernity, although he may be a tragicomic hero not fit for a Greek legend, he is the god of his age. At one point in the film, a female photographer who has been taking Jim's picture tells him, "They want you, worship you, love you, adore you. Jim, the god of rock and cock." While she continues to photograph Morrison, he drunkenly reels around the room chugging from a bottle of whiskey and mugging for the camera. The final images in this scene are of Morrison squinting at himself in a mirror, a close-up of his face, and a lap-dissolve from his face to the marble head of a Greek statue.

Parallels between Morrison and the Greek gods of the Golden Age are made repeatedly in *The Doors*. Early in the film, for example, Morrison declares to his fellow band member Ray Manzarek, "There ought to be great orgies, man. Like when Dionysus arrived in Greece. He made all the women mad. Leaving their homes and dancing off into the mountains. There should be great golden copulations in the streets of L.A., man." Morrison, "the god of rock and cock," in Stone's film is also the Greek god Dionysus. One critic commented, "Morrison once referred to The Doors as 'erotic politicians,' and their platform was explicitly Dionysian—a program of liberation based on intoxication of the senses."[16] Morrison, at one point in the film, echoes this sentiment when he says, "I believe in a long, prolonged derangement of the senses to attain the unknown. I live in the subconscious. Our pale reason hides the infinite from us."

The legend of Dionysus is more than a tale of intoxication to achieve enlightenment through altered states, however; it has a much darker strain of violent death. Later in the film, backstage at a Doors concert, Morrison's lover, Patricia Keneelly, asks him, "Do you hear them out there? Are you listening to them? It's you they want now, it's not The Doors. It's not your mother's or your father's child. It's you." We hear the growing chanting from the auditorium: "Jim! Jim! Jim!" Morrison replies, "They don't want me, they want my death—ripped to pieces." Kauffman called this scene the classic "performer as Christ being crucified for his audience."[17] More than the crucified performer/Christ, Morrison is the Greek god Dionysus, sacrificed by vivisection in a drunken orgy of ecstasy by his worshipers. Paradoxically, from the perspective of perennial philosophy, Morrison "the king" must die so that the king can live. Morrison is willing to sacrifice/slay himself in order to achieve a transcendent self of higher consciousness.

Although Morrison is fearful of death, like Christ he is willing to die for the people. After a fight with his girlfriend Pam, he climbs out on a window ledge and threatens suicide. As she tries desperately to get him back inside, he asks her, "Will you die for me? Will you die for me?" She responds, "No! Will you die for me?" Retorts Jim, "Sure, I'd die for anybody." Like Christ, Morrison is ultimately prepared to die for his followers, without discrimination, and like Christ, he leads a life in Stone's film that moves him relentlessly toward that destination.

This is most evident near the end of the film when Morrison is once again seen recording reflections on his life. Sporting Christ-like long hair and a full beard, wearing a football jersey with the number 66 on it (which is close to 666, the sign of the Antichrist), and speaking from behind the glassed-in walls of a dimly lit recording booth, he appears as the personification of a messiah cut off from his worshipers. Morrison, the Christ/anti-Christ, reflects sardonically on his life's meaning:

> Let's just say I was testing the bounds of reality, that I was curious. I kind of always preferred to be hated, like Erich Von Stroheim in the movies—the man you love to hate. It's meant to be ironic—like courage wants to laugh, essentially a stupid situation. You go on the stage and howl for people. Me, they see exactly what they want to see. Some say Lizard King, whatever that means, or some black-clad leather demon, whatever that means. But really, I think of myself as a sensitive, intelligent human being with the soul of a clown that always forces me to blow it at the most crucial moment—a fake hero—a joke the gods played on me.

Jim Morrison, the "fake hero," the antihero, the hero of the Iron Age, the "joke [of] the gods," the sensitive clown and the noble buffoon, is also the philosopher king interpreting the shadow play upon the wall—the shaman who dreams visions of a more perfect world, a world where the "doors of perception" will be cleansed so that we can see things as they truly are.

The Doors' lead singer Jim Morrison (Val Kilmer) holds the audience in the palm of his hand in another mesmerizing concert performance in *The Doors*. Copyright © 1991 Tri-Star Pictures, Inc.

But is his death meaningful? First, Stone clearly shows the excesses of Morrison's generation and demonstrates that the Lizard King was the epitome of that excess. Second, Morrison, through his own admission and in Stone's caricature of him, is portrayed as a reduced or clownish hero or perhaps as a Nietzschean antihero who worships death and excess as much as he does spiritual enlightenment (but maybe, for Stone, hero and antihero are one and the same, since Nietzsche was paradoxically a deeply religious figure, wailing, "God is dead" in the anguish of such a loss for modernity). Stone's final message may be that such excess used to pursue enlightenment may have made Morrison's death worthwhile. Morrison, like his band, according to Stone, was self-consciously aware of his mythic status and the power that adhered to it. Fellow band member Ray says to Morrison at one point in the film, "Things are about to explode, Jim. You can feel it in the air. People want to fight or fuck. Love or kill. Vietnam is right out there. Sides are being chosen. Everything's gonna flame. The planet is screaming for change, Morrison. We gotta make the myths."

According to Stone's film, Morrison's short life of twenty-seven years stood for something mythic. *The Doors* ends with a slow pan of Père Lachèse cemetery in Paris where Morrison is buried. We not only see Morrison's "shrine," surrounded by such tokens of esteem and love as flowers, mementos, and letters, but we also read the names on the graves of such other cultural visionaries as Honoré de Balzac, Oscar Wilde, Jean-Baptiste Molière, and Marcel Proust. Maybe despite Morrison's clowning and confused attempts as godhead, he, like many of his generation, was trying to achieve the transconsciousness promised by perennial philosophy. And this is what all generations must do. Yes, there is betrayal, in the invasion of Cambodia, in Watergate, in Iran-Contra, in Kennedy's death, in El Salvador and Central America. Although the days of Camelot eclipsed with Kennedy's death and although the promises of the new wine—the new covenant—have lost their sparkle, we must still try, Stone says, to reconfigure the Garden—to kiss the snake of knowledge and not be afraid to open our eyes to the fearful self-revelations that this newfound consciousness may bring. We should neither slay the snake of rationality nor worship it, but instead, find a way to integrate it into our psyche and achieve transcendent wholeness. We must learn to see ourselves as we truly are. When "the doors of perception are cleansed," when the covenant is restored, when the Garden is recultivated, "he who has ears will hear and he who has eyes will see." Morrison, like the prophets of old, like John the Baptist, like Jim Garrison in *JFK*, is a voice crying out in the wilderness.

Oliver Stone, the filmmaker, like Jim Morrison, the musician, is also a searcher for the truth and the means to attain that truth, someone who attempts, with every film, to cleanse the doors of perception. In *JFK*, District Attorney Jim Garrison says to his people, "We're through-the-looking-glass people here." Stone, like Morrison and Garrison, is also a searcher who realizes that in this world "white" is sometimes "black" and things are not as they appear. Stone, the idealist, searches for the truth in the belief that the truth comes through knowledge and that the truth shall set us free. His films imply that the Platonic ideal of a perfect communion seemingly possible before the Fall is possible again. But Stone seems to wail in his rage, How long must we wait?—the covenant is broken, and all that remains is the desire to taste the new wine. Are drugs the door to consciousness? Is sex? Violence? Mere mortals, Stone tells us, can only see the shadow play upon the wall of Plato's cave; the sunlight of pure truth above ground is too blinding for us, yet despite this we must continually search for heroes who can bear the pain of kissing the snake of knowledge in order to "break on through to the other side" with the hope of bringing us with them. If the old Eden was ignorance, the new Eden, according to Stone, comes through informed innocence. Jim Morrison, the artist after the pure, like Jim Garrison, the detective after the truth, both stand in for Stone. Stone, in each of his films, asks us to walk the ledge with him, to "dive into the impure with a certainty that the pure [lies] somewhere within,"[18] to suffer, perhaps as Morrison suffered, a "long, prolonged derangement of the senses" in order "to attain the unknown."

Salvador (1986)

Salvador, released in 1986, is Oliver Stone's first feature-length film. Co-scripted by Stone and journalist Richard Boyle, the film provides an account of Boyle's experiences during the 1980–1981 civil war in El Salvador. Characterized as Stone's "breakthrough" film, *Salvador* was likened to such films about the political situation in Latin America as *Missing,* set in Chile, and *Under Fire,* set in Nicaragua. The film also provoked comparisons with Roland Joffe's *The Killing Fields* and Haskell Wexler's *Latino.* Politically liberal in its politics, *Salvador* overtly condemns U.S. policy in Central America. It portrays the Salvadoran rebels as part of an indigenous peasant revolt rather than as communist-backed Russian puppets—as was often claimed by the Reagan administration—and argues that U.S. support for the right-wing Salvadoran army aided and abetted the massacre of thousands of Salvadoran peasants.

The film's politics, however, coupled with its unsavory protagonist and Stone's unproven track record as a director, made the project untouchable in Hollywood. Unable to find American financing for the film, Stone eventually secured backing from Hemdale Films, a British production company. It was the film's British backing, according to Stone, that allowed him to state his political views so strongly: "They view the situation in Central America with a little more irony than the American people do. It would not have been made had it not been for the English."[19] Working with a $6 million budget, Stone endeared himself to Hemdale by bringing the film in at $4.5 million. Shot in fifty-six days in California, Nevada, and Mexico, *Salvador* opened to limited commercial release in March 1986.

Critics primarily noted the film's energy and uncompromising liberal, leftist position on America's involvement in El Salvador. For example, one critic noted, "Even with its flaws, *Salvador* came on like a hammer blow, showing the influences of a comic-fantastical Borges, a high-steam Scorsese, and a polemical Godard . . . Stone's film was a bitter pill of truth about the suppressed story *behind* the story down there."[20] Another critic called *Salvador* "remarkable, if only for its drive and sense of attack, its willingness to deal in current politics as directly as it does."[21]

Although the film's primary message is an overt critique of U.S. policy in Central America, *Salvador,* as is apparent from the title, is also about an individual and a country "desperately in need of saving."[22] Commenting on the religious significance of the film's title, Stone said, "I did plan to call it *South of the Border* at one point, but *Salvador* to me meant both the country and Salvation."[23] The film's central protagonist, Richard Boyle, "a self-demolishing jerk who careens through Central America in search of a story and some spiritual salvation,"[24] is indeed a character in need of saving. A "has-been" journalist who still knows a few names, he has lost the confidence of every newspaper, magazine, or news service for which he ever worked. His primary reason for going to El Salvador is that he needs money badly, his wife and child have left him, and he has jumped bail to avoid the law. At least at the outset, then, Salvador represents for Boyle (James Woods) and his traveling companion, Dr. Rock (James Belushi), not salvation, but cheap sex, unlimited drugs and booze, and a country where anything goes. We soon realize, however, that Boyle is desperately searching for either a cause worth fighting for or a soft place to lay his aching head. Before he finds the cause, he finds the soft place in the arms of a Salvadoran peasant woman, Maria, who promises to marry him only if he confesses his sins and seeks absolution. In an achingly humorous scene, Boyle confesses his transgressions to a Catholic priest and is surprised at the ease with which he is granted forgiveness. While receiving communion, however, Boyle also stumbles upon a cause worth fighting for and a possibility for true redemption when Archbishop Romero, a strong advocate for peasant rights and a harsh critic of government repression, is gunned down during the Holy Communion service by a government assassin. Boyle awakes to political consciousness and for the remainder of the film becomes the type of journalist he may once have been, cleaning up his act, seeking evidence of government repression, and acting as the voice of American liberal public opinion. However, he is a reluctant hero and must be taught to search out the truth and not accept at face value U.S. government lies about America's involvement in places like El Salvador, Nicaragua, Chile, and Vietnam.

In *Salvador,* Stone developed the docudrama style that he later put to even more effective use in *JFK*—a style that includes the use of historical reenactment, historical footage, graphics, and handheld camera work. This docudrama framework is established from the first shot of *Salvador,* a graphic that reads: "This film is based on events that occurred in 1980–1981. Characters have been fictionalized." The graphic is followed by television news footage of fighting that is presumably taking place in El Salvador. A female newscaster in voice-over proclaims, "In the wake of the Nicaraguan Revolution, chaos has descended on tiny El Salvador in Central

America. Today eighteen people were killed and thirty wounded in a fierce gun battle between antigovernment demonstrators and the national police." The next shot is a medium shot of journalist Richard Boyle, lying in bed and smoking a cigarette, watching the newscast on television. Despite the film's opening "fictional" disclaimer, the use of television news footage immediately creates a nonfiction feeling, implying that the events in this film really happened.

Documentary conventions are continued throughout the film. Later in the film, for example, when Boyle and fellow photojournalist John Cassady make a trip to a noted mass-grave site used by right-wing death squads, a graphic is superimposed over the location that reads: "El Playon—dump site for death squad victims." This convention is continued whenever locations of note in Central America are visited by the main characters. The same technique is also used to identify U.S. and Salvadoran military and intelligence personnel by name and title. The graphics, in combination with the reenactment of historical events, such as the assassination of Catholic Archbishop Romero and the Nicaraguan Catholic nuns, and the use of news footage of Reagan's presidential election, lend *Salvador* the same air of authenticity that later brought Stone praise in *Platoon* and such severe criticism in *JFK*.

Stone's use of the handheld camera in *Salvador* not only lends the film a cinema-verité feeling of veracity and immediacy, it also creates the sense of urgency and confusion that marks both Boyle's and American experiences generally in El Salvador. In the scene of the assassination of Archbishop Romero, for example, the mayhem and confusion that follows the abrupt outbreak of violence is heightened by erratic and dizzying camera work. The camera, like the witnesses to the assassination, is jostled by the crowd and "disoriented" by the rapid unfolding of events. George Kimball called this a "stunning use of frenetic camera movement as a visual correlative for the mass insanity being dramatized."[25]

But more important, Stone's camera in *Salvador* is a metaphor for our experience of the entire film. We, like the camera and Boyle, are searching for coherence—some explanation not only for what just occurred in the assassination scene but also for what is happening in El Salvador. Stone's obsessive camera, like a lion on the prowl, is searching for the elusive truth. It is, according to Kimball, a "restless almost tormented camera that seems never to stop hunting through the unfolding scenes of chaos as if frantically searching for some 'truth' it believes must be there but simply cannot find."[26]

Salvador's film style is not only a metaphor for our experience of the film, it is also a glimpse of Stone's view of the artist-filmmaker's role in society. Film, like all art, according to Stone's *Salvador*, should wake and shock culture out of its political complacency and self-satisfied stupor. It should send us on a dizzying and spinning search for the truth, a journey that although sometimes disorienting and certainly dangerous, is essential if we are ever to evolve as a nation and a race. This is a film style and a message that Stone continued to make his own after *Salvador* and that became the visual and philosophical trademark of all his work.

Salvador's reflexive commentary on the artist-filmmaker is most evident in a scene in which the photojournalists Boyle and Cassady document the horrors of El Playon, a Salvadoran death-squad dump site. After scrambling over piles of both fresh and rotting corpses and trudging across a steamy and smoke-filled purgatorylike landscape, Cassady exclaims, "You know what made photographers great, Rich? They weren't after money—they captured the nobility of human suffering. That's what Capra caught. He caught that moment of death. He didn't just catch the death—he caught the reason why they died. You got to get close, Rich, to get the truth—you get too close you die. Someday I want a shot like Capra. Someday. Someday." As he speaks, we hear the swelling of religious choral music in the background.

The true artist is able to get closer to the truth than mere mortals; the artist is able to leave Plato's cave of veiled sight and ascend into the light of day, risking blindness or death in an uncompromising search for the truth. Cassady, if he is to be a dedicated artist, must not simply portray death or human suffering—he needs to interpret the reasons for that death and suffering.

Later in the film, Cassady gets his wish to look truth in the eyes. But in the capturing of that Capraesque moment, as his prophetic words warned, he is gunned down by aircraft fire. In his search for the truth, Cassady, like Kennedy in *JFK,* Champlain in *Talk Radio,* and Morrison in *The Doors,* gets too close to the "truth" and pays with his life. Walking the razor edge of consciousness or enlightenment comes at a price. In perennial philosophy this sacrifice is the ego death of the hero, but for Cassady and Morrison it is possibly also a transcendent death of the self in a return to the spirit. Both Cassady and Morrison die, in Stone's films, with a smile on their face—as if the "truth" was worth it, after all.

Although there are mythopoetic elements in *Salvador,* they are secondary to the film's political critique, a critique that makes *Salvador* the most politically outspoken and also the most raw-edged of any of Stone's films.[27] The film's most overt statement regarding U.S. policy in Central America comes from an extended soliloquy by Boyle to a U.S. colonel and an American intelligence officer, both of whom have been prodding Boyle for photographic evidence of Marxist backing for the rebel forces. Boyle's conversation with these two men epitomizes Stone's larger political thesis regarding America's disgrace after Kennedy's death, when the nation became mired in the ethical and political mud of places like Vietnam, Chile, and Central America, all in the name of fighting the specter of communism. Boyle, angry at the U.S. government's attempts to justify U.S. support for the Contras by constructing a communist-takeover scenario, explains, "They're in shit shape [the rebel forces]; they're getting nothing. Come on, Jack, when are you going to believe what your eyes see and not what military intelligence lets you think." The colonel replies, "Listen, Boyle, we've got AWACS [airborne warning and control system], infrareds, statements from defecting . . . commandants and enough military intel to prove 10,000 percent that this ain't no civil war, but outright commie aggression." Boyle responds by providing an eloquent, if somewhat pedantic, statement of the liberal perspective on U.S. support for the Salvadoran army as well as on U.S. military and economic policy in Chile and Vietnam:

> You guys have been lying about it from the beginning. You have not presented one shred of proof to the American public that this is anything other than a legitimate peasant revolution. So please don't start telling me about the sanctity of military intelligence, not after Chile, not after Vietnam. I was there, remember? . . . You've been lying about the number of advisers here; you've been lying about the trainers here on TDY [temporary duty]; you've been lying about switching so-called humanitarian assistance to Salvadoran military coffers, and you've been lying saying that this war can be won militarily, which it can't.

The colonel responds, "I'm not going to listen to this whining journalist left-wing commie crap, Jack. Now we know where this guy's sympathies lie. I don't even know why we're talking to him." Boyle's final exchange with the colonel not only offers a further challenge to U.S. government policy in Central America, but it also captures the central philosophical perspective of all of Stone's film protagonists, and perhaps even that of Stone himself:

> *Boyle.* Left-wing, Colonel? Well, maybe. But I'm not a communist. You guys never ever seem to be able to tell the difference. . . . You know, I love my country as much as you do. That may surprise you. . . . What are the death squads but the brainchild of the CIA. But you'll run with them because they're anti-Moscow. You let them close down the universities; you let them wipe out the best minds in the country. You let them kill whoever they want. You let them wipe out the Catholic Church and you let them do it all because they aren't commies and that's bullshit! You've created a major Frankenstein.
> *Intelligence Officer.* Yeah, well we can control him.
> *Boyle.* All I know is that some campesino who can't read or write or feed his own family has to watch his kids die of malnutrition. Do you think he gives a shit about Marxism or capitalism?
> *Colonel.* It was that kind of crap thinking that got us into Vietnam—this guilt shit. You liberal assholes, what the hell do you think the KGB's doing? Huh?
> *Boyle.* Is that why you guys are here? Some kind of post-Vietnam experience, like you need a rerun or something? You pour 120 million bucks into this

place, you turn it into a military zone. Why? So you can have chopper parades in the sky? All you're doing is bringing misery to these people, Jack. I don't want to see another Vietnam. I don't want to see America get another bad rap. I lost my hearing in this ear over there. What do you think I did this for? Fifteen dollars a photo from Pacific News Service? I did it because I believe in America. I believe that we stand for something—for a constitution, for human rights, not just for a few people, but for everybody on this planet. Jack, you've got to think of the people first, in the name of human decency—something we Americans are supposed to believe in. You got to at least try to make something of a just society here.

Salvador, like *Wall Street* and *Talk Radio,* are films about the post-Vietnam malaise. For Stone, they mark this country's continued betrayal by a government that cares more about feeding the military-industrial complex and ensuring geopolitical dominance than it does about the deaths of innocent peasants and American soldiers. Stone's protagonists, neither radical nor Marxist, are loyal Americans who still believe that their country can and should stand for something. Jim Garrison in *JFK,* at the moment he learns of Kennedy's assassination, asserts, "I'm ashamed to be an American today." Boyle, a patriot like Garrison, is also appalled by the actions of his government.

Stone's own views on U.S. involvement in Central America during the late 1980s were apparently vehement and well known. Speaking to Alexander Cockburn in 1987 about Latin America and the film *Salvador* and sounding remarkably like Richard Boyle, Stone explained:

> I'm beginning to think that the only solution is a war that involves Americans, because it's the only way this country is going to wake up to what is really going on down there. I think America has to bleed. I think the corpses have to pile up. I think American boys have to die again. Let the mothers weep and mourn. Let the mothers fucking wake up to what's going on. Because they don't give a shit about the one hundred thousand Guatemalans that got killed because of our technology, but when an American gets killed in Honduras, they're going to get upset.[28]

Although not stated explicitly in *Salvador,* the film's underlying premise is that U.S. involvement in El Salvador is a direct result of the geopolitical mentality and the military infrastructure that developed in Vietnam. The U.S. support for the Salvadoran Contras, in other words, was born out of the same misguided anticommunist foreign policy that made the U.S. government support South Vietnam against communist North Vietnam. Vietnam, once again, is Stone's, and our, frame of reference in *Salvador.* El Salvador, the film implies, like Vietnam, was another no-win situation.

The deeper message of the film, however, is that if President John F. Kennedy had lived, then American troops would have been withdrawn from Vietnam. The Vietnam War as we know it would not have occurred.

Vietnam allowed the confluence of interests, labeled the "military-industrial complex" by President Dwight D. Eisenhower, to gain an even stronger foothold in America. Vietnam also caused the deepening of Cold War animosity between the United States and the Soviet Union. It was this Cold War mentality that resulted in American foreign policy in Central America, more specifically, in El Salvador.

Stone's protagonist in *Salvador*, Richard Boyle, provides a wake-up call to the American people about the downward slide in government that has led to this current state of affairs. Boyle, neither radical nor Marxist, is instead a loyal American, willing to stand up and fight for what his country still means to him.

As Boyle experiences a political reawakening, cleaning up his act and becoming the type of journalist he may once have been, the audience is invited to do likewise. Boyle, like the apathetic Americans who are the film's target audience, is a reluctant hero who must be taught to search out the truth about America's involvement in places like El Salvador, Nicaragua, Chile, and Vietnam. As a result, *Salvador*, like *The Doors* and *Talk Radio*, reflexively ruminates on the artist-journalist's responsibility to take a stance on issues and events of sociopolitical importance, while also acknowledging the difficulty of doing so in a world seemingly turned upside down.

Talk Radio (1988)

Oliver Stone's *Talk Radio*, financed by Cineplex Odeon Films and released by Universal Studios in 1988, was based in part upon Stephen Singular's *Talked to Death: The Life and Murder of Alan Berg*, a book about a Denver DJ murdered by neo-Nazis in 1984. Stone combined this with a theater piece, written and performed by Eric Bogosian in 1987 for Joseph Papp's New York Public Theater. The play, like Stone's film, is a ninety-minute battle of wits waged between a talk-show host as agent provocateur and his bitter and outrageous call-in listeners.

A great deal of the film's contemporary feel springs from its reliance on the burgeoning market for "shock radio," a genre of broadcasting popularized in the 1980s by such notables as Howard Stern and Morton Downing, Jr. According to Beaver, this genre's rise in popularity resulted

> from the call-in host's willingness to engage in challenging, often hostile dialogue with listeners on the most controversial of issues—religion, sex, race, politics, societal frustration. The confrontational nature of the programming—with the host serving as calculated provocateur—worked to raise both ire and broadcast rating. It also challenged the limits of First Amendment free speech protection.[29]

Barry Champlain, Stone's protagonist in *Talk Radio*, is more than just a "calculated provocateur" intent on shocking his audience; he is a "lightning rod for our national psychosis," a prophet for "the raw-nerved, solipsistic, paranoid '80s."[30] In Stone's view, even though Champlain is not the medicine we want, he is the medicine we need. Like his counterparts Jim Morrison and Richard Boyle, he is a voice crying out against the sins of the ego-driven, greed-obsessed modern age. Explains Barry to his fans, "I'm not afraid to see. I come in here every night. I make my case. I make my point. I say what I believe in. I tell you what you are. I have to; I have to; I have no choice. You frighten me." Like Jim Garrison in *JFK*, Jim Morrison in *The Doors*, and Richard Boyle in *Salvador*, Champlain has "cleansed vision." He "sees" what no one else does, and he speaks the truth. But as a result, like Kennedy, he is assassinated for it. One critic remarked, "Here is another American film in which Dallas, the pride of Texas, is presented as hell on earth."[31]

It is hard to believe that the choice of Dallas for the film's setting was accidental, since Alan Berg's story could have as easily been set in his hometown of Denver, Colorado. Stone's choice of Dallas invites the Kennedy assassination comparison. Once again, a "prophet," a "visionary," is gunned down in this Texas town for speaking his mind, for telling the people what they do not want to hear. Just as Kennedy had to be stopped for refusing to

Talk Radio's Barry Champlain (Eric Bogosian), sending out his prophetic messages of doom into the darkened Dallas night. Copyright © 1988 Universal Studios, Inc. Courtesy of MCA Publishing Rights, a Division of MCA Inc. All rights reserved. Photo by Joyce Rudolph.

play politics the way the military-industrial complex and his own foreign policy advisers wanted it played, just as Christ had to be turned over to Pontius Pilate and was ultimately crucified for aggravating the state and arousing the people's consciousness, so Champlain needs to be stopped for telling America what it does not want to hear: that America is a deeply bigoted, hateful, stupid, and blind society. "Words cause permanent damage" is one of Champlain's slogans. And Champlain, like J.F.K. and Christ, is murdered because of his words.

Talk Radio tells a story—almost identical to that in *The Doors*—of the performer crucified for his fans. Both Morrison and Champlain, prophetic visionaries for their respective eras, are doomed to be destroyed by the very excesses and stupidity that they rail against. As in *The Doors,* the messianic allegory is overt. The foreshadowing of Champlain's assassination by a crazed neo-Nazi is set up almost from the beginning of the film. Whenever Champlain invites comments from his radio listeners, for example, his standard line is "The door is open, hit me with your best shot." This phrase, repeated again and again, foreshadows what happens when one of his listeners interprets this offer literally. That Champlain is a persecuted Jew, like Christ, and is crucified for his views, also like Christ, makes the analogy even clearer.

Stone claims to have seen *Talk Radio* as a "technical challenge." As he said, "It was a bit of an exercise to stretch myself and to try new ways of shooting, working with a very small cast: severe discipline, six people and a limited set, like a submarine film or an elevator film. How to deal with a limited amount of space was very challenging to me after having worked large canvases. It was like doing a chamber piece."[32] Despite *Talk Radio's* smaller "canvas," the film's camera technique was similar to that used in both *Salvador* and *The Doors.* Although still a lion on the prowl, Stone's camera in *Talk Radio* has become a big-game cat trapped within the confines of a small radio broadcasting studio. As a result, the camera work is even angrier and more frenetic. Sometimes on the hunt, as when Champlain is "out for blood" and needs to crucify one of his on-air callers for the sins and stupidities of modern-day America, the camera also often cowers on the defensive, as when Champlain finds himself the trapped and pacing target of a racial hatred so strong he is rendered powerless against it.

Barry Champlain, talk-show host, like Oliver Stone, director, "calls them like he sees them" and is unafraid to warn society of the seriousness of its excesses. The first lines of dialogue in the film are Champlain's opening words in one evening's radio talk show. *Talk Radio,* in other words, like *The Doors,* reflexively begins as a play within a play:

> The worst news of the night is that three out of four people in this country say they'd rather watch TV than have sex with their spouse. The second-worst news is that some kids needed money for crack last night, so you know what

they did? They stuck a knife in the throat of an eighty-year-old grandmother down on Highland Avenue, here in Dallas. One night, in one American city, multiply that by hundreds of cities and what do you got? A country where culture means pornography and slasher films; where ethics means payoffs, graft, insider trading; where integrity means lying, whoring, and intoxication. This country is in deep trouble, People. This country is rotten to the core and somebody better do something about it.

Like a latter-day John the Baptist, Champlain, like Oliver Stone, is a voice crying in the wilderness telling society to make straight its crooked paths, to clean up its act. Champlain's words, going out into the darkened Dallas night, just as Stone's projected film images go out into the darkened theaters of this country, have a strange sort of prophetic wisdom for his nameless and faceless audience, an audience that simultaneously loves and hates him. As one critic noted, "For most of this engrossing, infuriating movie, [Champlain] sits in a radio studio and just talks, a shaman sparking his listeners around the communal campfire. It is a spellbinding turn."[33] The same assessment could be made of Oliver Stone as filmmaker.

Champlain, however, like Morrison, is a lesser Christ, or possibly an Iron Age sort of hero, because over the course of the film, he comes to doubt whether his worshipers are even worth the sacrifice. *Talk Radio* seems to imply that America may be so far gone that it is beyond salvation. During his last night on the radio before his assassination, Barry screams at his listeners:

> You're pathetic. I despise each and every one of you. You've got nothing, no brains, no power, no future, no God. The only thing you believe in is me. What are you if you don't have me? . . . I come in here every night; I abuse you, I insult you; you just keep coming back for more . . . bunch of yellow-bellied, spineless, bigoted, quivering, drunken, insomniac, paranoid, disgusting, perverted, obscene little phone callers, that's what you are. Well, the hell with you. I don't need your fear and your stupidity. You don't get it. It's wasted on you—pearls before swine.

Champlain, the disillusioned messiah, comes to realize that his prophetic warnings of society's impending damnation, in biblical terms, are "pearls" cast before uncomprehending and unworthy "swine."

The image of a disillusioned messiah is poignantly portrayed when Barry finally realizes who his real audience is—not enlightened striving intellectuals with hearts, but rather mind-numbed drug-crazed "Generation X-ers." For perhaps the first time, Champlain is confronted with a "live specimen," a talk-show guest in the flesh: Kent, an acid rocker whose brain, if he ever had one, has been completely destroyed by the excesses of his generation. No longer can Champlain paint imaginary pictures of his potentially virtuous anonymous call-in listeners. The real thing sits before him. Comments

Champlain to Kent, "If you represent the future of this country, then we're in sad shape."

Desperate to salvage his mission—his purpose for continuing as an on-air messiah—Champlain turns away from Kent to the phone lines for affirmation. He finds none.

> *Julia.* I've been listening to your show for five years straight, Barry. I love you and your show. Your show's terrific! I don't know what else to say.
> *Barry.* Well, tell me something Julia, since you listen all the time. What is it you like about the show?
> *Julia.* Well, I don't know. A lot of things.
> *Barry.* Well, what for instance?
> *Julia.* Well, I love you Barr'.
> *Barry.* Uh-huh, that's a given. OK, what about me do you love?
> *Julia.* Well, you're very funny and I love to hear you talk about all the things you have to say.
> *Barry.* Yeah, yeah. OK, let's get back to the show. The show must serve some kind of purpose for you?
> *Julia.* Well, now, I wouldn't say that.
> *Barry.* Well, what would you say?
> *Julia.* Well, I don't know.

This Pinteresque dialogue may strike us, as it does Champlain, with the profound meaninglessness and stupidity of the current radio and television talk-show age. We sense the seeming purposelessness of the modern age with a mind-numbing angst—an angst compounded by the realization that Champlain is not only disillusioned with his followers but also remains skeptical of the existence of his God. Champlain's coworker, for example, after Champlain's death, muses on air, "He always wondered if there was a God. Barry said that he had to wait until the evidence was in. Now you know, Barry, now you know."

Like Morrison in *The Doors,* Champlain may be a sorry shaman and a shoddy savior, but he is the god of his age. One of his listeners, desperate for Barry to explain it all, to put meaning into his life, cries out in his despair: "Barry, I don't know much about God and I never was very religious, but you can't help feeling like something is wrong—like nobody's driving the train—the system. There's too many people getting sick. The traffic is just jamming up and even the weather's not so good lately. Barry, I just don't know." Champlain is unable to respond to this caller as he has just opened his mail and found what amounts to a death threat, a blood-spattered publicity photo of himself upon which is scrawled "the only good Jew is a dead Jew." A much-reduced Christ, possibly faced with the foreknowledge of his impending assassination, Champlain is powerless to comfort this bewildered and confused follower. Kent, Champlain's acid-rocker guest, fills the "dead-air" void by screaming an answer to the caller's anguish, "You don't get it, wimp. Here's what you get: a dollar fifty-nine. You go down to the drugstore, buy yourself a pack of razor blades, and slash your fucking wrists, pinhead!" Although Kent is thrown out of the studio for his outburst, his presence hangs over the studio like a deathly pall, casting a spell of gloom and hopelessness. We are forced to realize that Kent may be a projection of what Champlain already is, in the words of Shakespeare's Macbeth, "a poor player that struts and frets his hour upon the stage and then is heard no more"; he is a screaming voice "full of sound and fury, signifying nothing" (*Macbeth* 5.5.19).

Champlain may also be an imperfect savior because although Christ, in Christian mythology, acknowledged humanity's many shortcomings, he loved people anyway, but Barry Champlain, a voice crying out in the urban wilderness of the Dallas night, can neither love his worshipers nor himself. One anonymous female caller challenges him with this: "The question is obvious. Why does an intelligent fellow like yourself spend so much energy hurting other people? Do you not love yourself? I think you're very lonely, Barry. I'm sorry for you because you don't know how to love." Champlain, for once, is struck speechless by this caller's comment, as if hit by some profound insight into his flawed character as talk-show savior.

Champlain's messianic complex and the foreshadowing of his sacrificial death continue throughout the film, but these elements are most evident in the words of Champlain's executive producer at the radio station. Infuriated by Champlain's self-destructive impulses, such as allowing unscheduled guests like Kent into the studio and failing to cooperate with the studio bigwigs, he warns Champlain to "pull it back just for a little bit. It's a job—that's all it is. . . . What do you think you're doing here? Changing the world? This is a talk show, Barry, and you're a talk-show host. I'm glad you take it all so seriously, Barry, but you gotta learn when to stop or it's gonna kill you." Champlain, of course, like Garrison in *JFK*, Morrison in *The Doors,* and Jesus Christ, despite the best advice of his disciples, *is* out to "change the world" and never learns to "pull it back," even though it ends up killing him.

Barry is also warned of his impending assassination by one of his crazed listeners, a woman who spouts judgment-day rhetoric seemingly straight from the Book of Revelations: "The day will come for you, Barry, and there will be a reckoning, an adding up and a totaling. Those who turn away will be turned upon, and I don't care what your story is, Barry. You are responsible, and there will be no confusion at your trial. It will be short and necks will crack. The whip will strip your back bare to the bone, and your children will cry for you as they are slaughtered before your eyes." As he listens to this religious fanatic's prophetic diatribe, rather than being angry—his usual response to venomous callers' attacks—Barry worriedly paces the studio like a caged or hunted animal. The camera circles him continuously.

He is helpless prey trapped behind the glassed-in walls of the sound booth. It seems that Barry heeds her words, however, and possibly for the first time, he takes his impending trial and crucifixion at the hands of "the people" seriously—the masses who called out for his "death" earlier in the film at a basketball game, just as Christ was decried in front of King Herod. Perhaps we also witness him coming to terms with his morally ambiguous status as a prophet of his era. Champlain responds:

> Believe it or not, you make perfect sense to me. I'm a hypocrite. I ask for sincerity and I lie. I denounce the system as I embrace it. I want money and power and prestige. I want ratings and success and I don't give a damn about you or the world. That's the truth. For this I could say I'm sorry, but I won't. Why should I? I mean, who the hell are you anyway, you audience? You're on me every night like a pack of wolves 'cause you can't stand facing what you are and what you've made. Yes, the world is a terrible place; yes, cancer and garbage disposals will get you; yes, a war's coming; yes, the world is shot to hell, and you're all goners. Everything is screwed up and you like it that way. You're fascinated by the gory details, you're mesmerized by your own fear. You revel in floods, car accidents, unstoppable diseases. You're happiest when others are in pain. That's where I come in isn't it? I'm here to lead you by the hand through the dark forest of your own hatred and anger and humiliation. I'm providing a public service. You're so scared you're like a little child under the covers. You're afraid of the boogie man but you can't live without him. Your fear—your own lives—have become your entertainment.

Champlain, in this last broadcast before his death, has become profoundly disillusioned with himself, his listeners, and his mission.

After the show Champlain confides his despair about his "flawed ministry" to his sound engineer, Stu, saying, "The show's a washout, Stu." Stu replies, "Give me a break, Barry; we're going national, man. Besides it's not that important. It's just one show." Retorts Champlain, "If it's not that important then why am I doing it?" Stu answers him: "I don't know, Barry. If you don't like the heights, don't climb the mountains." Champlain's talk show is more than just a talk show to him. Although he cynically rails against his listeners' stupidity and hopelessness and acknowledges his own hypocrisy and lies, he believes both he and his audience can be saved and that his prophetic words, his personal brand of "wake-up radio," like Stone's "wake-up cinema," might be the only thing that can save them all. Champlain, like Stone, like the biblical Moses, can't keep himself from "climb[ing] the mountains," scaling the heights, or walking along the ledge, like Jim Morrison in *The Doors*. Although it is precarious, although one's chances of falling off, or failing, increase the closer one gets to the peak or the edge, for Stone and for his protagonists it is the only game in town. Like Moses, if you want the tablets, you have to climb the mountains to get them; if you want true wisdom, you must ascend from the cave of veiled sight; and if you want the truth, as Cassady in *Salvador* says, "You've got to get close, but if you get too close you die." Did Champlain get too close? Or not close enough?

Critics have noted Champlain's strange mix of cynicism and idealism. One critic called him "a classic Stone antihero: cynical, selfish, aggressive, insensitive to women, yet somehow saved by a vestigial idealism, a product of the worst and the best in American society."[34] In the opinion of another critic: "Champlain is the same mixture of honest and sleaze, high aspiration and character as James Woods's reporter in Stone's *Salvador*. Like that character, Champlain is a catalyst; he drags out the truth, the dark side. But he's become a beast in public to win his rating. And he's become a beast in private as well. He tears his life and his ideas to shreds. Honesty becomes a gig and cynicism a crutch."[35]

In *Talk Radio*'s final scene, Champlain is gunned down in the parking lot by a neo-Nazi assassin masquerading as an autograph-seeking fan. Champlain's body, repeatedly riddled with bullets, slumps to the floor of his car. In a final freeze-frame close-up of his face, the shot is slowly overexposed until his face glows with a messianic white light. The camera slowly tilts up from his body into the night sky as it follows the projectory of a massive radio tower "crucifix," alive with pulsing blood-red lights, like a heartbeat or an electronic pulpit that continues to live on, despite Champlain's death, as it sends out its messages into the darkened Dallas night.

But what accounts for *Talk Radio*'s cynicism? Why, for example, are Richard Boyle in *Salvador*, Jim Morrison in *The Doors,* and Barry Champlain in *Talk Radio* such unappealing protagonists? Both *Talk Radio* and *The Doors* end in death, whereas *Salvador* ends in defeat. Champlain, his "Christ-like" glow in death aside, is assassinated by a ranting and raving neo-Nazi; Jim Morrison, despite his mission to "break on through to the other side" of consciousness, overdoses on drugs and alcohol in a cheap Paris apartment; Boyle, although he makes it back to the States alive, is helpless to stop his girlfriend Maria's possible deportation back to El Salvador and certain death.

The cynicism, in one interpretation, is a hopelessness either about getting to the bottom of things and finding the truth itself or about locating heroes who can convey the truth to the people. Stone's *Salvador,* for example, implies that the Salvadoran rebels are just as culpable for the death and destruction in El Salvador as are the right-wing Salvadoran government and the American administration that supported them. Likewise, Boyle and Champlain are a mixture of both good and evil impulses without resolution. As such, they are hardly ideal models of heroism. Boyle, Morrison, and Champlain are flawed heroes—heroes who wail and gnash their teeth at the injustices of American politics and modern consciousness as they watch each of the plagues in Pandora's box—greed, deceit, murder, betrayal—enacted before them. They remain uncertain, however, as do we who live in the postmodern world, whether transcendence beyond this "vale of tears," this "will to power," is even possible.

In another interpretation, however, the cynicism is merely a temporary roadblock, a necessary first step in bridging the gap from one era of consciousness to the other, in forming the models from which future heroes will be made. Stone's heroes, after all, can only be shaped from the existing postmodern bricolage that lies scattered around them like crumbled rubble from the temple proper. Although this may be the only building material available, it may be what causes such violent reactions to Stone's films. By transporting the viewer across levels of psychomythic reality rather than within a given level, Stone's films may enrage, whereas "straight" mythic interpretations like *Star Wars* and *E.T.* only endear. Stone's films refuse to simply romanticize bygone eras with the "archaic" language of myth; rather, they challenge the current age by telling mythic tales in the language of postmodernity.

Maybe the master narratives no longer make sense. Perhaps the hero quest for "(higher) truth, justice, and the American way" is nothing more than a vain and idle pursuit. The road to the new Jerusalem, or Camelot, could be nothing more than a wrong turn down a blind alley. And maybe the filmmaker's job is to forget the search for Platonic truths, to accept human fallibility and the complexities of good and evil, and to settle for small moments of illumination—quite situational truths in the miasma of the postmodern condition. But maybe, just maybe, Stone's protagonists, like Stone's films, are so maddeningly interesting and appealing because they challenge postmodern arguments against coherence and truth by using the very weapons of postmodernity. Speaking the language of postmodernism like a native, Stone's films use the disparate pieces of self-conscious postmodernity to tap into a repressed or forgotten preconscious reality whose mythic unity appears to have been destroyed by the general fragmentation of the postmodern world. The "flaw" in Stone's films and in his protagonists may be that models for transconsciousness do not yet exist. This means that Stone's heroes, crying out against the sins of the modern age, can identify the problem but only hint at the solution. As this is the case, the sacrifices of their bodies can only become the material from which to forge the bridge to transconsciousness that future generations might walk across.

Notes

1. Russell Miller, "Rider on the Storm," *Sunday Times Magazine* (London), 14 February 1991, 20.

2. Glenn Collins, "Oliver Stone Is Ready to Move on from Vietnam," *New York Times,* 2 January 1990, sec. 3, 20.

3. Frank Beaver, *Oliver Stone: Wakeup Cinema* (New York: Twayne Publishers, 1994), 151.

4. This scene may also provide an autobiographical reference to Stone's own father since both Morrison and Stone in their youth, according to Elizabeth Stone, were "poets, both rebelled against their strict fathers. [Morrison's] father was an admiral—and against the suburban life of the Sixties. Oliver saw himself as very much of a rebel" (Miller, "Rider on the Storm," 21). Stone's films are often about young men pitted in spiritual wars with their fathers, for example, Bud Fox in *Wall Street*, Chris Taylor in *Platoon*, Ron Kovic in *Born on the Fourth of July*, and Jim Morrison in *The Doors*. These young men often rebel against their fathers and what they represent.

5. Martin Medhurst, "The Rhetorical Structure of Oliver Stone's *JFK*," *Critical Studies in Mass Communication* 10 (1993):128–143.

6. Isa. 24:7–11 King James Version.

7. Joel 1:5, 1:10 King James Version.

8. Stuart Klawans, review of *"The Doors,"* *Nation,* 25 March 1991, 390.

9. Paul Baumann, "Sex, Drugs, and Rock n' Roll," *Commonweal,* 3 May 1991, 294.

10. Mark Rafferty, "The Current Cinema," *New Yorker,* 11 March 1991, 82.

11. Mark Rowland, "Stone Unturned," *American Film* 16 (March 1991):42.

12. Klawans, review of *"The Doors,"* 391.

13. David Ansen, "Your Not So Basic Showbiz Bio," *Newsweek,* 18 March 1991, 57.

14. Jim Morrison, in real life, wanted to be a filmmaker, claiming he was "interested in film because to me it's the closest approximation in art form that we have to the actual flow of consciousness, in both dreamlife and the everyday perception of the world" (Robert Horton, "Riders on the Storm," *Film Comment* 27 [May/June 1991]:61).

15. Rowland, "Stone Unturned," 43.

16. Rafferty, "Current Cinema," 82.

17. Stanley Kauffman, "Stanley Kauffman on Films," *New Republic,* 1 April 1991, 28.

18. Ibid.

19. Elizabeth Gordon, *"Salvador:* Too Hot for U.S. Distribs," *Film Journal* 89 (1986):40.

20. Patrick McGilligan, "Point Man," *Film Comment* 23 (February 1987):12.

21. Richard Coombs, "Beating God to the Draw," *Sight and Sound* 56 (spring 1987):137.

22. Horton, "Riders on the Storm," 57.

23. Coombs, "Beating God to the Draw," 137.

24. Horton, "Riders on the Storm," 57.

25. George Kimball, review of *"Salvador,"* *Films and Filming* 388 (January 1987):42.

26. Ibid.

27. In fact, as Stone has matured as a filmmaker, the balance between the mythic and the political has tipped—some critics might claim to his films' detriment—in favor of the mythic.

28. Alexander Cockburn, "Oliver Stone Takes Stock," *American Film* 13 (December 1987):25.

29. Beaver, *Oliver Stone: Wakeup Cinema,* 113.

30. David Ansen, review of *"Talk Radio,"* *Newsweek,* 9 January 1989, 54.

31. Suzanne Moore, "It's Only Words," *New Statesman and Society* (September 1989):43.

32. Oliver Stone, as quoted in Beaver's *Oliver Stone: Wakeup Cinema,* 10.

33. Richard Corliss, review of *"Talk Radio,"* *Time,* 19 December 1988, 79.

34. Pam Cook, review of *"Talk Radio,"* *Monthly Film Bulletin* 56 (September 1989):285.

35. Michael Wilmington, "Dangerous Games for Power and Fame: *Talk Radio* Takes a Savage Look Under Society's Surface," *Los Angeles Times Calendar,* 21 December 1988, 8.

five

Meeting the Shadow
and the Journey Home

The point is, Ladies and Gentlemen, that greed, for lack of a better word, is good. Greed is right, greed works, greed clarifies—cuts through and captures the essence of the evolutionary spirit. Greed, in all its forms—greed for life, for money, for love, knowledge—has marked the upward surge of mankind.

—Gordon Gekko, in *Wall Street*

There is a deep doctrine in the legend of the Fall: It is that expression of a dim presentiment that the emancipation of ego consciousness was a Luciferian deed.

—Carl Jung[1]

That's your shadow on the wall. Can't get rid of your shadow, can you, Wayne?

—Mickey Knox to Wayne Gale, in *Natural Born Killers*

Wall Street, released in 1987, and *Natural Born Killers,* released in 1994, represent two different views of the teleological development of humanity. Although *Wall Street,* on the surface, seems to provide the more optimistic appraisal of the potential for redemption in a world driven by ego excess, it is actually *Natural Born Killers,* the seemingly darker of the two films, that offers hope of transcendence through the redemptive powers of love. Although *Wall Street*'s Bud Fox is seduced by the world of corrupt corporate finance, learns his lesson, and ultimately redeems himself by rejecting Gordon Gekko and that for which he stands, Fox remains a much weaker character sketch than Gordon Gekko. Gekko, from the perspective of perennial philosophy, represents society's central stumbling block on its journey toward

Posing for a commemorative photo, *Natural Born Killers'* Mallory (Juliette Lewis) and Mickey (Woody Harrelson) show off their hardware. Copyright © 1994 Warner Bros. Productions Ltd. and Monarchy Enterprises C.V. Photo by Sidney Baldwin.

transcendence—he is the epitome of ego consciousness in the modern age. His belief in life as a zero-sum game is a central metaphor for Stone's vision of life in the 1980s—a winner-take-all world where success is defined by excess. By contrast, although Mickey and Mallory Knox, the protagonists of *Natural Born Killers*, view life as "a will to power," they seem to yearn for something more than this "vale of tears," as is evidenced by their attraction to the Indian shaman and their remorse at his death. As a result, they remain more complex characters than either Bud Fox or Gordon Gekko, primarily because, like Chris Taylor in *Platoon,* they seem to be aware, however dimly, that growth requires a balancing of opposites, an acknowledgment of the human capacity not only to love but also to hate and destroy. Mickey and Mallory are different from Gekko because even in the face of their shadow, they are learning to love. Gekko, a stranger to love, only knows destruction in the pursuit of ego excess. Mickey and Mallory, by their recognition of the transcendent possibilities manifest through love, in however twisted a fashion, may represent a glimmer of the next phase in the teleological development of Stone's protagonists.

Wall Street (1987)

Reading like the real-life story of insider trader Ivan Boesky, Oliver Stone's prophetic *Wall Street,* released in 1987, seemed to presage the stock market crash in October of that year. With *Wall Street* Stone had once again turned his camera on another corrupt American institution, the world of corporate finance. And despite the radically different setting of *Wall Street* from his previous film *Platoon,* Stone, according to critics, was telling the same story by simply replacing one jungle for another. In the words of one critic, "*Wall Street is Platoon* in civvies. Instead of jungle warfare, there's the financial jungle, where man eats man rather than shoots man."[2] Another concurred, "The plot is almost identical in the two films: young men, both played by Charlie Sheen, are torn between a good and bad man. Both end with the young man turning on the bad man and destroying him."[3]

More often than not, however, critics compared *Wall Street* to Hollywood morality plays of the 1930s and 1940s. One critic noted that "underneath the shiny, contemporary surface is a musty old Hollywood movie about good and evil, full of stock characters and clichés."[4] Stanley Kauffman agreed, claiming that "the action in Stone's new picture, for all the dexterous direction and satiric reproduction of ultramod behavior, is a 1930s Warner Brothers morality drama."[5] According to another critic, the film

> could have been written and directed by one of the Hollywood Ten in the late 1940s. . . . The very fact that *Wall Street*'s last shot is a panoramic view of New York City's skyscrapers with the "Halls of Justice" at the bottom of the frame and a huge, imposing "The End" at the top of the frame seems to indicate that Stone meant to harken back to the old films that ended in just such a manner—the big "Crime Doesn't Pay" finish.[6]

Critics who did not make the liberal morality play comparison often drew a Mephistopheles connection instead, calling Gordon Gekko a "modern day Mephistopheles,"[7] "a manic Mephistopheles. . . . a loathsome Satan [with] a fascinating personality."[8] Oliver Stone, however, preferred to liken *Wall Street* to *Pilgrim's Progress,* noting that the film "is basically a

Pilgrim's Progress of a boy who is seduced, corrupted, by the allure of easy money. And in the third act, he sets out to redeem himself. He goes back to an essential decency that he rediscovers in himself—very much like some of us do in life."[9]

Whether critics compared *Wall Street* to a Hollywood morality play or to a literary classic, what emerged was the sense that Stone had gone for the large-scale perspective or the sweeping statement and had sacrificed the individual character.[10] For many critics, this was the film's central flaw, since symbols and metaphors are much less interesting to play than people. One critic complained, "The elder Sheen's great talent is nearly wasted; his paint-by-numbers character has been created as a symbol not a person. . . . Gekko is a mesmerizing apostle for the amoral but because the good guys are never really a match for him, Stone can't pull together a plausible resolution for his fable."[11]

Wall Street, in many ways, is a Hollywood morality play—a Paradise Lost, a Pilgrim's Progress, a rite of passage film. But perhaps its dullness for some results from its being a less well-told morality play than, for example, *Platoon* or *JFK.* All of Stone's characters are allegorical because all of Stone's films embody the perennial philosopher's call to move to the next stage of consciousness. Many of Stone's heroes, like Boyle in *Salvador,* Morrison in *The Doors,* and Champlain in *Talk Radio,* are repositories of both the good and the bad instincts of humanity and thus embody the complexities of life. *Wall Street* is perhaps Stone's least well-made film because it fails to grapple with these complexities and instead takes an unproblematic view of good and evil in 1980s America.

However unsubtle the film, *Wall Street* "serves as a political-economical allegory of America in the 1980s."[12] It is the story of how America sold its soul to the devil of corporate greed. Like Bud Fox (Charlie Sheen), 1980s America became seduced by fast money and a slippery-slope morality. Now is the time to wake up, the film screams, and realize what we have done. *Wall Street* is our cleansing, our rite of passage. Like Bud, we must descend into the "heart of darkness" that is corporate greed and shallow ego-worship and wrestle with the devils we meet there—the Gordon Gekkos and Michael Milkens of this world. Only then can we emerge, possibly scarred, like many Stone protagonists, though wiser and better for the experience.

Wall Street, like every film Stone has ever made, is a story of corruption and betrayal. Bud Fox is the victim not only of the power broker Gordon Gekko but also of a money-hungry society that values success over integrity. Once seduced by the corrupt world of high finance, Bud Fox also creates victims of the smaller fish in the corporate pond, upon whom he and Gekko feed. Fox betrays his father, his friends, his value system, and ultimately, Gordon Gekko, the man who first betrays him. But betrayal in *Wall Street* runs even deeper than this. Just as Jim Morrison's and Ron

Kovic's generation was betrayed in Vietnam; just as Jim Garrison's generation was deceived in the cover-up of the Kennedy assassination; just as Richard Boyle's generation was lied to in El Salvador, so middle-class America has been lured by the false promises of the free market economy in the 1980s. America's embarrassments, such as Black Friday on Wall Street and the savings and loan banking scandal, simply add fodder, in some cases retrospectively, to Stone's argument in *Wall Street* that all that glitters is not gold.

Although *Wall Street* will most likely be remembered as one of Stone's minor works, it remains critically interesting not only as a document of the greedy 1980s but also as a central metaphor for the age of ego consciousness epitomized by Gordon Gekko (a role that garnered Michael Douglas an Academy Award for Best Actor). Gekko is both one of Stone's most dangerously seductive characters and his most clearly drawn portrait of the evil with which Stone's prototypical heroes do battle. Most important, however, Gordon Gekko, from the perspective of perennial philosophy, represents society's central stumbling block on the journey toward transcendence.

Gordon Gekko, a "lizard" of ego consciousness in the modern age and in the "me" decade of the 1980s, is a man who marks his worth by the money he makes, the infamy he garners, and the possessions he has accumulated. This philosophy of greed is best displayed in an exchange between Gekko and Bud Fox, after glimmers of Bud's consciousness have begun to emerge. "Tell me, Gordon, when does it all end?" Bud queries. "How many yachts can you waterski behind. How much is enough?" Gekko replies: "It's not a question of enough, pal. It's a zero-sum game—somebody wins, somebody loses. Money itself is not lost or made, it's simply transferred from one perception to another like magic. See this painting here? I bought it ten years ago for sixty thousand. I could sell it today for six hundred [thousand]. The illusion has become real, and the more real it becomes, the more desperately they want it—capitalism at its finest." When asked again by Bud, "How much is enough?" Gekko, after another extended sermon on the value of corporate greed, concludes, "I create nothing, I own." For Gekko, enlightenment comes through ownership. Defined by what he can possess, he is the epitome of ego consciousness, a reflection of 1980s excess.

This is best demonstrated in Gekko's tribute to greed: a speech he delivers at a stockholder's meeting for a company in which he is the major stockholder. Addressing a crowded auditorium, Gekko intones: "The point is, Ladies and Gentlemen, that greed, for lack of a better word, is good. Greed is right, greed works, greed clarifies—cuts through and captures the essence of the evolutionary spirit. Greed, in all its forms—greed for life, for money, for love, knowledge—has marked the upward surge of mankind. And greed will not only save Teldine Paper but that other malfunctioning corporation called the U.S.A." For Gekko, the "upward surge of mankind," or our teleological

Wall Street's Bud Fox (Charlie Sheen) learning the tricks of the insider trading business from the master, Gordon Gekko (Michael Douglas). Copyright © 1987 Twentieth Century Fox Film Corp. Photo by Andrew Schwartz.

development, is nothing more than a Darwinist rat race paced by the greediest rats in the pack.

This is not to say that Gekko does not possess emotions or aesthetic sensibilities. We learn of his appreciation of fine art and attractive women, an appreciation, however, that is at the level of ownership and ego consciousness. Gekko, for example, sends a high-class prostitute to Bud Fox's apartment as a present for helping him on a stock deal. Gekko "gives" his former mistress Darian (Daryl Hannah) to Bud after he is finished with her. Darian, like the paintings on Gekko's walls, goes with the status and the power of being a "player"—so much so that when Bud Fox breaks rank with Gekko, he must "give" Darian back. Despite her fond feelings for Bud, she also knows that she is "owned" by Gekko and the status and power he commands. She, like Gekko, has sold herself, body and soul, to the company store.

Darian is not only Gekko's mistress and Fox's girlfriend, however; she is also the interior decorator primarily responsible for decorating the nihilistic modern-day Sodom in which these archetypal characters, like preening peacocks, roam. Gekko's office and home, like Bud Fox's new apartment when he finally makes it into the "big time" like Gordon, are a metaphor for the overrich and underclassed twentieth-century city dweller for whom "chic" means sledgehammer-exposed brick walls, sharp angles, garish colors, and cold steel. Stone's camera frequently prowls around this devastated world, detailing the cages that trap these shallow ego-worshipers.

Although Gekko is able to see himself reflected at twice his size in every painting or woman he owns, he is frustratingly unable to extend this feeling of ownership to the natural environment. Standing in a black velour bathrobe on a deserted, predawn beach and talking on a cellular telephone to Bud Fox back in New York, Gekko philosophizes on greed and ownership. The sight of the rising sun, however, causes him to interrupt his litany and interject, "Ah, Jesus—I wish you could see this—lights coming up. I've never seen a painting that captures the beauty of the ocean at a moment like this. [Pause.] I'm gonna make you rich, Bud Fox, rich enough you can afford a girl like Darian." Gekko's rapture for the beauty of the ocean at sunrise is connected to his sadness at his inability to own the view in the same way, perhaps, that he can own paintings of such views. He wants to "capture" the ocean and the sky, just as he wants Bud Fox to be able to "afford" to own a woman like Darian. Rather than seeing nature as a reminder of the transcendent—the next phase in teleological development in which ownership is meaningless—Gekko wants to tame and possess it by reducing it to ego size or by expanding his ego consciousness until it can contain the whole of the universe itself.

As seductive as Gekko's proclamations that "greed is good" and "life [is] a zero-sum game" are for an audience—particularly in the late 1980s—Stone reminds us of the error of our thinking. *Wall Street* is, after all, a morality play. As Gekko finishes his conversation with Bud, the camera slowly zooms out to a long shot of the entire beach. Gekko has become nothing more than an insignificant black dot in a vast ocean-filled screen. His multimillion-dollar deals, his fifteen minutes of fame, are nothing more than a tick in the clock of eternity, a grain of sand in the vastness of the universe. Lack of humility, perhaps, is Gordon Gekko's tragic flaw.

Stone continually reminds us in *Wall Street* of the error of Gekko's ways by opposing him with the voice of reason, represented by Bud's father, Carl Fox, and Bud's fellow stockbroker, Lou Manneheim. Carl Fox, a hardworking union representative from a midsize airline, like Lou, is from the "old school" when it comes to ethics and integrity. Early in the film when Bud is forced to ask his father for money, despite making more of it than his father, Carl Fox questions his son's high-rolling lifestyle and his inability to live within his means. Bud responds, "There's no nobility in poverty anymore, Dad. One day you're gonna be proud of me, you'll see." Carl Fox's reply echoes the film's central lesson, "It's yourself you gotta be proud of, Huckleberry."

If Gordon Gekko represents the amoral high-rolling player, Lou Manneheim, even more so than Bud's father, represents the ethically conscientious stayer. Perhaps the oldest broker in the firm, Lou claims to have weathered the storms of over thirty years of both bull and bear markets by "sticking to fundamentals." Lou complains to his younger counterparts at one point: "Jesus, you can't make a buck in this market. The country's going to hell faster than when that son of a bitch Roosevelt was in charge. Too much cheap money sloshing around the world. Worst mistake we ever made was letting Nixon get off the gold standard. Putney Drug—you boys might want to take a look at it." A young broker replies, "No—take five years for that company to come around." Lou continues, "But they got a good new drug. Stick to the fundamentals. That's how IBM and Hilton were built. Good things—sometimes—take time."

It is hard not to draw comparisons between Lou Stone, Oliver's Wall Street stockbroker father, and Lou Manneheim, Bud Fox's "father figure" colleague. Although many critics have argued that the film's central battle for Bud's soul is waged between Bud's father and Gordon Gekko, a far more interesting and compelling conflict exists between the opposing ethical systems of Gordon Gekko and Lou Manneheim. As a voice of reason and balance, Lou is the stockbroker to whom Bud seems to defer and about whom he is most solicitous. Bud seems to respect Lou, possibly for some of the same reasons he admires his father—for his integrity, hard work, and sense of fair play. Later in the film, for example, when Bud Fox is seduced by the lure of easy money made from shady stock deals, he still thinks of Lou and gives him a tip about a company he calls "a sure thing." Lou retorts, "There's no such thing except death and taxes. Not a good company anymore, no fundamentals. What's going on, Bud? You know something? Remember there are no shortcuts, son—quick buck artists come and go, but the steady players make it through the bear markets. You're a part of something here, Bud. The money you make for people creates science and research jobs. Don't sell that out." Bud replies, "You're right, Lou, but you gotta get to the big time first, then you can be a pillar and do good things." Lou responds, "You can't get a little bit pregnant, son." An ethical individual, like a pregnancy, is uncompromisingly straightforward—either you are or you are not. Just as it is impossible to be a little bit pregnant, so it is impossible to be a little bit unethical. Ethical infractions invite a slippery-slope morality. For Lou, and for an identifying audience, the question is simple: When you wake up in the morning and look in the mirror, can you live with the person you see reflected there?

This message of integrity before all else is echoed near the end of the film as Bud is about to be arrested for violating the Securities and Exchange Commission's rules against insider trading. Just before his arrest, Bud's colleague Lou stops him in the hall, grips him by the arm, and solemnly reminds him, "Bud, man looks in the abyss. There's nothing staring back at him. At that moment man finds his character and that's what keeps him out of the abyss." The individual, the film seems to imply, separated from the trappings of ego consciousness—fame, fortune, possessions, reputation—is in peril of becoming entirely lost, unless, at that moment, a new consciousness of the Self emerges, as a result of some inner strength of character, which allows the individual to explore or at least acknowledge the abyss and in losing the self, find the Self again. A new consciousness will only emerge, however, in the ethically sound individual, the one who has inner fortitude and, perhaps, vision. Gordon Gekko, in contrast to Lou, sees life as a "zero-sum" game. As he says, you are either "a player or nothing." If faced with the abyss and separated from the trappings of ego consciousness, Gordon Gekko would have to leap in.

Natural Born Killers (1994)

Natural Born Killers, released in September 1994, is, in many ways, Oliver Stone's *Wall Street* for the 1990s. This time, however, "Gordon Gekko" is the protagonist. If Gekko represents ego consciousness and the greed and excess of the 1980s, then Mickey and Mallory Knox (Woody Harrelson and Juliette Lewis), the "Generation X" protagonists of *Natural Born Killers*, epitomize that same ego consciousness and greed, reborn as 1990s nihilism and hyperexcess. If Gordon Gekko's unfulfilled fetish is to own the vast beauty of the natural world and his personal tragedy is the realization that he cannot—because his voracious appetite to possess and use all that he sees is stymied in the face of eternity—then no such tragedy exists for Mickey. Mickey is the god of his world, and unlike Jim Morrison of *The Doors*, this mantle sits lightly, almost unperceived, on his shoulders.

Mickey's messianic complex, for example, is most apparent on his and Mallory's "wedding day," when the couple exchange serpent rings and fidelity vows, sealed appropriately in their own blood. We see them in a medium shot, standing on a canyon bridge and looking down over the coursing river perhaps one-half mile below. After Mickey slashes both of their palms to seal their blood wedding, they join hands and peer over the edge of this vast abyss to watch their blood drip down to the river below. As Mallory's makeshift wedding veil blows off and floats slowly into the chasm, Mickey boldly proclaims to the wind, "God, before you and this river and this mountain and everything we don't know about: Mallory, do you take Mickey?" After Mallory replies in the affirmative, they exchange rings designed in the shape of entwined serpents as Mickey concludes, "By the power vested in me as the God of my world, I pronounce us husband and wife." Ego excess is complete. Mickey Knox is king and god of all he surveys. The intense fear and dread generated by *Natural Born Killers* comes, in part, from the realization that Mickey and Mallory, faced with the abyss, have long since jumped in. The abyss, in fact, is where they live.

America's newest pop icons Mallory (Juliette Lewis) and Mickey (Woody Harrelson) demonstrate their technique in *Natural Born Killers*, Oliver Stone's 1994 satire on violence and the American media. Copyright © 1994 Warner Bros. Productions Ltd. and Monarchy Enterprises C.V. Photo by Sidney Baldwin.

Natural Born Killers' portrait of America, with the notable exception of *Talk Radio,* is, on the one hand, the most pessimistic indictment Stone has yet to make of our potential for humanist advancement. On the other hand, as twisted and as seemingly without conscience as Mickey and Mallory are, they offer a glimmer of the transcendent future possibilities of love even in the destructive present of hate. Mickey and Mallory, teleologically speaking, are two of the most advanced Stone protagonists. Mickey, in particular, seems to possess a secret that is at the heart of his fascination for Wayne Gale and Gale's television audience. Mickey seems to know that whether reviled or revered, our shadow must be sought out; it must be faced and explored. The problem that Mickey and Mallory face is that although they are unafraid to face their shadows—their alter egos—they act out this exploration by committing violent crimes against others and thus remain stuck at the shadow level. Their descent into the unconscious, in other words, is not followed by an ascent into enlightenment. They prefer to dwell in the darkness of their shadow self and, if possible, to bring others down with them.

Wayne Gale, the host of the sensationalist television show *American Maniacs,* for example, cannot escape his shadow as he is lured by Mickey and Mallory into the realm of his darker nature. When Mickey and Mallory seize upon a chance to escape from jail during the prison riot sparked by Mickey's interview with Gale, they take Gale with them as hostage. Despite his hostage status, Gale gets caught up in the excitement of the escape and soon feels released from the constraints of a socially defined and confined life. After trading his television camera for a gun and telling his wife via cellular phone that their marriage is over, a bloody but triumphant Gale proclaims, "Oh man, I'm alive for the first fucking time in my life and I want to thank you Mickey. Let's kill all these motherfuckers." Like Mickey, his new role model, Gale has become submerged in his shadow and for the first time begins to revel in death and destruction for the sheer animal "high" of the experience.

Natural Born Killers invites the audience to both embrace and distance itself from Mickey and Mallory. In some ways admirable because of their willingness to explore their shadow, they remain detestable in most others. Although they have made strides in their journey toward transconsciousness, they do not go far enough. Placed within the context of Stone's other films, *Natural Born Killers* implies that if we run from our shadow we cannot grow—this is the lesson we learn from Mickey and Mallory. If we become seduced or consumed by it, however, like Mickey and Mallory, we become the embodiment of dread. If we face our shadow—our ability to *create* monsters like Mickey and Mallory—only then can we emerge transcendent, with psyches held together by a seemingly paradoxical balance between ignorance and knowledge, spirit and flesh, and darkness and light.

This is the lesson, as we will see, that the Indian knows and tries unsuccessfully to teach to both Mickey and Mallory.

Natural Born Killers was shot in fifty-four days at a cost of $34 million. Coscripted by Oliver Stone, David Veloz, and Richard Rutowski, the story began as a script by Quentin Tarantino, director of *Reservoir Dogs* and the Oscar-nominated *Pulp Fiction*. Tarantino, however, ended up taking story credit rather than screenwriting credit in the final version. Because of its extensive violence and foul language, Stone was forced to trim or remove over one hundred fifty shots from the film and make five trips to the Motion Picture Association of America (MPAA) board before he secured an R rating.[13] Said Stone of his editing efforts to win the R rating, "We didn't try to play hardball about it, and some of what they said made the film better, more accessible. We didn't lose the basic idea."[14] After editing sessions that lasted for a grueling eleven months, the film was finally released in September 1994 by Fine Line Cinema, a division of Warner Brothers.

Stone was once again accused of going "over the top" with *Natural Born Killers,* but for many critics "over the top" was just where he needed to be. As one reviewer put it, Stone "[rubs] our noses in our own lust for excess, and some viewers are bound to say that he's gone too far. Yet this may be one case where too far is just far enough—where a gifted filmmaker has transformed his own attraction to violence into an art of depraved catharsis."[15] Corliss called the film "a Stone-crazed parable of greed and abuse. Shake well, pull the pin, and stand back. Except, of course, that Stone doesn't let you stand back. . . . The ride is fun, too, daredevil; fun of the sort that only Stone seems willing to provide in this timid film era."[16] Concluded Corliss, "*Natural Born Killers* is an explosive device for the sleepy movie audience, a wake-up call in the form of a frag bomb."[17] Another critic called the film "feverish, psychedelic, insanely bloody. . . . It seems to have exploded directly from the filmmaker's psyche, a gonzo-poetic head trip about America's escalating culture of ultraviolence."[18] "A big, dazzling, monstrously violent comedy that is probably the most extreme movie ever made in Hollywood," asserted another critic. "Psychedelic and assaultive, it's like a fever dream snatched from the skull of Charles Manson."[19]

As usual, critics seemed divided in their assessment of the film's impact on audiences. In the words of one critic, *Natural Born Killers* "may turn out to be the love-it-or-hate-it film of the decade. Either you go with the flow of Stone's scabrous, seductive images or you don't."[20] The issue for many critics was the film's treatment of violence. Those who loved it often saw it as a successful parody of violent America. Those who did not were often fearful of its effects on young moviegoers, in particular. Claimed one critic:

It will almost certainly appall older audiences, who will decry its seeming nihilism, and will probably thrill wised-up urban viewers (especially young men), who will see it as a killer ride—a movie hip to the nonstop epileptic seizure that is our media culture. Both responses strike me as perfectly reasonable. *Natural Born Killers* is the most sensationalist attack ever made on sensationalism, and it left me amazed and aghast. I only hope the Beavises and Butt-heads in the audience realize that the movie's a grisly joke and not a self-help manual.[21]

This critic's response struck at the heart of the film's dilemma: As an indictment of the mass media's sensationalizing of violence, the question arose, does the film itself fall prey to the very sensationalizing it satirizes? The film's sensationalist potential was acknowledged, for example, by Juliette Lewis, who plays Mallory. Noted Lewis, "Halfway through the movie, I felt myself getting excited by it. And, like, if it had cut off there, we would have left the theatre and been . . . like, it might have enticed people to do something they never would have done." Lewis dismissed this sensationalist possibility, however, by concluding that the film "goes on and on, and by the end you don't want to go out and act crazy. . . . You want to just go home and be with someone you love."[22]

Critics who liked the film often recognized its indictment of both the mass media and a culture that thrives on the violent images the media pump out. In one critic's opinion, "The film is saying that the more we become full-time image receptors (even when the images are banal), the more life itself seems a collection of raw sensations divorced from empathy or meaning. . . . The film isn't blaming violence in society on violence in the media. It's saying that they've become symbiotic, part of an apocalyptic chicken-and-egg cycle."[23]

Stone's response to critics' assessment of his film was to use the age-old argument that filmmakers simply reflect back to culture what they see around them. As Stone saw it, "I am celebrating what I see, a Beavis and Butt-head crimescape in the 1990s—enormous crime, violence, and the celebration of that in the media. My mirror goes up and I reflect without judgment. Kubrick didn't make a judgment in *A Clockwork Orange* . . . If you are an honest filmmaker, you don't care about the consequences. You take what is around you in the world, transform it in your particular way, and then show it back."[24] Stone came down the hardest on the mass media, however, claiming that despite a zero increase in violent crime over the past twenty years, the media's sensationalizing of violence has made it "the No. 1 enemy" in America. Stone explained, "Every night on the news it's back-to-back murder and body bags. Even the national news is perverted . . . It's the old yellow journalism. Now that communism is dead, they need new demons. This virus has infected us all—the demon's within us and among us."[25] Although Mickey and Mallory Knox (whose names throughout the film are abbreviated in a sickly sweet satiric commentary as "M & M") may be wholly without redeeming qualities, Stone asserts that characters such as television journalist Wayne Gale, "who represent the Establishment, are by contrast wholly perverted. And our Establishment is perverted and corrupt."[26]

The film must be placed in the context of modern America's fascination with the celebrity killer-criminal, on the one hand, and on the other, the mass murderer–serial killer who becomes a celebrity as a result of his or her actions. *Natural Born Killers,* for example, through a single shot of former football star O. J. Simpson, makes reference to Simpson's 1995 trial for the murders of his former wife, Nicole Simpson, and her friend Ron Goldman in her house in Los Angeles. A shot of ice-skater Tonya Harding also invokes America's twisted fascination with famous figures brought low by crime and violence. Quick shots of Lorena Bobbitt (found guilty of severing her husband's penis but acquitted of charges surrounding the incident due to her countercharges of marital rape and spousal abuse); the Waco, Texas, conflagration; and the Menendez brothers' trial (two brothers who murdered their parents after claiming years of physical and psychological abuse) also invoke Americans' macabre fascination with horrendous crimes. Speaking of his film's eerie clairvoyance, Stone asserts that when he started *Natural Born Killers,* it "was a surreal piece. Now, thanks to Bobbitt and Menendez and Tonya Harding, it has become satire. By the time I'd finished, fact had caught up to fiction. O. J. is the final blowout."[27]

Not only is Stone's film an interesting example of art imitating life, the media's response to Stone's film also hinted at the possibility of life imitating art. After the arrest of two Ohio boys in September 1994 for a cross-country murder spree that left at least three dead, a *New York Times* article speculated that the boys' motive for committing the crimes might have been their emulation of Mickey and Mallory.[28] A second murder case in Avon, Massachusetts, in June 1995, was labeled the "Natural Born Killer Stabbing" by the *Boston Globe* after one of the three young suspects reportedly told a friend after the stabbing, "Haven't you seen 'Natural Born Killers' before?"[29] When the murder trial received wide media coverage in Massachusetts, Senate Majority Leader Robert Dole used *Natural Born Killers* as an example of movies' negative impact on young audiences.

Whether film critics hated or loved *Natural Born Killers,* there was almost universal agreement that the film was a stylistic tour de force—"MTV on drugs," said one critic, the "visual equivalent of gansta rap, with bits of everything—sampled, parodied, or pried loose from their original cultural contexts to create a horrifying whole."[30] Woody Harrelson characterized the film as "definitely a trip, no question about that. If I were attending this thing, I wouldn't do any drugs. Drugs would be redundant."[31]

Stone used a number of different film stocks, formats, styles, and techniques in making the film, including Super-8, 16 millimeter, and video cameras; Technicolor and black-and-white film; and styles and techniques involving rear projection, slow motion, animation, pixillation, oblique camera angles, and rapid-fire cutting. Despite the seemingly random quality of the finished product, however, the film was apparently carefully orchestrated. Explains coeditor Hank Corwin, "We wanted an impressionistic feeling, but there was no randomness. Every two-frame flash was thought out. This style can work on anything. It could be one of the futures of filmmaking."[32] The result of Stone's cinematic tour de force in *Natural Born Killers* is that "at any given moment, Mickey and Mallory's story has the texture of a home movie, a documentary, a lush Hollywood romance, a slapdash reenactment on a TV crime show, or an image caught by a surveillance camera."[33] Noted one critic, "NBK plunders every visual trick of avant-garde and mainstream cinema . . . and, for two delirious hours, pushes them in your face like a Cagney grapefruit. The actors go hyper-hyper, the camera is ever on the bias, the garish colors converge and collide, and you're caught in this Excedrin vision of America in heat."[34]

The production set of *Natural Born Killers* imitated the frenzied intensity for which Stone was aiming in the film. As Woody Harrelson recalled, "The set was intense and exciting. Oliver played an incessant barrage of wild music to get you going. The crew would jam the music, then fire shotguns into the air."[35] Stone's favorite cinematographer, Robert Richardson, described the shoot as "extraordinarily angst-ridden because it was anarchy in style. It wasn't planned out in the traditional sense. It was more like throwing paint at the canvas—you didn't know if you were making art. The only rule was that you could change your mind."[36]

Woody Harrelson interpreted the experience of playing Mickey as "a journey into the heart of darkness. It affected all of us. When I was doing it I was very much in the head space of the character. Surrounded myself with books and videos about serial killers, interviews with the likes of Manson. I don't think I've ever been more consumed by anything." Harrelson referred to Jung's idea of the shadow to describe the therapeutic quality of playing Mickey. He explained, "I went into my own shadow, my own rage. All of this stuff was opened up that I'd been repressing. I used to be quite violent. I'd gotten a handle on it. So, by opening it up it was like opening up a wound."[37] Harrelson's father was convicted for murdering a U.S. judge. Stone, aware of Harrelson's family past, admitted drawing on it in his work with Harrelson in the film. As Stone put it, "I know he had that history. I looked into his eyes the moment I met him and knew this was a man who has violence in him, and he was starting to be in touch with that . . . Woody has a lot of genetic violence. I can feel it. That's why he's good."[38]

Although snakes, shamans, and drugs are motifs that appear in a number of Stone's films, most notably in *The Doors* and *Platoon,* their most interesting and complex use appears in *Natural Born Killers. The Doors* invites a number of interpretations of the snake, most notably its function in goddess fertility cults and its pivotal role in tempting Adam and Eve with knowledge and prompting humanity's fall from grace, but *Natural Born Killers* offers the most thematically revealing interpretations of the snake of any of Stone's films. The snake motif in *Natural Born Killers* stands as a condensation symbol for the central thematic structure developed in all of Stone's films. Snakes, along with drugs and the shaman, most clearly articulate the idea that psychological growth and transcendence are only possible when a culture descends into its collective unconscious, acknowledges its shadow, and learns to embrace the precarious balance between darkness and light, goodness and evil, and spirit and flesh.

Snakes and dragons (the Chinese variation on the snake motif), and particularly entwined snakes, as in the caduceus, appear throughout *Natural Born Killers*. At their blood wedding on the canyon bridge, Mickey and Mallory exchange entwined serpent rings to seal their marriage vows. As their joined blood drips down to the river below, Stone uses cartoon animation to turn the blood drops into two entwined red serpents. Later in a hotel room when Mallory removes her serpent wedding ring, Mickey tells her to never take it off, warning her that "everything good that we ever do starts with these." As they entwine hands we see a close-up of their matched rings. Besides having the yin-yang symbol tattooed on his arm, Mickey also has an entwined serpent tattooed on his chest. We see another shot of entwined snakes on the dashboard of Mickey and Mallory's car. This caduceus symbol appears again on the ghostly green neon marquee of the drugstore where Mickey and Mallory search for anti-snakebite venom to counteract the effect of numerous rattlesnake bites. Throughout the film we frequently hear nonsynchronous use of the hiss and rattle of a rattlesnake, as for example, when Mallory, angry with Mickey for desiring the female hostage they abducted, leaves the hotel and drives through the desert night. Although there are many images of animals seen throughout the film, eight-headed Chinese dragons also appear numerous times.

From the beginning of recorded time, the snake or serpent, regardless of cultural variations in interpretation, remains the most universal and most ambivalent of archetypes. A mythological symbol in both Western and Eastern cultures, snakes have variously represented the forces of good and evil and, in some cases, as in the Navaho Beauty Chant, the precarious balance between them. Male, female, or self-created,[39] the snake may represent the sun or the moon, life or death, salvation or sin, healing or poison, evil or good. It is often depicted as "a mediator between the three worlds, the sky, in that it resembles solar rays and lightning, the earth and the primordial waters, from which all creation emerges, and the underworld, in which it lives. It is often depicted as encircling the world—the Ouroboros."[40] But most important, from the perspective of *Natural Born Killers,* the snake represents wisdom—both good and evil, resurrection, immortality, healing, and the unconscious.

The snake is a wisdom archetype for many Eastern and Western cultures. In Egyptian mythology, for example, the royal serpent Uraeus, a cobra, was worn on the Sun God Ra's head to represent Ra's divine power and wisdom. In Greek lore, the serpent was sacred to Athena, the goddess of wisdom, where it acted as the guardian spirit of her temple at the Acropolis in Athens. In Christian symbolism, the snake can represent Christ as wisdom, as when "raised on the Cross (the Tree of Life), it is Christ's sacrifice for the healing and salvation of the world."[41] Christ himself refers to the wisdom of snakes when he charges his disciples to "be as shrewd as snakes and as innocent as doves."[42]

The ambivalence of the snake as wisdom, however, is typified in Greek mythological figures such as Medusa and Graia, who have serpents for hair and who represent "the powers of enchantment and magic connected with the wisdom and guile of the serpent."[43] Wisdom as evil is apparent in the Judeo-Christian representation of the snake in the Garden of Eden story. Here, the snake tempts and seduces Eve, convincing her to eat with Adam from the tree of knowledge. This creates an awareness of sin, which causes their expulsion from Paradise. From the perspective of perennial philosophy, the snake in the Garden also represents the catalyst for our separation from Edenic innocence, just as the expulsion from the Garden represents our first step toward ego consciousness.

In addition to wisdom, the snake symbolizes resurrection and transformation. In ancient Crete, for example, the serpent was often depicted on burial stones. In Greek mythology, the soul was said to leave the body in the form of a snake, thus emphasizing its connection with the afterlife or immortality. The *Physiologus* says that when the serpent "grow[s] old it fasts forty days, goes into a crevice and casts its skin to renew its youth. So must man put off the Old Adam and pass through the straight gate."[44] In Campbell's interpretation of the Buddha legend, the serpent or dragon resides beneath the navel of the world, where it is "symbolical of the waters of the abyss, which are the divine life-creative energy and substance of the demiurge, the world-generative aspect of immortal being."[45]

Besides wisdom, resurrection, and transformation, the snake is also a symbol of healing. Buddha is said to change himself into a snake to heal his people during times of famine and disease. Snakes were often kept as pets in Cretan, Greek, and Roman households because of their association with healing and fertility. Asclepios, the son of Apollo and the god of medicine, was associated with the snake in whose shape he appeared to Romans during the plague. Hippocrates was also depicted as a snake when he delivered Athens from the plague. Modern Western medicine and pharmacology retain the symbolism of the snake in the caduceus, which depicts two snakes entwined around a herald's staff.

Although snakes and dragons appear frequently in *Natural Born Killers,* the most obvious and significant use of the snake motif appears in the scene in which Mickey and Mallory encounter and ultimately murder the Navaho Indian shaman in his ritual house-hogan in the southwestern desert. Significantly, the Indian is the only victim in Mickey and Mallory's murderous rampage for whom they feel any remorse. He is also the only person that tries to heal them of the evil "soul-sickness" that causes them to commit murder. The Indian, who can see the future and can read Mickey and Mallory's souls, knows what they will do to him even before it happens.

We learn of the Indian's premonitions regarding Mickey and Mallory when he first recognizes the demon within them—their consumption by their shadows. As they enter the hogan, Mickey asks, "Feel the demon here, Mal?" She replies, "I think we're the demons." As they speak, the words "Demon" and "Too much TV" are surrealistically projected across their chests. The Indian's grandson asks him if Mallory is crazy, to which the Indian replies, "She has sad sickness. Lost in a world of ghosts." When the boy asks if his grandfather can help them, he responds, "Maybe they don't want to be helped." The Indian then tells a story that reveals the true nature of snakes and explains why Mickey and Mallory may be beyond help: "Once upon a time a woman was picking up firewood. She came upon a poisonous snake frozen in the snow. She took the snake home and nursed it back to health. When it was well, the snake bit her on the cheek. As she lay dying, she asked the snake why. 'Why have you done this to me?' and the snake answered, 'Dumb bitch, you knew I was a snake.'" As the Indian tells the story, we see him continually stroking a rattlesnake held in his lap. When he finishes his story, he rises, moves to the door of the hogan, and releases the snake, saying, "Old man, go be a snake."

Despite the Indian's knowledge of the true nature of snakes, whether hearth pets or serial killers, and despite his premonitions about his impending death at Mickey's hand, the shaman still tries to heal these "snakes." In a ritualistic trance in which we are treated to the nightmares of the sleeping Mickey and Mallory, the Indian intones what may be the Navaho Beauty Chant over their sleeping bodies.

In the Navaho tradition, the Beauty Chant—the story of Bear-man and Snake-man—is used by shamans in healing rituals. Like all chants of the Navaho people, the Beauty Chant is a type of psychotherapy used to heal patients' "divided spirit or to reclaim their missing soul (for sickness was thought of more as a matter of spirit than of the body)."[46] When the chant is completed, the shaman ritualistically shocks the sick person by appearing to them in the shape of the returning Snake-man to help effect the cure.[47]

It is worth recounting the story of the Beauty Chant in some detail since it seems to be the basis for Mickey and Mallory's encounter with the Navaho Indian shaman in his house-hogan. Here is a brief summary:

Bear and Snake win a shooting competition for which they are promised two young maidens from an Indian village. Angry at their success, the villagers refuse to deliver up the two maidens. Not easily daunted, Bear and Snake set up camp close by in a shelter made of sage-brush. The two maidens, unable to resist the strange and wonderful scent of the sage, are lured to Bear-man's and Snake-man's camp where they are offered fragrant tobacco pipes and beautiful jewelry. Overwhelmed by their kindness and youthful beauty the girls fall in love with them. After smoking the pipe, however, they fall into a deep unconsciousness from which they wake to find Bear and Snake ugly old men who have tied them to themselves at the ankle. The younger girl, Glispa, manages to escape and reaches the door only to be confronted by a field of hissing snakes. The snakes, sensing her fear of them, begin to hiss louder. Controlling her terror, however, she threads her way between them only to find Snake-man chasing her. Wading down the river to elude capture she comes ashore in the land of the Snake-people who take her in and feed her. Living with the Snake-people she once again falls in love with Snake-man, who appears at the Snake-people's feast as young and handsome once again. Snake explains to Glispa that he is a powerful shaman who can teach her healing chants and the accompanying sand painting rituals. After living with them for two years, Glispa eventually returns to her village where she teaches the healing rituals she has learned to her brother. He eventually becomes a great shaman himself with powers to heal and to initiate others into the healing ways.[48]

In this story the snake is both good and evil, enemy and friend, dangerous threat and comforting healer. Snake-man's knowledge of healing and transcendence, although dangerous, is seductive. It is a wisdom that if feared (like the shadow) cannot be mastered. But if embraced, this knowledge can heal an entire tribe of its soul-sickness and open the way toward a future path of teleological development—a movement toward a new Garden of consciousness.

As the Indian in *Natural Born Killers* recites what may be the Navaho Beauty Chant, he dances around an apparently hypnotized rattlesnake, smokes what is possibly a drug-laced pipe, and calls on the snake's spirit for help. Here we have all three of Stone's motifs brought together in one instant: drugs, the shaman, and snakes. As he finishes the chant, the Indian performs the ritual shock in order to effect the cure of his soul-sick patients. Mickey, startled by the Indian's actions, awakens from his nightmare and instinctively grabs his gun and shoots the Indian in the chest. Mallory, also awakened, like Glispa, from a druglike sleep, sees what Mickey has done and repeatedly screams, "Bad, bad, bad, bad!" For perhaps the first time in their ethically anchorless life, both Mickey and Mallory experience remorse. Without knowing why, they intuit that the Indian represented something different—a chance, perhaps, at transcendence. As the Indian lies dying, he gasps, "Twenty years ago I saw the demon in my dreams. I was waiting for you." Mickey and Mallory have bitten the hand of the only person who ever nurtured them. The murder of this befriended shaman not only represents their betrayal of him but also a betrayal of their own potential for growth and transcendence.

Despite their remorse, all is now lost for Mickey and Mallory; they start to run out of the hogan, pursued only by the horror of what they have done. As they reach the door of the Indian's hut, however, like Glispa in the myth, they are confronted by seemingly hundreds of hissing rattlesnakes. Unlike Glispa, they are bitten numerous times. Having received no healing from the Indian shaman, who was unable to exorcise the demons from their souls or return their lost souls to them, Mickey and Mallory are afraid of the snakes, afraid of the knowledge they represent. The snakes, "sensing their fear" (as Jim Morrison in *The Doors* notes), bite them without mercy. Unable to achieve healing from Navaho wisdom, the two flee in search of modern medicine's remedy for their sickness. They search out a drugstore for a snakebite antidote.

In their search, Mickey and Mallory come upon a drugstore called the DrugZone, a vast sterile pharmacy lit by glaring and sickly green neon lights. In this "house of healing," the healer, the pharmacist-clerk, is protected and separated from the patients by bulletproof glass. This pharmacy—representing modern medicine—is as cold and alienating as the shaman's hogan—lit by the red glow of a hearth fire—was inviting and warm. The drugstore is unable to provide Mickey and Mallory with a cure, however—they are out of "snakebite juice." Western medicine, despite the neon caduceus displayed on the pharmacy's marquee, offers no healing for either the body or the soul. The age of modern rationality and ego consciousness knows no cure for the soul-sickness that ails Mickey and Mallory. Such relief is only to be found in the transcendent possibilities offered by the "alternative medicines" of the Indian. Mickey thus feels no remorse over killing this obese and cowering drugstore medicine man, as he did when he killed the Indian shaman.

In an operatically choreographed dance of violence, somewhat reminiscent of the scene in *Clockwork Orange* where Alex bludgeons the "cat woman" to death with a giant phallus to the strains of Beethoven, we see Mickey brought down by Detective Jack Scagnetti and half a dozen police officers who have finally caught up with them outside of the DrugZone. Repeatedly kicked, punched, and spit on, Mickey is "subdued," while a female Japanese television reporter, miraculously appearing at the scene, looks on. She comments to her video camera about Mickey's virility, his large gun, and his being rendered "impotent" by the police. The scene recalls the Rodney King beating by three Los Angeles policemen in 1992, also captured forever on a bystander's video camera. The message? In a mass-mediated world, violence begets violence. We may feel both anger and sorrow toward Mickey and Mallory as both perpetrators and victims of violence. Just as John F. Kennedy in *JFK* is a victim of the whims of the military-industrial complex, just as Jim Garrison, in his attempts to reveal the truth regarding J.F.K.'s assassination, is himself victimized by a scornful and laughing mass media, so Mickey and Mallory are victims of a corrupt family environment and a mass-mediated culture that either condones or outright celebrates violence and sexual deviance. They, in turn, create victims of the people around them through random acts of violence. Detective Jack Scagnetti, the man enlisted by Mickey and Mallory's prison warden to quietly eliminate them and who, in this scene, beats Mickey unconscious, is himself a victim of violence. As a child he watched his mother gunned down by the Texas mass murderer Charles Whitman. And like Mickey and Mallory, Scagnetti is also a victimizer. Both desirous of and angry at Mallory for evading him, for example, he later sexually victimizes her in her small jail cell, just as he punishes a Mallory "look-alike," hired to slake his libidinous thirst earlier in the film. As the camera slowly zooms out on the gruesome scene of Mickey's repeated bludgeoning by the police at the DrugZone, the camera tilts up to reveal the neon marquee, the entwined serpents of the caduceus glowing brightly in the darkened night. Where, the film asks, is our healing?

In *Natural Born Killers* the snake is neither wholly good nor wholly evil. As in *The Doors,* it is to be both trusted and feared, reviled and revered. In Jungian terms, the snake is an individuation archetype, representing the coalescing of opposites. Serpents, according to Joseph Campbell, "seem to incarnate the elementary mystery of life wherever apparent opposites are conjoined."[49] As Jim Morrison in *The Doors* urges his disciples, "Kiss the snake on the tongue. But if it senses fear, it'll eat us instantly. But if we kiss it without fear, it will take us through the Garden, through the gate, to the other side." Whether reviled or revered, the "snake," archetype of the unconscious, must be sought out and explored, like Jung's shadow. If we run from it, if we fear it, we cannot grow beyond the realm of ego consciousness. If we become seduced by it, however, and consumed by it, like Mickey and Mallory, we become the incarnation of evil and dread.

The Indian shaman, for example, even though aware of the true nature of snakes, is not afraid of them. In fact, he keeps one at his hearth side, as did the ancient Greeks, perhaps to represent his role as healer but also to signify his searching for wisdom and possibly his lack of fear of his own shadow, his own unconscious, and the knowledge of his impending death.

The Indian's snake, in this sense, symbolizes enlightened consciousness—a portal to the spiritual realm and the unconscious. That Mickey and Mallory wear snake rings, tattoo them on their bodies, revere the Indian Snakeman, regret his death, and swear to kill no more after murdering him indicates their yearning for healing and an enlightened consciousness. But it also indicates their inability, due to their lower "snake natures"—their tendency to be consumed by their shadow (which the Indian saw)—to move beyond their shadow into the realm of the unconscious. Such transformation is a double bind, however, because although the individual desires transcendence, this transcendence implies the "death" of the isolated self—the giving up of ego identity: "In order to satisfy the self's greatest desires one must sacrifice that very desiring self."[50]

Mickey, in however strained an interpretation of its meaning, is aware of this perennial paradox when he says to Wayne Gale in his prophetic interview, "Except a corn of wheat falleth to the ground and die it abideth alone. But if it die it bringeth forth much fruit." The paradox is that life is renewed in the surrendering of life, as is self in the forgetting of self. Mickey, however, interprets this in his own warped fashion to justify murdering scores of innocent victims. We see this, for example, when he is asked by Gale how he could possibly murder fifty-two innocent people. Mickey replies, "Innocent? Who's innocent, Wayne? You innocent? . . . It's just murder, man, all God's creatures do it in some form or another. I mean you look in the forest—you've got species killing other species, our species killing all species, including the forest, and we just call it industry, not murder." This social Darwinism theme is further echoed throughout the film by numerous shots of predators and prey: lions bringing down deer, a praying mantis eating its mate, a car crushing a scorpion, fruit decaying and being consumed by mold, and young seedlings pushing up from the soil.

The film's final song, Leonard Cohen's "The Future," fatalistically echoes this Darwinist theme. Over the credits and a compilation of images from the film, we hear:

> You don't know me from the wind/You never will, you never did/I'm the little Jew that wrote the Bible/I've seen the nations rise and fall/I've heard their stories, heard them all/But love's the only engine of survival . . . He has been told to say it clear, to say it cold/It's over, it ain't goin' any further/And now the wheels of heaven stop/You feel the devil's riding crop/Get ready for the future, it is murder/When they said repent, repent/I wondered what they meant.

This song seems like a pessimistic indictment of our chances for teleological evolution—as Mickey says to justify his killing of innocent victims, "It's just murder." If the future is murder, what hope remains? Are we destined, like Gordon Gekko, to destroy ourselves and our frail planet in a drive to own and consume all that we see? With the Devil at our backs and the doors of Heaven seemingly closed, is it truly over? Is "the little Jew that wrote the Bible," who has "seen the nations rise and fall," so disappointed in his creatures that even repentance is no longer possible? Or is one slim possibility, one last chance for humanity to be found in love, the "engine of survival"? And if love is our survival, then will a failure to love be our doom?

As Dr. Frankenstein designed the monster so that mortality could touch immortality—could see the face of God mirrored in human-created human flesh—so Frankenstein was doomed to failure, not by his creation of the monster, but by his inability to love it. When Wayne Gale pleads for his life at the end of the film, Mickey explains to him why he must die, saying, "If we let you go, we'd be just like everybody else—killing you and what you represent is a statement. I'm not 100 percent sure exactly what kind it's saying but, you know, Frankenstein killed Dr. Frankenstein." Mickey and Mallory are Wayne Gale's—and society's—Frankenstein. And like the creature, they are unloved. (Stone emphasizes the Frankenstein motif by using numerous clips from the film *Frankenstein* throughout *Natural Born Killers.*) When Wayne Gale pleads for his life claiming he has developed a bond with Mickey and Mallory during their interview and subsequent murderous rampage, Mickey replies, "No, not really. You're scum, Wayne; you did it for rating. You don't give a shit about us or about anybody except yourself. That's why nobody gives a shit about you." Mickey and Mallory, like Gale, are the creatures of a loveless, greed-driven egomaniacal society. Unloved creatures made of mud remain mud creatures. Frankenstein, a badly stitched-together and roughly animated corpse given intelligence but never love, like Mickey and Mallory, is the haphazard product of an uncaring and abusive society.

Unlike *Wall Street,* where a central force of the film is its depiction of social Darwinism at work in the age of ego consciousness, *Natural Born Killers* goes further, like *The Doors,* but in a more sophisticated fashion, to hint at a solution to the problem that creatures of mud—humans—face when they try to attain godhead by creating Frankensteins in their own image and ultimately fail because their creatures turn against them. The solution? We must learn to embrace our creations—our demons—learn to love them, take them to our bosom, take responsibility for them, even knowing that they, like us, are creatures of the mud, possessing a snakelike nature that might ultimately destroy us but that might potentially liberate us as well.

This is the lesson the Indian already knew when he petted his hearth snake and embraced the demons that were Mickey and Mallory and offered them shelter, food, and healing—a lesson that taught not to become like them, but neither to run from them. "What does not destroy me makes me stronger," said Nietzsche, as quoted by Stone in *The Doors.* More than a Nietzscheian "will to power," however, the procedure is instead an act of balancing opposites, of coming to terms with our shadow, of wrestling with our collective unconsciousness, and of acknowledging, even loving, the demon in ourselves and in others. Only then might we love them out of existence. Mickey, speaking on camera in response to Wayne Gale's query about what makes someone capable of fifty-two murders, responds: "I don't think I'm any scarier than you are. I'm extremes, dark and light. *You* know that. [We see a shot of the yin-yang symbol on his forearm.] I'm right with Mao [he slaps the tattoo], Mao. That's *your* shadow on the wall. Can't get rid of your shadow, can you, Wayne? You know the only thing that kills the demon?—love. That's why I know that Mallory is my salvation. She was teaching me how to love." In a dreamlike voice-over, we hear Mallory say, "I forgive you, baby." Mickey continues, "It was just like being in the Garden of Eden." Love "beats the demon." Love forgives all. The one thing that Frankenstein longs for is love. But love is the one thing that Dr. Frankenstein, his creator, cannot give. He cannot acknowledge his own demon, his own shadow, his own hubris Tower of Babel, manifested before him in the form of his monster creation.

To get ourselves back to the Garden of Eden (Mickey's words), or in perennial philosophy, to move toward transconsciousness in the new Garden of enlightenment, we must move through our shadows and work out our own demons. Like the snake that sheds its skin, we must shed our old nature to become the new Adam. In Jungian terms, we must learn to plumb the depths of our collective unconscious for the lessons to be learned there. But we must not simply return to a pre-egoic state, the idealized realm of preconsciousness, however, since such a return to innocence is no longer possible. Encouraged by the snake, we have eaten of the fruit of knowledge and have known sin. The only salvation left, and perhaps the superior salvation, since it represents movement forward rather than backward, is to no longer fear our sin, to no longer run from our knowledge (our ability to make Frankensteins in our own image), but rather to "kiss the snake of knowledge on the mouth and ride it through to the other side." We must learn, in other words, to embrace our monsters—our shadow selves—not to become them, but rather to acknowledge the necessarily paradoxical and dynamic balancing of opposites that the entwined snakes and the yin-yang symbol represent. We must balance the opposites—earth and sky, darkness and light, goodness and evil, salvation and sin, spirit and flesh—as we move forward, armed with love, toward the new Eden, our home, the place, paradoxically, where we may have always been.

Notes

1. Carl Jung, *The Archetypes and the Collective Unconscious*, trans. R. F. Hull (Princeton: Princeton University Press, 1990), 230.

2. John Simon, review of "*Wall Street*," *National Review*, 22 January 1988, 66.

3. Sean French, review of "*Wall Street*," *Sight and Sound* (spring 1988):136.

4. Cathleen McGuigan with Michael Reese, "A Bull Market in Sin," *Newsweek*, 14 December 1987, 78.

5. Stanley Kauffman, "Stanley Kauffman on Films," *New Republic*, 4 and 11 January 1988, 24.

6. *The Motion Picture Guide: The Films of 1987,* ed. Jay Nash and Stanley Ross (Evanston, IL: Cine Books, 1988), 319–320.

7. Kauffman, "On Films," 24.

8. Blake Richards, "Dead End Street," *America,* 30 January 1988, 100.

9. Alexander Cockburn, "Oliver Stone Takes Stock," *American Film* 13 (1987): 22.

10. James Lardner, review of *"Wall Street," Nation,* 23 January 1988, 97.

11. McGuigan with Reese, "Bull Market," 78.

12. Jack Boozer, Jr., *"Wall Street," Journal of Popular Film and Television* 17 (fall 1989):99.

13. An R rating is very much more desirable than an N-17 (no children under 17 allowed), since many theatres will not play an N-17 film. N-17 films cannot be advertised on television, and it is often hard to place ads for them in newspapers.

14. Corie Brown, "American Maniacs," *Premiere,* August 1994, 42.

15. Owen Gleiberman, "American Psychos," *Entertainment Weekly,* 26 August 1994, 91.

16. Richard Corliss, "Stone Crazy," *Time,* 29 August 1994, 66.

17. Ibid., 68.

18. Gleiberman, "American Psychos," 90.

19. John Powers, "Lost Innocence," *Vogue,* September 1994, 293.

20. Gleiberman, "American Psychos," 90.

21. Powers, "Lost Innocence," 296.

22. Brown, "American Maniacs," 43.

23. Gleiberman, "American Psychos," 93.

24. Brown, "American Maniacs," 43.

25. Corliss, "Stone Crazy," 66.

26. Brown, "American Maniacs," 42.

27. Corliss, "Stone Crazy," 66.

28. Sam Howe Verhovek, "2 Ohioans Arrested in a Series of Slayings," *New York Times,* 7 September 1994, A1.

29. Ellen O'Brien and Patricia Nealon, "Suspect Caught in Avon Slaying: Third Suspect Caught in 'Natural Born Killers' Stabbing Case," *Boston Globe,* 30 June 1995, 1, 26.

30. Brown, "American Maniacs," 42.

31. Ibid., 43.

32. Corliss, "Stone Crazy," 68.

33. Gleiberman, "American Psychos," 93.

34. Corliss, "Stone Crazy," 66.

35. Ibid., 68.

36. Ibid.

37. Brown, "American Maniacs," 43.

38. Ibid., 42.

39. As a symbol of fertility and seduction, the snake can be masculine, feminine, or androgynous. Eve yields to the serpent—as phallic and masculine, the "husband of all women"—whereas the Virgin Mary is often depicted as crushing its head. Zeus, the Greek Father God, "has the serpent as a phallic symbol and it appears with him in his many different aspects as Zeus/Ammoin, Zeus/Chthonios and

Zeus/Meilichios" (J. C. Cooper, *Symbolic and Mythological Animals* [London: Aquarian/Thorsons (HarperCollins) 1992], 204–205). As feminine, the snake is central to goddess worship, in which it represents intuitive wisdom and female fertility. The Great Mother-Goddess Ishtar, for example, is frequently shown either accompanied by serpents or with them emerging from her shoulders. In Celtic myth, the serpent also represents the Great Mother, the Celtic Bride, who was worshiped during festivals as the Snake Goddess and was later adopted by Christians as Saint Brigid. In Hinduism, the snake represents both male and female fertility: "Vishnu sleeps on the coiled serpent of the primordial waters, the unpolarized state before creation; his two serpents, or nagas—whose bodies intertwine—depict the fertilization of the waters; from their union rises the Earth Goddess" (ibid., 207). In Chinese legend, serpents are also both masculine and feminine fertility and creation symbols. The sea serpents Lakhmu and Lakhamu, for example, "give birth to the male and female principles of heaven and earth" (ibid., 203).

40. Ibid.

41. Ibid., 206.

42. Matt. 10:16 New International Version.

43. Cooper, *Symbolic Animals*, 205.

44. Ibid., 206.

45. Joseph Campbell, *The Hero with a Thousand Faces,* Bollingen Series 17 (Princeton: Princeton University Press, 1973), 41.

46. Cottie Burland, *North American Indian Mythology* (Hamlyn Publishing Group, 1968), 105.

47. Ibid., 101.

48. Ibid., 102–105.

49. Cooper, *Symbolic Animals*, 203.

50. Janice Hocker Rushing, "*E.T.* as Rhetorical Transcendence," *Quarterly Journal of Speech* 71 (1985):191.

SIX

Final Thoughts

We are heading toward a new era in the twenty-first century, I hope, of total consciousness. People of all colors will be sharing this planet. It's necessary for us to get out of our skins and cross this spiritual and divisive gulf that people have formed.

—Oliver Stone[1]

When the Ten Thousand things are viewed in their oneness, we return to the Origin and remain where we have always been.

—Sen T'sen

Oliver Stone is one of the most successful directors currently working in Hollywood. Able to balance political critique with character-centered dramas, he has found a way to sustain both a popular and controversial vision of America. His major-release films, from *Salvador* to *Natural Born Killers*, tell the story of America's fall from grace after the death of John F. Kennedy, our descent into the hell that was Vietnam, our confrontation with our shadow selves in the 1980s and 1990s of ego excess, and our search, even now, for new visions that will render life, and possibly death, meaningful once more. Medhurst, speaking of Stone, says that "what [D. W.] Griffith was to the first quarter of the twentieth century, Stone is to the last—the principal chronicler of the spiritual angst of a people."[2] As we have seen, President John F. Kennedy's death and the start of the Vietnam War—seminal events for millions of Americans—provide the framework for audience interpretation of Stone's angst-ridden chronicle of thirty years of American life.

The story of Stone's films, however, is also the story of his developing protagonists, archetypal heroes who act as philosophical test pilots for an

147

entire generation as they try out the next phase of teleological development. These heroes are often artist-visionaries, such as Barry Champlain in *Talk Radio,* Richard Boyle in *Salvador,* and Jim Morrison in *The Doors,* individuals willing to take a stance on issues of sociopolitical importance and provide prophetic vision for the people. Such artists, according to *Salvador,* attempt to wake and shock cultures out of their politically complacent stupor. They invite us to go on a dizzying search for the truth, a journey that although sometimes arduous and certainly dangerous is essential if we are to grow as a culture and a race. Artist-visionaries such as Richard Boyle and Jim Morrison, for example, are able to get closer to the truth than mere mortals. Willing to leave Plato's cave of veiled sight and ascend into the blinding light of day, they risk blindness or even death in an uncompromising search for the truth.

Often complex and less than perfect, Stone's heroes are set apart by their ability to live life in the extreme. Whether in a war zone or on the edge of the psyche's internal abyss, they often test themselves in a battle with the most terrible adversary of all—themselves. *Platoon,* for example, invites the audience into a mythic arena where battles between archetypal heroes are waged in a struggle for an individual's soul. As hero, Chris Taylor's dilemma over the course of the film is to construct himself not simply by rejecting the evil that is Sergeant Barnes and embracing the goodness that is Sergeant Elias, but his task is rather to integrate both in a precarious balancing act that acknowledges his capacity for both good and evil. Chris must confront his internal Barnes—his shadow—in order to realize his Elias potential. Chris Taylor is continually referred to as a "cherry," a virgin in combat. Taylor's shedding of innocence thus represents what we Americans did when we broke our cherry on the hard reality that was Vietnam. Vietnam became our heart of darkness, our passage from a pre-Edenic innocence to a post-Armageddon knowledge. Even though Taylor's battle for self-knowledge begins in a leech-infested swamp in Vietnam, the film's conclusion hints that the future direction for Stone's heroes is internal and that the most significant human battles are those of the soul.

This theme is elaborated in both *Born on the Fourth of July* and *Heaven and Earth.* Kovic, in *Born on the Fourth of July,* for example, like Taylor, realizes that Vietnam and its lasting effects on his body represent an internal battle to uncover the truth about himself and about Vietnam. His boon is to share such knowledge with the American people—a people charged with the responsibility of carrying the torch passed to them by the previous generation. *Heaven and Earth,* the third film in Stone's Vietnam trilogy, also asserts an increasing sense of the hero's journey as spiritual and inward rather than rational and outward. Le Ly Hayslip, the film's protagonist, invites us to see that the true battlefield was not in Vietnam but in the hearts and minds of the people who survived that war.

The battlefield of the soul, however, is difficult terrain to negotiate in a postmodern and post-Vietnam world, built on shifting grounds for truth, value, and right. As a result, Stone's protagonists often seem torn between Platonic and relativist views of the truth. For one thing, they are pro-claimers of the truth, philosopher kings whose role is to enlighten the masses about the truth in America, Vietnam, Central America, and the world. Yet as relativists, they often acknowledge that reality is in the eye of the beholder and that the belief in perennial advancement may be an ideal-istic dream.

Stone's controversial film *JFK* represents the heart of this dilemma. On the one hand, *JFK*'s argument for a conspiracy in the assassination of John F. Kennedy provides unequivocal support for this version of the truth. *JFK* is Stone's argument regarding America's betrayal by our leaders and our expulsion from the Garden that was Camelot. Kennedy as a messianic fig-ure is redeemed by Jim Garrison, another messianic figure, who despite persecution and ridicule will not rest until the lies and distortions surround-ing Kennedy's death are exposed and the truth is told. Kevin Costner, through his squeaky-clean portrayal of Jim Garrison as a Capraesque cru-sader for the truth, invites a Platonic assessment of such a search. On the other hand, *JFK*'s "postmodern" film style, coupled with the audience's re-alization that the definitive truth regarding the Kennedy murder may never be known, forces the film to acknowledge that there may be many truths regarding the events surrounding Kennedy's death and that Stone's version is just one more thesis of the probable. The *JFK* debate, as we have seen, highlights this dilemma regarding conflicting views of truth, history, and representation.

Although Jim Garrison is certain of the truth about JFK's assassination, Stone's protagonists are usually uncertain prophets of the "truth." They are doomsday visionaries of the current era of rationality, and many of them remain unconvinced that movement beyond this age is even possible. They may intuit the way, but they often remain skeptical about whether they themselves, or others, will be able or willing to follow. For example, both Jim Morrison, the "shaman of sensuous panic," and Barry Champlain, a latter-day John the Baptist crying out in the wilderness of the darkened Dal-las night, feel heartache at the loss of God in the current age of reason. De-spite their doubts, both Morrison and Champlain live life on the edge in order to push the envelope of possibilities and their followers crucify them both for their overly zealous lifestyles. Paradoxically, from the perspective of perennial philosophy, despite the uncertainty of their attempts at god-head, both artists must die to self in order to be resurrected to a higher con-sciousness. As a messianic figure, each artist must also die so that the peo-ple can likewise "die" to an earthly self in order to be reunited with the divine through their savior's sacrifice.

Stone's films, then, can be viewed as an anomaly in that they offer a unified mythic vision of humanity's perennial journey toward the self in the midst of postmodern fragmentation. But rather than being merely archaic or easily dismissed, as are many contemporary mythic interpretations, Stone's films draw on perennial philosophy, Jungian psychology, and world mythology in order to critique and extend social constructions of the postmodern condition. Responding to the felt fragmentation of the current age—a result of our failure, in Jungian terms, to tap the collective unconscious—Stone's films, in Jung's words, "dream the myth outward." They offer archetypal stories that continually reinterpret humanity's struggle with its collective unconscious. Stone's films depict heroes who descend into the unconscious, pass the gate of their shadow, and spend some time in the womb of sleep, silence, or passivity in order to receive the pearl of wisdom they find there. This journey often requires slaying the monsters of modern rationality, which frequently means "slaying" themselves in either an ego death or a messianic sacrifice for the people. The precious gift, the "boon" that they then share with the culture, is this: They present us with the ability to explore our own shadow, to plumb the depths of our collective unconscious (without dwelling there indefinitely) in order to know the truth—often interpreted as transconsciousness or glimpses of a future unity with the divine Ground of our being. *Natural Born Killers,* for example, which appears on the surface to be one of the most pessimistic assessments of culture's potential for humanist advancement, portrays two protagonists who, although stuck at the shadow level, are at least willing to explore the collective unconscious and do battle with the demons they find there—even when those demons are in themselves.

Stone's protagonists' odyssey of the self is explored in both *Natural Born Killers* and *Wall Street. Wall Street,* Stone's parable of greed and ego consciousness in the "me" decade of the 1980s, offers up morality lessons in the form of Gordon Gekko. A much more fascinating character study than the film's protagonist, Bud Fox, Gekko, driven by ego excess, represents society's central stumbling block in its journey toward transconsciousness. *Natural Born Killers,* in many ways a Wall Street parable for the 1990s, asserts that society's failure to embrace both Mickey and Mallory as its Frankensteins—products of a mass media– and violence-obsessed society— also represents its central stumbling block in a journey toward transconsciousness. The lesson we are invited to learn from *Natural Born Killers* is that love, the "only engine of survival," requires embracing our creatures— the Frankensteins made in our own image—whether they manifest themselves as "Mickeys and Mallorys," Western imperialism in places like El Salvador or Vietnam, the lies and manipulations of the military-industrial complex in the assassination of a U.S. president, or the rampant greed of unchecked capitalism. We must take these Frankensteins to our bosom even knowing that they, like the snake, have the potential to destroy us; but possibly, through the knowledge they possess, they can liberate us as well. Our certain doom, however, lies in denying their existence.

Stone's Vietnam trilogy, *Heaven and Earth, Platoon,* and *Born on the Fourth of July,* despite differences in their interpretation of the hero quest, also invites us to explore and embrace America's collective shadow. The larger assessment that emerges from all three films is that Americans must learn to love their country—but with judgment rather than innocence—loving it not out of blind patriotism but with the knowledge that its actions are sometimes wrong. We have gone through trial by fire in Vietnam and must not forget the mistakes we have made or the lessons we have learned. From the perspective of perennial philosophy, the lesson is this: If we truly want to be at home in the universe, we need to accept who we are; we should not seek a return to the Edenic paradise, which is no longer possible in a post-modern, post-Vietnam world, but rather fashion a new world (a new Garden) built upon our mistakes. We must construct our house by starting with the "cornerstone that the builders rejected" and acknowledge who we are in our quest to discover what we can become.

All of Oliver Stone's films, then, call for a kind of informed innocence, not represented by a preconscious paradise before the Fall but rather by a transconscious identity shaped by acknowledging and integrating our shadow selves and exploring our collective unconscious together.

Stone's current film project, *Nixon,* will most likely continue this search. Produced by Clayton Townsend, with coproducer Eric Hamburg, the script was written by Christopher Wilkinson, Steven J. Rivele, and Oliver Stone. The film, starring Anthony Hopkins in the lead role, was shot over two months in summer 1995 and is due for release in December 1995 by Disney's Hollywood Pictures and Cinergi Productions.

Although *Nixon* has not been released as of this writing, working versions of the script were leaked to the press as early as March 1995. According to a March 14, 1995, report in *Daily Variety,* one of Oliver Stone's enemies may have actively dispersed multiple copies of the script in order to kill the film with bad publicity. The article also speculated that Stone himself leaked a version of the script in order to heighten expectations about the film. According to the article, however, sources close to Stone claimed that Stone was "blindsided" by the early release of the script and did not want to debate the merits of a work in progress before it had even begun production.

Regardless of how early versions of the screenplay were released, they managed to stir up some of the same controversies Stone faced with *JFK.* As one critic explained it, "News of the script has started an immediate debate on historical authenticity."[3] The attacks on Stone's script for *Nixon* primarily focused on speculations raised in a March 20 *Time Magazine* article that the film involves Vice President Richard M. Nixon in a plot to kill the Cuban dictator Fidel Castro. In the words of one journalist, "Stone weaves a tale in which Nixon, then Eisenhower's Vice President, commands an operation which puts together a CIA-Mafia-FBI team to assassinate Castro."[4] According to the *Time* article, Nixon's hit squad is also later involved in the assassination of President John F. Kennedy. One critic claimed that out of fear of a libel suit, Stone waited until Nixon's April 1994 death to make such accusations.[5] Critics' responses to Stone's *Nixon* script were often reminiscent of the scathing indictments Stone received for *JFK* and hinted that Stone, in his defense of *Nixon*, may be in for the same type of controversy he encountered with *JFK*. Speaking directly to Stone, one critic asserted:

> It's hard not to feel that you and the late President Nixon were in some sense made for each other. Both intelligent and talented—he could have been a great president, you could have been a great film director—you were both handicapped by an indifference to the facts. I understand that there is a substantive difference. Nixon broke the law and ignored the Constitution. You have broken only the laws of historical filmmaking. Yet both of you are guilty of corrupting the minds of Americans.[6]

According to some journalists, Stone's lack of public comment about the criticisms of his *Nixon* script only prompted further speculation, "leaving the filmmaker scrambling to deny most of what is printed."[7] Stone eventually called the Nixon report in *Time* "ridiculous," adding, "The sensationalized stories on 'Nixon,' based on very early drafts of the script, totally misrepresent the film we are trying to make. If the media will allow us to finish writing the script, then shoot and edit the movie and present it to the public, I believe that we will be able to offer our audience an exciting and sympathetic portrait of the most controversial president in our history."[8]

Nixon apparently interprets Richard M. Nixon's career, focusing on the influences and impulses that ultimately led to his political suicide. Although the script focuses primarily on the Nixon presidency, it includes glimpses of Nixon's childhood and early political career. It begins, for example, with the Watergate break-in and then flashes back to events in Nixon's youth in conservative Orange County, California, his early California campaigns for public office, and his response to claims of misuse of campaign funds in his now-famous "Checkers" speech.

Those who read early versions of the *Nixon* script claimed that Stone portrays Nixon as a complex, tragic, and conflicted figure, not unlike a character in a Shakespearean play.[9] One journalist noted that "a reading of the closely guarded script, and conversations with Mr. Stone and some of the actors, suggests that the film seeks to portray Nixon in a variety of ways: demonic but also tragic, obsessed with his past, vulnerable and charismatic, frightened and hard."[10] However, a Stone source countered this assessment, saying, "It would be wrong to say that this will be either a sympathetic portrayal or some liberal diatribe . . . He doesn't come off looking very good. But it's not a one-dimensional screed against Nixon."[11] Describing his portrait of Nixon, Stone himself explained, "He's a classic tragic character, probably the most dominant politician in America in the last half-century after Roosevelt. . . . The toughness that it took for him to rise to the top as an outsider and take the knocks were the very qualities that made him cynical and bitter and defeated him."[12] Anthony Hopkins, speaking of the Nixon character he plays, seemed to confirm Stone's interpretation: "I sense I know him. I sense he was run out of his job by his own demons. I understand the rejection he felt, the isolation. And I feel compassion for this man."[13]

Thus, from all accounts it seems that Stone's second film about a contemporary U.S. president will once again raise the type of controversy, criticism, and speculation that Stone faced with *JFK*. Stone's choice of former President Richard M. Nixon as his subject matter also seems to ensure his continued commitment to investigating the issues and individuals that have shaped the past thirty years of American life. The film's promised portrayal of Nixon as a complex character, most likely driven by both good and evil impulses and constantly faced with his own shadow, also speaks to Stone's continued exploration of the collective demons of the unconscious that drive culture and continually prod us to assess who we are in the quest to discover what we can become. Regardless of the critical and popular reception of Stone's version of Nixon's life, one thing remains certain: with $40 million per film at his disposal and with a commitment to continually exploring the tragedies and triumphs of the human condition, Oliver Stone, like Barry Champlain in *Talk Radio*, is "not afraid to see." Like Champlain, Stone "makes his case," says "what [he] believe[s] in," and tells us "who we are" because he has to—because, in Champlain's words, "he has no other choice."

Notes

1. Michael Singer, *The Making of Oliver Stone's Heaven and Earth* (Boston: Charles E. Tuttle Co., 1993), 146.

2. Martin Medhurst, "The Rhetorical Structure of Oliver Stone's *JFK*," *Critical Studies in Mass Communication* 10 (1993):128.

3. Charles Lawrence, "Stone Casts Nixon in Plot to Kill Castro," *Daily Telegraph*, 14 March 1995, 10.

4. Ibid.

5. Mark Lawson, "Dear Oliver Stone: Nixon the Movie?" *Independent*, 15 March 1995, 21.

6. Ibid.

7. Valerie Kuklenski, "People," *United Press International,* 14 March 1995, BC cycle.

8. Ibid.

9. Lois Romano, "The Reliable Source: Nixon in Hollywood," *Washington Post*, 23 February 1995, C3.

10. Bernard Weinraub, "Stone's Nixon Is a Blend of Demonic and Tragic," *New York Times*, 30 May 1995, C13.

11. Romano, "Reliable Source," C3.

12. Weinraub, "Stone's Nixon," C13.

13. Ibid.

Filmography

SEIZURE (1974)

Producers: Garrard Glenn and Jeffrey Kapelmann
Director: Oliver Stone
Screenplay: Edward Mann and Oliver Stone (based on a story by Oliver Stone)
Photography: Roger Racine
Music: Lee Gagnon
Cast: Jonathan Frid, Martine Beswick, Joe Sirola, Christina Pickles, Roger de Koven, Mary Woronov, Hervé Villechaize, Richard Cox, Henry Baker, Timothy Ousey, Lucy Bingham, Alexis Kirk, Emil Meola
Released by Cinerama and American International Pictures

THE HAND (1981)

Producer: Edward R. Pressman
Director: Oliver Stone
Screenplay: Oliver Stone (from the novel *The Lizard's Tail* by Marc Brandel)
Photography: King Baggot
Music: James Horner
Cast: Michael Caine, Andrea Marcovicci, Annie McEnroe, Bruce McGill, Viveca Lindfors, Rosemary Murphy, Mara Hobel, Pat Corley, Bill Marshall, Charles Fletcher
Released by Orion Pictures and Warner Brothers
Running Time: 104 minutes, color

SALVADOR (1986)

Executive Producers: John Daly and Derek Gibson
Producers: Gerald Green and Oliver Stone
Director: Oliver Stone
Screenplay: Oliver Stone and Richard Boyle (based on Richard Boyle's unpublished accounts of his trips into El Salvador)
Photography: Robert Richardson and Leon Sanchez Ruis

Editor: Claire Simpson
Music: George Delerue
Cast: James Woods, James Belushi, Elepedia Carrillo, Michael Murphy,
    John Savage, Tony Plana, Cynthia Gibb, Colby Chester, Will MacMillan,
    Jorge Luke, Valerie Wilman, José Carlos Ruiz, Juan Gernandez
Released by Hemdale and Virgin Films
Running Time: 122 minutes, color

PLATOON (1986)

Executive Producers: John Daly and Derek Gibson
Producer: Arnold Kopelson
Director: Oliver Stone
Screenplay: Oliver Stone
Photography: Robert Richardson
Editor: Claire Simpson
Music: George Delerue
Cast: Tom Berenger, Willem Dafoe, Charlie Sheen, Forrest Whitaker,
    Francesco Quinn, John C. McGinley, Richard Edson, Kevin Dillon,
    Reggie Johnson, Keith David, Johnny Depp, David Neidorf, Mark
    Moses, Chris Pedersen, Corkey Ford, Corey Glover, Bob Orwig
Released by Hemdale and Orion Pictures
Running Time: 111 minutes, color

WALL STREET (1987)

Producer: Edward R. Pressman
Director: Oliver Stone
Screenplay: Oliver Stone and Stanley Weiser
Photography: Robert Richardson
Editor: Claire Simpson
Music: Stewart Copeland
Cast: Michael Douglas, Charlie Sheen, Daryl Hannah, Martin Sheen,
    Terence Stamp, James Spader, Sean Young, Millie Perkins, John C.
    McGinley, Hal Holbrook, Tamara Tunie, Franklin Cover, Sylvia Miles,
    Sean Stone
Released by American Entertainment/20th Century Fox
Running Time: 124 minutes, color

TALK RADIO (1988)

Producers: Edward R. Pressman and A. Kitman Ho
Director: Oliver Stone

Screenplay: Eric Bogosian and Oliver Stone (based on the play by Bogosian and the book *Talked to Death: The Life and Murder of Alan Berg* by Stephen Singular)
Photography: Robert Richardson
Editor: David Brenner
Music: Stewart Copeland
Cast: Eric Bogosian, Ellen Greene, Leslie Hope, Alec Baldwin, John C. McGinley, John Pankow, Michael Wincott, Linda Atkinson, Robert Trebar, Zach Grenier, Anna Levine, Rockets Redglare, Tony Frank, Harlan Jordan
Released by Cineplex Odeon Films and Universal Pictures
Running Time: 110 minutes, color

BORN ON THE FOURTH OF JULY (1989)

Producers: A. Kitman Ho and Oliver Stone
Director: Oliver Stone
Screenplay: Oliver Stone and Ron Kovic (based on the book by Ron Kovic, *Born on the Fourth of July*)
Photography: Rob Richardson
Editors: David Brenner and Joe Hutshing
Music: John Williams
Cast: Tom Cruise, Kyra Sedgwick, Caroline Kava, Raymond J. Barry, Jerry Levine, Frank Whaley, Willem Dafoe, Tom Berenger, Bryan Larkin, Josh Evans, Tony Frank, Jayne Hayes
Released by Universal Pictures
Running Time: 145 minutes, color

THE DOORS (1991)

Executive Producers: Mario Kassar, Nicholas Clainos, and Brian Grazer
Producers: Sasha Harari, Bill Graham, and A. Kitman Ho
Associate Producers: Clayton Townsend and Joseph Reidy
Director: Oliver Stone
Screenplay: Oliver Stone, J. Randall Johnson, Randy Johnson, and Ralph Thomas (from the book *Riders on the Storm* by John Densmore)
Photography: Robert Richardson
Editors: David Brenner and Joe Hutshing
Executive Music Producer: Budd Car
Cast: Val Kilmer, Meg Ryan, Kevin Dillon, Kyle MacLachlan, Frank Whaley, Michael Madsen, Kathleen Quinlan, Michael Wincott, Dennis Burkley, Josh Evans, Paul Williams, Kristina Fulton, Crispin Glover
Released by Imagine Films Entertainment and Carolco Pictures–Tri-Star
Running Time: 141 minutes, color

JFK (1991)

Executive Producer: Arnon Milchan
Producers: A. Kitman Ho, Oliver Stone
Associate Producer: Clayton Williams
Director: Oliver Stone
Screenplay: Oliver Stone and Zachary Sklar (based on the books *On the Trail of the Assassins* by Jim Garrison and *Crossfire: The Plot That Killed Kennedy* by Jim Marrs)
Photography: Robert Richardson
Editors: Joe Hutshing and Pietro Scalia
Production Designer: Victor Kempster
Music: John Williams
Cast: Kevin Costner, Sissy Spacek, Joe Pesci, Tommy Lee Jones, Gary Oldman, Beata Pozniak, Joe O. Sanders, Laurie Metcalf, Michael Rooker, Jack Lemmon, Walter Matthau, Donald Sutherland, Kevin Bacon, Edward Asner, Brian Doyle-Murray, Gary Grubbs, Wayne Knight, Jo Anderson, Vincent D'Onofrio, Pruitt Taylor Vince, Jim Garrison
Released by Warner Brothers, in association with Regency Enterprises, Le Studio Canal+, and Alcor Films
Running Time: 189 minutes, color

HEAVEN AND EARTH (1993)

Executive Producer: Mario Kassar
Producers: Oliver Stone, Arnon Milchan, Robert Kline, A. Kitman Ho
Associate Producer: Clayton Townsend
Director: Oliver Stone
Screenplay: Oliver Stone (from the books *The Day Heaven and Earth Changed Places* by Le Ly Hayslip with Jay Wurts and *Child of War, Woman of Peace* by Le Ly Hayslip with James Hayslip)
Photography: Robert Richardson
Editors: David Brenner and Sally Menke
Production Designer: Victor Kempster
Music: Kitaro
Cast: Hiep Thi Le, Joan Chen, Tommy Lee Jones, Haing S. Ngor, Debbie Reynolds, Dustin Nguyen, Lan Nguyen Calderon, Mai Le Ho, Conchata Ferrell, Vivian Wu, Dale Dye, Liem Whatley, Robert Burke, Michael Paul Chang
Released by Warner Brothers, in association with Regency Enterprises, Le Studio Canal+, and Alcor Films
Running Time: 142 minutes, color

NATURAL BORN KILLERS (1994)

Executive Producers: Arnon Milchan and Thom Mount
Producers: Jane Hamsher, Don Murphy, and Clayton Townsend
Associate Producer: Rand Vossler
Director: Oliver Stone
Story: Quentin Tarantino
Screenplay: David Veloz, Richard Rutowski, and Oliver Stone
Photography: Robert Richardson
Editors: Hank Corwin and Brian Berdan
Production Designer: Victor Kempster
Cast: Woody Harrelson, Juliette Lewis, Robert Downey, Jr., Tommy Lee
   Jones, Rodney Dangerfield
Released by Warner Brothers, in association with Regency Enterprises, Le
Studio Canal+, and Alcor Films
Running Time: 118 minutes, color

Oliver Stone also has the following screenplays to his credit:
Midnight Express, 1978, directed by Alan Parker
Conan the Barbarian, 1982, coscripted with John Milius, directed by John
   Milius
Scarface, 1983, directed by Brian De Palma
The Year of the Dragon, 1985, coscripted with Michael Cimino, directed
   by Michael Cimino
Eight Million Ways to Die, 1986, coscripted with David Lee Henry, di-
   rected by Hal Ashby

About the Book and Author

This book represents an illustrated, critical analysis of filmmaker Oliver Stone and his works, placing him in the tradition of American political artists.

Oliver Stone—polemicist, leftist, artist, and—surprisingly for politically conservative America—mainstream director—is one of the most controversial American filmmakers in Hollywood. His films include *JFK, Platoon, Born on the Fourth of July, Heaven and Earth, The Doors, Salvador, Talk Radio, Natural Born Killers,* and *Nixon*—all political, passionate, and disturbing. This book embraces Stone's work, analyzes his films, and places him inside the tradition of American political filmmaking.

Mackey-Kallis argues that Stone's films are mythological constructions based on historical events and personae which draw upon "the inevitable tension between social actuality and film form." Not simply an aesthetic contemplation, this book analyzes Oliver Stone's films as artistically structured instruments for public communication. Ample illustrations illuminate her discussions.

Susan Mackey-Kallis was born in San Diego, California, in 1961 and was educated at the University of California–San Diego (B.A.), West Virginia University (M.A.), and The Pennsylvania State University (Ph.D.). Mackey-Kallis has focused her research on political rhetoric and the sociopolitical role of fiction film in America and has published articles on such topics as the Reagan and Bush administrations' campaigns against drugs, the Reagan reelection campaign film, political values in advertising, and popular music and politics. She is currently an assistant professor in the Communication Arts Department at Villanova University and lives with her husband, Kyriakos Kallis, and their two dogs, Elsa and Dooney, in Haverford, Pennsylvania.

Index

Abyss, 128, 129
Academy Awards, 13, 65, 74, 125
Alcohol, 71, 93
Allegory, 25, 26. *See also* Myths
Allen, Woody, 64
American Dream, 48, 54, 79
Anderson, Carolyn, 5(n9)
Anima, 70
Ansen, David, 39, 64, 75, 95–96
Anson, Robert, 34
Apocalypse Now, 62, 63
Appy, Christina, 25, 75
Audiences, 4, 32(n79), 36, 96, 97, 113, 116, 134
Archetypes, 3, 9, 16, 19, 20, 21, 30(nn 30, 32), 67, 70, 73, 95, 98, 136, 141

Beatty, Warren, 13
Beaver, Frank, 66, 89(n41), 110
Benson, Thomas, 5(n9), 32(n79)
Berenger, Tom, 65
Betrayal, 27, 33, 34, 71–72, 93, 103, 109, 124–125, 149
Blake, William, 67, 95, 98
Bogosian, Eric, 110
Born on the Fourth of July, 3–4, 8, 9, 12, 13, 25, 26, 27, 35, 37, 59, 60, 73–82, 119(n4), 148, 151
Boyle, Richard, 104, 105
Bregman, Mark, 65
Buddhism, 70, 84, 85, 87
Budgets. *See* Films, financing
Bush, George, 43–44

Camera work, 106, 112, 117, 127, 135, 141
Campbell, Joseph, 7, 19–20, 69, 70, 72, 81, 137, 141
Capitalism, 27, 35, 47, 125, 150
Capra, Frank, 107
Castro, Fidel, 45, 152
Cave image, 19, 69, 70. *See also* Plato, cave allegory
Cawley, Leo, 62

Central Intelligence Agency (CIA), 43, 44, 45, 46, 47, 50
Chaplin, Charlie, 13
Characters, 15, 25, 26, 29, 37
Child of War, Woman of Peace (Hayslip), 82–83
Christ, 8, 32(n95), 36, 48, 49, 51, 53, 69, 71–72, 75, 78, 79, 94, 97, 98, 99–100, 101, 112, 115, 137
Christensen, Terry, 14
CIA. *See* Central Intelligence Agency
Cockburn, Alexander, 34, 39
Cohen, Leonard, 142
Cold War, 11, 110
Collective unconscious, 16, 18, 19, 20, 136, 143, 144, 150, 151
Coming Home, 62, 73
Commonweal, 75
Communication, 2
Conan the Barbarian, 12
Coombs, Richard, 63, 64
Corliss, Richard, 24–25, 35, 36, 37, 64, 132
Corruption, 35, 124
Corwin, Hank, 135
Critics/criticism, 2–3, 4, 5(n9), 25, 26, 39–44, 64–65, 72, 74–75, 84, 104, 117, 123, 124, 132–133, 134, 152
Cuba, 45–46, 152
Cutter's Way, 73
Cynicism, 117–118

Dafoe, Willem, 65
Daily Variety, 151
Daly, John, 65
Death, 21, 68, 85, 95, 101, 107, 109, 117, 142
December 7th, 42
Deer Hunter, The, 62, 63, 73
Democracy, 34, 54
Denby, David, 26
Denton, Robert, 31(n71)
De Palma, Brian, 64
Deserts, 77, 79–80, 97–98, 138